GUESS I'M LUCKY

GUESS I'M LUCKY

My Life in Horse Racing

BY
WOODY STEPHENS
AND
JAMES BROUGH

DOUBLEDAY & COMPANY, INC.
GARDEN CITY, NEW YORK
1985

PHOTO ACKNOWLEDGMENTS

The photographs reproduced in this book are primarily from the author's personal collection. We are grateful to the New York Racing Association for supplying additional photographs. The photographs of Devil's Bag courtesy UPI/Bettmann Newsphotos; Soli, Canadian Winter, and Contredance courtesy Creative Graphics/William Kuebler.

Library of Congress Cataloging in Publication Data
Stephens, Woody.
    Guess I'm lucky.
      1. Stephens, Woody. 2. Racehorse trainers—Kentucky—Biography. I. Brough, James, 1918– . II. Title.
SF336.S73A34   1985   798.4′0092′4 [B]
ISBN 0-385-19568-0
Library of Congress Catalog Card Number: 85-6991

Copyright © 1985 by Woody Stephens and James Brough
ALL RIGHTS RESERVED
PRINTED IN THE UNITED STATES OF AMERICA
FIRST EDITION

To Lucille

Contents

1 Just as the Sun Was Rising 1
2 From Dark to Dark 15
3 The Weighting Game 28
4 Making or Breaking 40
5 The Speed Boys 52
6 The Rules of the Game 65
7 The Captain's Stable 79
8 The Nature of the Business 92
9 The Horse Has the Right of Way 107
10 All in the Blood 120
11 The Sweet Scent of Roses 131
12 How Much Makes Too Many? 149
13 August in Saratoga 161
14 You Don't Win 'Em All 175
15 The Big Money 190
16 One of These Days 204
   Woody's Stakes Winners 215
   Major Events in Woody's Career 228

GUESS I'M LUCKY

1
Just as the Sun Was Rising

Five o'clock sharp, rain or shine, is the time I'm usually getting myself out of bed seven days a week, twelve months of the year, and I don't allow three minutes either side of that. It isn't hard to do when it's as natural as breathing and a habit that comes from working with horses.

I started waking up ahead of the roosters when I was a kid on a Kentucky farm, with my heart set on being a jockey. I had horses on my mind back then, and for more than fifty years I've had my hands on horses, a few of them mine, most of them owned by other people bent on seeing them out on the racetrack creaming the competition.

I've never kept count of how many I've had in my barns, but I've sent them out to win Kentucky Derbies and most other big stakes in the country. So it's fair to say that horses made me, and I reckon that in training them I made those horses. Anyway you look at it, I've been lucky.

Time takes over and writes the rules when you're training a thoroughbred for racing. You measure its promise and then its performance with a stopwatch registering split seconds. That's one rule. Another tells you when it's time to climb out of the hay and get to work, lucky or not—at five o'clock every morning.

This particular Sunday morning was no exception, and I was starting true to form. I had myself a bite to eat and a swallow of Sanka, always black, then backed out the Mercedes to drive the three miles that lie between Belmont Park and the little house in Franklin Square, Elmont, New York, that's been ours—my wife, Lucille's, and mine—since we bought it, the first we ever owned, in 1952, the year I reached the age of thirty-nine.

Now I was seventy. This was Sunday, June 17, 1984, a few days short of midsummer. The sky was already bright when I swung in off Hempstead Turnpike through the open gates to the backstretch of Belmont Park. On the far side of the street, the pizza parlors, the car wash, the offtrack betting joint, and everything else—all asleep and quiet as the top of Kentucky's Big Black Mountain.

Going in slow over the bump set in the road, I watched the yellow barrier tilt up in front of the guardhouse. The Pinkerton man on duty had the look of a state trooper in the big felt hat and blue shirt they get to wear on the job.

"Hi, Woody. How you doing?"

"Good. How's it with you?"

"Can't complain. When you figure on running Swale again?"

"No sooner than the fall. A horse that's took the Derby and then the Belmont has earned vacation time."

"Anything you recommend for today?"

I shook my head. "I'm taking off on vacation myself. First time in thirty years." The Pinkerton waved me through.

I'd been scheduled to leave for Hot Springs, Arkansas, Saturday night. Earlier on in the year, I'd landed in a hospital bed after running into several sorts of trouble, some of it brought on by my own fretting maybe, and we'd suffered a death in the family, too. I was feeling in better condition than I had been then, but it wasn't hard to recognize there was room left for improvement. Next birthday, three months away, I'd be seventy-one years old, and that was proving a handicap to making a quick recovery.

The remedy might lie in Hot Springs, where the Indians are supposed to be the first ones to take the cure. I knew, because I'd tried it before, that some long soaks in the water that flows clear as crystal down there in the Ozarks could do me a world of good.

But bringing yourself to leave isn't easy when you're training thoroughbreds worth millions of almighty dollars, specially when you've got one of them you thought so highly of as Swale, son of Seattle Slew. When you have a really good horse, you never want to walk away. You say to yourself, "What if I go and then something happens to him?"

And in this business there's so much can go wrong, so much to watch out for, in and out of your control. A horse may be put out of action by hives or a hairline crack in a bone, by fever in a knee, or a fistula on the withers—there's no end to the list of ailments.

If the track isn't watered right and it gets too hard, a horse can hurt itself easy in a workout. It's a delicate animal, constructed for speed, that weighs in at around one thousand pounds. At a gallop, the weight bears down on each leg in turn, with the forelegs taking most of the punishment. There's a tremendous amount of pressure when the going is close to forty miles an hour.

A virus can sweep through a barn and catch everybody off balance, including the veterinarians, who don't deny there's a lot to be learned about the diseases of horses and the best way to treat them. Landaluce was a case in point, the champion two-year-old filly of 1982 trained by Wayne Lukas; in November of that year, he watched her wilt and die of an infection that nobody could explain.

Stepping on a stone the size of a pecan shell can cause damage, which happened once to a favorite of mine, Devil's Bag. And even good intentions can stir things up, like a pony girl who worked for me not so long ago at Hialeah, Florida. She thought she'd go to the infield to pick some sweet, fresh grass as a treat for the horses. Now, a pony will eat most anything and thrive on it, but a blood horse has a different constitution. The grass she fed them brought one or two of them down with colic.

But my mind was clear of the thought of trouble that Sunday morning when I was heading along the road to my barns on the backstretch, where the horse is still king and the filly is queen, and there's a thousand of them stabled there. The fifteen-mile-an-hour speed limit signs spell it out: "Horses have the right of way."

There were horses everywhere you turned, some with riders going out for exercise, some being walked by their grooms on the inside ring which circles the stalls. I felt I was lucky to have maybe the best of the lot in Swale, the dark bay colt that had won the Kentucky Derby for me in May and then, as if that wasn't enough, taken the Belmont Stakes only nine days ago, to make it three years in a row for me to celebrate—1982, 1983, and 1984—a first for any trainer.

In all the time since he was brought to me in Hialeah, Swale had never been sick or needed as much as an aspirin. He was a sound, healthy three year old who did his best in every race he ran. He'd run enough of them by now to earn a million and a half dollars, sometimes by a nose, but he was always determined because he put his heart right into it.

Just last night he'd been looked over by Seth Hancock, who on paper was only one of a half dozen owners of Swale, joined in a partnership called Raceland Stable, though Seth regarded Swale as *his* horse and his favorite. Then Seth caught a flight back to Kentucky, which is his home and still, to my way of thinking, mine.

Swale was conceived and foaled on Claiborne Farm, owned for the most part by Seth, along with his sisters Dell and Nancy. It's a beautiful place: thirty-two hundred acres standing near the little town of Paris, with its population of seven or eight thousand people, maybe thirty miles from where I was born myself. I knew it from the time I was a young kid, breaking horses for Seth's father, A. B. Hancock, known as "Bull." Out of a total of sixty-five mares down there now, five belonged to me.

It was Bull who developed the idea of putting together a syndicate to buy a horse for breeding. After cancer killed Bull in 1972, Seth took over at the age of twenty-three and carried on with syndicating, over the years putting deals together that add up now to around a hundred million dollars.

It seemed there was nothing to hold Swale back from winning again and again. At that time, no trainer in history had ever had a stable with horses earning five million in purses in a single year, but maybe my number was coming up. If the sun kept shining for this colt, his syndication price could hit well over fifty million, which would be something else for the history books.

Swale broke one record when he earned $537,000 in the Kentucky Derby, which was $108,150 more than the previous mark set in '82 by Gato Del Sol. Winning at Churchill Downs was the job Swale was bred for by Seth, who's an upright, stand-up feller and a millionaire too.

Bull Hancock tried for years to produce a Derby winner, but he failed. The failure soured him so much that in the will he wrote he wanted Claiborne Farm to get out of racing altogether and concentrate on breeding. He couldn't see burdening his two sons, Seth and Arthur, with the doubts and risks of the game that Bull had been in since 1954. Soon after he died, Claiborne's racing stock went under the auction hammer in a Belmont sale, and the orange silks of Claiborne, some of the oldest registered with the Jockey Club, disappeared from the tracks.

But Arthur had gone into business with his own Stone Farm, which is close by, the year before his father passed on, and he started racing his own colors, yellow and gray. In February of '73 he left Seth to operate Claiborne without him. In 1980 he sold his interest in the family trust to his younger brother and his sisters.

A fire at Stone Farm the following year killed eleven horses worth four hundred thousand dollars, among them an eighteen-year-old mare, Theonia, that he'd just bought for something near half that figure. But he still had Gato Del Sol, the horse that took him into the winner's circle in Louisville in 1982.

I don't know if there was real rivalry between the brothers, but by then Seth had already decided on racing, not on selling Claiborne's yearling colts—the fillies had been earmarked for the track three or four years earlier. Seth set out to breed his own Derby winner.

One of Claiborne's mares was Tuerta, a Spanish name meaning "blind in one eye." Bull Hancock saw her born that way in the foaling barn in April 1970. He had been hoping for a colt, because he had plenty of fillies, and it's rare for a filly to race first under the wire at the Kentucky Derby. Yet Tuerta turned out to be a good stakes winner and the last of them to carry the silks in the lifetime of Bull, who'd had no time for her the day she was born. Seth wanted foals from Tuerta.

Seth had a hand as an adviser in the mating that resulted in the foaling in April 1974 of Seattle Slew at Ben Castleman's White Horse Acres, another farm in bluegrass Kentucky; the sire was Bold Reasoning, a great-great-grandson of Nasrullah, the stallion Bull Hancock had imported nearly a quarter of a century ago; the dam was My Charmer, a Fair Grounds winner. Slew sold for $17,500 to Mr. and Mrs. Mickey Taylor and Dr. and Mrs. Jim Hill, who operated Tayhill Stable as a team. Shares in the stallion sell today for as much as three million dollars apiece, give or take a hundred thousand.

He was the first horse ever to win the Triple Crown—the Kentucky Derby, the Preakness, and the Belmont Stakes—without a previous defeat. By the time he was retired to the stud at Brownell and Leslie Combs's Spendthrift Farm, he'd earned $1,208,726 and lost only three of his seventeen races.

His first crop of foals came along in 1979—one of them was the doomed filly Landaluce. Tuerta, a sweet, plain-looking bay, was bred to him the next time around, and that's how Swale entered the picture.

In the fifty years I've been at the racetracks, I've seen the game grow into an industry, but among the best of the people involved in it, there's a sense of fairer play than you'll find in Detroit or Hollywood. When Seth conceived the Raceland Stable partnership, the agreement called for an annual drawing of lots to decide which of the yearling colts they bought every year should go to which individual partner.

Seth's mother, Mrs. Wardell Hancock, drew their names, and fifth choice of the colts fell to him. The yearling he picked didn't look like anything special. Mrs. Hancock named him Swale, which means "a hollow or depression, especially one in wet, marshy ground."

I was sent Swale in December '82 when he came to Hialeah with two other colts, Devil's Bag and Vision, and I trained them easy all winter. All of them were well-bred horses, and I had no idea which might be the best.

Then early in '83, I shipped them to New York, began to school them, and got serious about them. I started to notice, when I was taking them to the gate, that Devil's Bag wasn't working as hard when I was running them all together as the other two were. They were driving, urged on by the riders, while he was breezing, taking it easier. I got to thinking Devil's Bag was something special, but the other two were really good horses.

Devil's Bag started in a six-furlong maiden test at Saratoga in August; Swale came out sooner, at Belmont in July at five furlongs. He went out of the gate as an odds-on favorite, but after leading into the stretch, he was second by two-and-a-half lengths. Odds-on again two weeks later, he led all the way to win.

In a dozen races he never finished worse than third, and that happened only twice; in six of them, all added-money events, he made first money. He didn't object to having slop kicked up in his eyes the way some horses do, as he proved by taking the Saratoga Special in the mud, but the surface at Keeneland for the Lexington Stakes in April was so sloppy he had trouble standing. He started the one-to-ten favorite in this final prep for the Kentucky Derby, but he finished a distant second, and some of the crowd booed him for that. A story went around that we were going to scratch him from the Derby because he'd been trained too soft; there wasn't a word of truth to it.

He was a sweet-natured horse with the will to win and the

promise of greatness in him, yet he stood in the shadow of Devil's Bag, who was superior to him in my judgment and everybody else's. The Devil was the grandest-looking horse I'd ever seen.

I said as much when I was delivered to my barn at Churchill Downs in a long black limousine, driven in by Dr. David Richardson from the Louisville hospital that he'd ordered me into more than a week ago. This was on April 30, Monday, five days before Saturday's Run for the Roses.

The entries for it had closed in February—there were more than three hundred of them—and that was the month my mother died. The pressure of my business was already building up again on every side, and it was already getting to me. I was tired to the bones, and I was bothered with emphysema, which lingers on in spite of giving up cigarettes fifteen years ago. Because I was slow in letting a doctor check me over, the result was pneumonia, but I'll save the details for later.

The outing to the barn didn't last long. I was soon back in the hospital, with some deciding to do. Did Devil's Bag have a chance of winning the Kentucky Derby? The distance is a mile and a quarter. The previous Saturday, in the Derby Trial Stakes, he'd tired and was going full drive to beat out a field of so-so horses. There was doubt about him in my mind, and it didn't get any weaker from thinking about it.

That night I spoke with the colt's jockey, Eddie Maple, and with the owner, Jimmy Mills. Seth Hancock came in, and after we'd chawed it over, the decision was left to me.

I said, "Well, if it's all the same to you and Mr. Mills, let's back off." I wanted Devil's Bag for the Preakness Prep and the Preakness Stakes, both of them shorter distances, which would be run in Baltimore a week after the Derby. Everybody felt this was the right thing to do.

If he ran badly or got himself hurt, that could mean he'd never run again. The next morning Dr. Richardson drove me back to Barn 41 at the Downs so I could make the announcement. Now Swale had to win the Derby for me if it was going to be a win. The early betting put him at seven-to-one. The clear favorites were a pair of fillies, Althea and Life's Magic, trained by Wayne Lukas, who has a stable three times the size of mine, with thirty horses in California and forty in New York. Barn 43 was his number, and that's where the TV cameras were.

Right up to the morning of Derby Day, it was Devil's Bag and not Swale that visitors wanted to see in Barn 41, though they were both there, the Devil lazy in stall eleven, Swale acting up some in stall seven. I took a quick look at them, but my worrying was about the weather. Rain had been coming down during the week, and the forecast called for showers in the afternoon, which could mean mud. My colt hadn't done well in the slop at Keeneland.

The rules these days keep the field of the Derby down to twenty, since there'd been some overcrowding with twenty-four horses in the past. For this hundred-and-tenth running, there were seventeen colts, a gelding, and Wayne's pair of fillies. The rain had held off, and the sun was turning the track harder and fast. A strong favorite was nowhere in sight, but the weight of the betting went on Althea.

Wayne, if he'd been anything but a trainer, maybe, would have been away on his honeymoon—he'd been a bridegroom early on in the week. But another filly of his, Lucky Lucky Lucky, had beat one of mine, Miss Oceana, in the Kentucky Oaks on this same racetrack the day before, Friday, and Wayne was eager to make this the best week he'd ever seen.

Laffit Pincay was my rider. Laffit hadn't won a Derby in ten previous tries; and the Hancocks, Bull and his sons, had never made it with a Claiborne Farm entry either. That left only me who'd been in the winner's circle before—with Cannonade in '74.

Mike Griffin from Claiborne, who'd been on the receiving end of the phone while I was in the hospital, walked with Swale, his groom, and his exercise rider in the procession to the paddock. Swale was settled down and calm when the saddle was cinched on him. I was feeling too washy myself, so Mike took care of the job. I rested my back against a wall of the stall and watched.

"This horse looks awful good, Mike." I was thinking that if I could have run Devil's Bag as an addition, we would maybe have turned out one and two. We shook hands as I left the stall.

I didn't count on going to the winner's circle; this time around I didn't feel up to tackling the crowd. I'd be better off in the directors' room, watching the TV with Lucille.

Pincay, who's one of the greats, didn't need to be told much. Don't let anybody get an easy lead on you. Let the colt run his own style. Lie close to the pace, move ahead on the turn, drive strong in the stretch.

Althea broke fast from the gate at the ring of the bell, shooting out from the number one slot while Swale was in fifteen. Without Devil's Bag, the pace was nothing much to talk about. First turn, and Swale was hot after her, pricking his ears and very strong at the quarter pole.

At the three-eighths, he was beginning to take over, which was just what we were looking for. "Beautiful" was most all I had to say. Down the backstretch, the colt inched ahead of the filly. At the top of the stretch, Pincay showed him the whip, and the lead opened up two lengths and then to five.

Althea was fading toward the back end of the field. Chris McCarron in the saddle eased up on her, which was what Wayne wanted, so she'd come out of it in good shape. The pace, never really fast, left Swale with plenty of steam. His final drive took him home to the wire to win by three-and-a-quarter, with Althea some thirty lengths behind him in nineteenth place.

The winner's circle was where I had to be. "I'm going," I told Lucille, "even if you have to carry me, or if I have to crawl on my hands and knees."

A blanket of roses covered Swale's withers. Laffit's smile was a mile wide, and his fist was up high in a salute. Bill Shoemaker, a good pal of his who'd finished ninth on Silent King, had tears in his eyes when he hugged him. The Hancocks were there in full strength—Seth, Arthur, and their mother—ready to pop the champagne. I waved a hand to answer the shouts of "Great job, Woody" and all the rest of it. "It was a cinch," I said, as clear as I could, holding the reins of the winner.

Just as the Sun Was Rising

I was remembering it all when I stopped the car outside the barn, ready to walk through for a look at every horse, which is the routine start of the day. But this wasn't to be a routine day. Sandy Bruno, the only girl among my assistants, was in a hurry to talk to me. "Woody, Swale fell over." Her face was white as cotton. When I got the story together, I guess I turned as pale as she was.

The colt had just come back after a light gallop over the Belmont track that lasted no more than ten minutes. His exercise rider, Ron McKenzie, noticed nothing out of the ordinary: "He went the way he always did, kind and willing."

He was led into the yard outside the barn, in a corner by a shade tree, close to where there's warm and cold water on tap. He was due for a warm wash from a bucket with iodine solution added as a precaution against skin disease. Every horse of mine gets this same treatment—a warm-water bath, not a cold-water hosing, from the grooms.

Some of the newspapers wrote afterward that he reared, but that wasn't the truth. He went over backward the way a horse does if he doesn't care for being rubbed so that he bites the shank in his mouth and scares himself; Caveat had this habit.

Sandy and Phil Gleaves, who was another assistant trainer on the payroll, went running to see what was wrong. Swale was hunched down like a dog as she patted his dark head. "You'll be all right," she kept whispering. "Just relax. You're going to be fine."

He struggled to get up, then flopped on his side. Sandy raced for the phone to call a vet; Phil took off to scour the place to see if there was a vet around; Billy Badgett, the third of my assistants, stuck by Swale. His breath was down to slow gasping, and his eyes were rolling back in his head.

Bob Fritz, his regular veterinarian, was there four minutes later to pronounce him dead with no evidence of great suffering. There was no point trying to bring him back with a shot of adrenaline. Dr. Fritz listed three possible causes: heart failure, a stroke or, "and I hate to say it, some toxic substance."

I went to my office to call Seth. Before I picked up the phone, I sat for a moment, feeling my mouth numb, as if I'd been given a shot, ready for a dentist to pull some teeth. Seth said, "Are you kidding me?" just not believing what I told him. Finally he said, "Well, these things happen," and he advised me to go on ahead to Hot Springs to try to stop the whole thing haunting my mind.

By now, as a mark of respect the colt was covered with the white nets lettered "Florida Derby 1984" that were a gift for him after he'd won it last March. There was a long wait ahead before he could be carried to Barn 64, where the testing is done at Belmont; the ambulance to take him there isn't allowed off the track while horses are running on it.

Bad news seems to travel as fast as light. In no time at all, the barn was surrounded with people. Reporters, photographers, and camera crews were trampling the flowers that Belmont puts in free of charge. Two specialists were flying in from Pennsylvania, from the New Bolton Center for Veterinary Medicine at the state university. Cameramen wanted a shot of Swale's empty stall, number three. But Sandy had led the pony in there, and she was too upset by everything to consider moving it.

It was one o'clock before Swale was in Barn 64 and the autopsy got going. The colt was opened up from chin to tail and all the parts lifted out for inspection, with Phil Gleaves standing by to watch and finding it "horrible," as he said. Everything was judged to be normal, including Swale's willing heart.

They sent back to New Bolton the organs they chose for further testing, along with samples of urine, blood, muscles, and intestines to check Dr. Fritz's question about "toxic substances." Seth had originally asked for only the head, hooves, and heart to be shipped to Kentucky for burial at Claiborne according to a Hancock tradition. Then he changed his mind and wanted the horse home where he'd been born, so a shrine could be built for him. Swale's carcass was stuffed with straw and sewn back together again. The brain was frozen for future study.

The next day, Monday, a different team of investigators came asking questions. The New York Racing Association and the State Racing Board were looking for clues that might help solve the mystery. Everybody who'd been in contact with the colt on Sunday morning was cross-examined, partly to settle the suspicion about a "toxic substance." A groom with a grudge who'd been fired off the job had supplied it, maybe? The answer was that the theory simply wouldn't hold water.

Could Swale have been killed for the insurance he carried? No dice again. The coverage amounted to about fifteen million dollars. Alive and syndicated as a stallion, he'd have been worth three times that and more, maybe as much as a hundred million, the way prices of shares go on rising.

The days went by, and the mystery was still a mystery. There was no valid explanation, no matter what kind of money was being spent by Seth to find one. Swale was gone. The vets clung to hoping they might find a reason sooner or later, but it was a slim hope; most all horses die without an autopsy being performed, so the vets' knowledge is limited.

I understand that the brain or part of it has been saved, frozen, so that if veterinary knowledge expands in the future, there will be something to work on and study, just the way it is with some men and women who've suffered from Alzheimer's disease.

I had a dog, a German shepherd runaway that turned up with a broken chain and attached herself to me. She had a funny way of holding her head to one side, so we called her Sidewinder. She figured she was my protector, so she'd nip the calves of anybody she thought was threatening me. She died the day after Swale. She lies buried a stone's throw from the spot by an old shade tree where he fell. He'll have his shrine at Claiborne. Her headstone's a piece of plank that says *Sidewinder —1984*.

I miss both of them sometimes, though I wasn't there when she went, and I didn't stick around for the autopsy on the colt. Hearing about everything that followed was more than enough when I ducked out to Hot Springs. They kept on my tail down there with the notebooks and cameras, and the hot line to Belmont Park barely stopped ringing.

Then the letters and cards came pouring in, two hundred of

them, sent from all over the country and places around the world, a lot from little kids, some with poems written in memory of the horse.

The loss was an awful blow to me. Thinking about it wasn't far different from getting kicked in the belly by a cranky mule. If there was consolation to be had, it was in a few words I've repeated to myself again and again over the years: "Let the sun come up tomorrow morning."

2

From Dark to Dark

If I hadn't made it as a horse trainer, I'd be back to being a groom, and some grooms don't have the price of a change of clothes. If it hadn't been for the horses, I'd have been a farmer like my dad, a tenant farmer sharecropping another man's land.

My dad was Lewis Stephens. Even in the best of times he couldn't earn any real money, and when the hard times came, we were downright poor. He had seven children to feed, and I was the third of them, born on the first of September in 1913, to my mother, named Helen. Two girls had arrived ahead of me; three more and another son came later.

The place was a plain little farmhouse near Stanton, Kentucky, which was home to no more than a couple of thousand people. In the fields outside, you could see the great spread of the forest set on the flanks of the Allegheny Mountains that honors the memory of Daniel Boone.

In that forest, when you followed trails that old Daniel himself might have trod, there was scenery to blow your breath away: Cave Run and Laurel River Lakes, Yahoo Falls, and natural arches and cliffs rising three hundred feet above your head in Red River Gorge.

But there wasn't a whole lot of time to spare for admiring the scenery when you lived on a tenant farm. Hogs had to be slopped, cows milked, chicken eggs picked up and washed for selling. The big patch of vegetables had to be hoed and the wood cut and split for the kitchen stove. As soon as one of us was old enough, we had chores to do.

The heaviest job of all, of course, was growing the tobacco that was the cash crop. They say the richest soil of any covers a circle of land stretching twenty miles around Lexington. We lay farther off than that, but my dad grew good burley tobacco by applying hard work and sweat.

Day after day without letup, work started before sunrise, and it went on hour after hour until nightfall, when there wasn't light left to see by; from dark to dark, we used to say. When the tobacco leaves were cut, I'd watch the field hands up on the roofs of the drying sheds spreading them out in the beating sun, then coming down to wring the sweat out of their overalls and go for a swim in the stream, where watermelons hung from strings in the water to keep them cool for eating.

My mother's work lasted longer than dark to dark. Every morning she was out of bed to cook another meal on the wood stove and make lunch for those of us who were in school. We kept a flock of three hundred chickens, and it was mostly her job to bring back the eggs in a wicker basket and sell them at maybe fifteen cents a dozen. And she'd be up at four-thirty.

I remember like yesterday the cotton bonnet she wore to go out and weed the acre of corn and beans and squash that was hers to plant and tend. I remember the milk bucket swinging against my dad's leg as he left to milk the cows in a barn that stood something like a mile away.

Then at night she'd be washing our clothes, when a washing machine was one of a long list of luxuries we couldn't afford. The shirts and overalls and such would dry on the line next day before she turned to mending and darning to keep us clean and neat when there wasn't money to buy new clothes.

Being poor might have been the cause of knitting us close as a family. I've no recollection of home where there wasn't happiness among us. Trouble was something you'd overcome if you tried. "Look on the sunny side" was a standard saying of my mother's. She and my dad both belonged to the First Christian Church, but it was a grandmother of mine who was better acquainted with the Bible.

I was named Woodford Cefis Stephens, and the "Cefis" was her choosing. It was a name in the Scriptures, she said, but I can't quote chapter or verse. When I got out into the world, I tried to hold it down to a *C* until a newspaper reporter dug out the truth, and then there was no use trying to hide it.

My grandmother may have been a hard-shell Baptist like a lot of people in those parts, stricter in the matter of faith than we were in the family, and I wasn't sorry for the difference. There's a tale told about a convert to that church who had to go through the process of being baptized. The preacher said, "Repeat after me, 'I do believe,'" then dunked him under the water. The man didn't have the breath to say anything when he came up. The preacher pushed him under again, but there wasn't a word out of him when he surfaced for air. On the third try, he gave his head a shake to clear his ears: "I do believe you're trying to drown me."

I didn't see too much of the inside of First Christian Church after I was five years old or thereabouts. On Sunday mornings, my dad would drive us all down there in the buggy and hitch the horse outside, next to the horses and rigs of the rest of the congregation. While everybody else went in to sing the hymns and listen to the preacher, I was allowed to stay out with the horses, where I used to reach up to stroke their heads and give their tails a tug.

Our mother was willing to sacrifice her time and personal pleasures out of love for all of us, but the pleasures she might have missed didn't include liquor, dice, or gambling. We were brought up strangers to all of those. I doubt whether anybody among us had placed a bet on a horse until I did, after I'd left home.

A time comes every year in that section of the world when you can't help but notice the beauty of the land, and it can clear your mind of most other things. The grass that grows in the Lexington plain spreads like a thick, green, pile carpet all year round, but for a week or two about the first half of June it blooms, and the color gave Kentucky its name, the Bluegrass

State. Limestone accounts for the blue and makes for strong bones in the people and the horses that are born there.

That pasture plus streams of pure water and a mild climate that keeps winters short made Lexington the thoroughbred breeding center of America when wagon trains were still pushing toward California. When I was a kid, starting to learn my way around, the stud farms were some of the greatest marvels of the scenery, the rich men's method of enjoying themselves and making money, too, maybe, even if they were absentees seldom seen in the barns.

The fences stretching out over thousands of acres were fresh with white paint. Foals stumbled after the mares in some of the fields, stallions fat with feeding cantered around in others. Between the fieldstone pillars, the roads I'd never set a foot on led up to trim buildings that could have been like the palaces of kings for all I knew, because I hadn't been inside any one of them.

The big-money crowd began to buy Bluegrass farms soon after the war between North and South, but at the time I was born, horse racing was in a state of decline. The Kentucky Derby that year was just a $5,000-added event. The Jockey Club had set up in business in 1871, when it cost no more than two dollars a head to register a blood horse, but the first of its presidents to see a Derby run was August Belmont II, who arrived at Churchill Downs from New York in 1913.

He was a banker whose money went to building the subway there, and Belmont Park carried his family name. But he took his time coming down to Louisville: he was sixty years old by then. He saw a win for Donerail, ridden by Roscoe Goose, a local boy who'd learned his trade aboard dray horses from a brewery, taking them to the blacksmith; Roscoe died a trainer in '71, with better than a million dollars to his name. A two-dollar bet on Donerail would have paid Mr. Belmont $184.90 that afternoon, but there's no knowing what he backed.

Breeding thoroughbreds held the interest of quite a few of the big-bankroll families that lived and hobnobbed together in New York City, which was where most of the money was. The bloodlines of the horses were usually longer than theirs.

Whitneys, Vanderbilts, Rockefellers, Darius Ogden Mills from California—they were all involved, and their next generation and the ones after that never lost interest in the game.

Whitney was the name that stuck in the mind of everybody who cared about racing, and it had been stuck there long before I ever set eyes on a racetrack. William C. Whitney, with his fortune made from New York streetcars, bought a racing stable that was handed down to his son; Harry Payne Whitney inherited racing fever. Like a lot of owners before and after him, he was hell-bent on winning the Kentucky Derby.

My second birthday was coming up when Harry entered his first horse to make the attempt, the filly, Regret, who'd been out three times and won three times over six furlongs at Saratoga. At Churchill Downs in 1915, there was some speculating about whether he'd scratch her the day before the race when the *Lusitania* went down off the Irish coast with a German torpedo in her hull and his brother-in-law, Alfred Gwynne Vanderbilt, was one of the thousand and more passengers who drowned.

Mr. Whitney wasn't backing off because of any such thing as that. Though every one of the fourteen fillies who'd run in previous Derbies had failed, and there always are doubts about their stamina against colts over a mile and a quarter, the betting favored Regret, in a lineup of fifteen males.

She took the lead from the start, and she stayed there 'til the end. "I am satisfied," said Mr. Whitney in the winner's circle. But he wasn't. The taste of victory was like a bit grabbed between his teeth.

He had two no-show horses in for the year following and one in the year after that. With money to burn, he went on trying right through to the fourteenth year of my life, when I was giving serious consideration to becoming a horseman myself. From 1916 to 1926, he'd run sixteen losers before he won again with Whiskery.

There were more Whitneys ready to take up the reins: his sister-in-law, Mrs. Payne Whitney; Mr. John Hay Whitney and his wife; Mr. and Mrs. Cornelius Vanderbilt Whitney, who are still the king and queen of Saratoga Springs when the season opens there every August and the partying goes on every night, though the time has come lately for me to leave early, or else I can't get up according to schedule in the morning.

I wasn't the tallest or the strongest child in my family; "delicate" was a word I heard used occasionally around the house. One of my older sisters, Nora, who died a while back, topped me by inches and weighed one hundred and thirty-five pounds when she was in high school playing on a basketball team that didn't lose a game.

One reason I developed a liking for horses early on might have been the fact that when my dad hoisted me up on one of them, or on the back of one of his mules, I was five or six feet higher off the ground, looking down at people instead of up. I got that boost up in the world from him, starting when I was three or four years old. He let me ride them as they pulled the hitch that did the plowing. It provided a lot more pleasure, I found out later, than hoeing tobacco for fifty cents a day. Dad used to say, "Woody's a born horseman," and I was happy to hear it, because I didn't want to be considered a born field hand.

When I started in school, I got my own pony given to me by my grandfather; I was six years old. I rode Bill the three miles there in the morning, taking feed for him and lunch for me. I'd keep him in a little livery stable, an open shed, while I was at my lessons, then at lunchtime I'd ride him half a mile down the road to a creek to give him a drink of water before I brought him back.

By the time I'd reached ten or thereabouts, my dad would trust me to take a wagon and a team of mules or horses by myself into town to be loaded with such things as lumber or feed. He always felt I could do it, so I did. I concluded that I liked horses an awful lot, the look of them when they were fed and cared for right, the way they responded after you'd learned how to handle them, the feel of them under your touch —and all of this before I'd had contact with any real good ones.

Kentucky was a state where traditions died hard, and one of them was bigotry, though my family was spared the worst of that. In my granddad's lifetime, both armies, North and South, drove in to fight there. A victory for the North at Perryville kept Kentucky out of the Confederacy, but the slaves weren't free for quite a while after Abraham Lincoln, born in what then was Hardin County, had declared them to be. Then the Ku Klux Klan sprang up to write its own rules and make them stick by beatings, shootings, and burning down houses.

History wasn't my best subject in school, but I had a lesson in one tradition riding to classes one morning. At a fork in the road, there was the body of a black man dangling by a wire strung from a tree. The story was that he'd broken into a warehouse stocked with barrels of bourbon whiskey and killed the night watchman. The Klan hauled him out of jail to string him up. I was in the company of some other young boys and, when we saw that dangling body, we didn't see fit to linger; we just kept right on going under his feet.

Bourbon whiskey is another Kentucky tradition, and distilling it is the oldest industry in our state. Prohibition, passed as the law of the land in 1919, was a terrible blow, but it spurred on the drys to take aim at a new target they regarded as another source of evil and corruption: legalized racetrack betting.

Though it had proved impossible to save bourbon from the lawmakers, the horsemen didn't intend to let the racing business suffer the same fate, since that could bring ruin to them and to Kentucky's reputation as the best of all breeding grounds of twentieth-century champions.

Tracks at that time had been closing by the dozens in the slump of a few years back, horses by the hundreds sold overseas for anything they would bring, and thousands of animals converted into pulling laundry wagons or maybe into dog food. But the tide had started to turn, and prospects looked promising.

Horsemen, politicians, and investors in the Bluegrass joined together in 1918 to create the Kentucky Jockey Club, a monopoly that owned every important racetrack in the state—Churchill Downs and Douglas Park in Louisville, Latonia in Covington, and the course called Keeneland in these days. The president was a millionaire breeder, Johnson N. Camden, who also served as chairman of the Kentucky State Racing Commission, which controlled every track, the racing dates, and all the betting.

One leader of the attackers was the United States Congressman from Paducah. Alben W. Barkley, who would be Harry Truman's running mate in the 1948 presidential election, had built up his following by speaking up loud and clear for Prohibition. Now he hoped to find more supporters by fixing his sights on the gamblers in the state.

The exchange of shots went on for years; I was in high school before it was over. It ended when a politician out to get the gamblers got steamrollered in a state election. Word got around that two million dollars had been put up to beat him. Assuming that was true, it was money spent in a good cause maybe. If racetrack betting had been outlawed in Kentucky, the chance might never have come my way to leave the farm and sign up to be a jockey.

It was a different farm from the one I was born on. In 1928 we'd made a move from Stanton to a place outside of the little village of Midway that sits in the Bluegrass country about a dozen miles from Lexington, with even fewer people living there than there were in Stanton.

I believe there were at least two reasons for the change. My dad by working was getting worn and starting to look old, though he was some distance away from being fifty. Machinery was cutting down the labor in other kinds of farming, but growing tobacco still needed a lot of personal attention and work by hand.

The seed is so fine it has to be mixed with sand or ashes before it's sown, and half an ounce of it can grow into maybe forty thousand plants ready to be set out in the fields, young and delicate, after they've been given plenty of water and shaded from the sun while they sprouted, a job that lasts five or six weeks.

During that time, which brings you into May, you've done the plowing and the fertilizing, laying the earth off into furrows three or four feet apart. In those furrows, you pile up little mounds of earth every couple of feet or so, a mound for each planting. Then, on his hands and knees, a man can set two full acres between dark and dark.

Chopping out weeds and fighting bugs are a *must* as a daily routine and those were two of my chores. You don't want more than eight or twelve leaves on a plant, so you top the flower buds off as soon as they show and do the same to the suckers.

A leaf is ripe when it turns from dark to a paler green, when it will either crack or crease between your fingers. You pick them one at a time as they ripen, which they do from the top down over a matter of days. Then the wagons carry them to the curing barns astride a pole. We'd unload them there and spread them on the roofs to dry before they were hung up from the beams inside, with slow fires burning to raise the temperature as high as one hundred and fifty degrees.

The curing can last anywhere from five days to six weeks, depending on the method you use, and the fires must be kept going. When it's over and done with, the leaf's too brittle for stripping and sorting. So it has to be moistened before it's twisted into bunches of six to a dozen, called "hands" in the trade, all tied together with another leaf around the lower end. As a final step, you take the leaves to the warehouse for "sweating," which means fermenting, to make them ready for market.

This was the business my dad was in; it was no wonder to me that old age was creeping up on him like the tide.

He had a second cause for worrying. The war that ended when I was five years old taught a lot of soldiers to smoke, and after they came home, smoking spread as a national habit. That might have been bad for the health of a lot of people, but it meant growing more tobacco and the biggest crops of it ever harvested. Then the market began to drop and prices of the leaf took a nosedive.

My dad's cash crop wasn't bringing in enough cash for us to live on and it was time to move on, to better land in the Bluegrass, where growing tobacco might be a touch more profitable. The goodbyes were said to the landlord, Vic Dodge, and we started again at Midway, closer to the bloodstock farms than we'd been before.

One of the big men in town was the banker, J. M. Parrish, whose office stood across the street from the railroad depot; he liked to look out his window to watch what was going on over there. He also owned the biggest building in Midway, a stylish house painted in his racing colors, and he owned a stable of thoroughbreds, too.

I'd reached the point where I was eager to ride anything with a mane and a tail, but I'd never been on board a blood horse until I met Mr. Parrish. That came about when I rode in one day and spotted a train pulling into the station. I reckoned I'd done a fair job training the pony, so I was eager to test how he'd respond to the hissing and clanging of a steam locomotive. I took him right up beside it, and he didn't turn a hair.

Mr. Parrish was at his window on the lookout. He called me over to ask a question. "Seems to me you're quite some rider. How would you like to break a few yearlings for me, son?"

"Would if my dad agreed."

"Guess I'll have a talk with him."

It was soon settled, and I'd get paid for a job I'd have paid for myself if I could have afforded it. I'd go after school and over weekends. I was as happy a thirteen-year-old kid as you'd find anywhere in Kentucky.

The overseer for the Parrish farm was Howard Rouse, who'd be manager of the big King Ranch in Lexington later on in his life. We broke three yearlings that summer, working them in a big field of wheat while I schooled myself along with the horses.

That's when I got to ride my first thoroughbreds, and I loved every minute I spent on their backs. The feeling must have been infectious: my little brother, Bill, nine years younger, got the idea that he'd take after me.

The one thing schooling a horse and growing tobacco have in common is that both require a lot of patience and a lot of time, which I was more than willing to apply to horses, but not to fifty or so acres of tobacco and everything that went with that way of living.

You could call the time spent with Howard Rouse step number three in learning about horses. I had experience in riding and then in handling a team. Now I was picking up knowledge about treating young thoroughbreds when they went into training.

I'd never been one to abuse a horse, and I knew in my bones that I never would be. A yearling is like a baby in that respect: If it's brought up wrong, it's next to impossible to heal it without a tremendous amount of trying.

I learned fast that one of the most important things was to take it slow and easy. Gentle handling from the start can save a carload of trouble later. The first move is to slip on a halter for leading the animal. Then on goes the bridle, consisting of three pieces: headstall, cheekpieces, and bit, with reins added. If you nip his ears in the course of operation, you may make him head shy. Some old-timers followed the practice of unbuckling the bridle into its pieces, so the headstall could be put as a separate item, the bit into his mouth next, and the cheekpieces strapped pretty tightly to prevent him getting it under his tongue, which he's bound to try to do.

All of this is done with a few soft words and no hurrying, over and over again until he's used to the experience. Next, he has to get accustomed to the feel of a surcingle cinched up an inch or two at a time to hold a saddle pad on his withers.

He's dressed now for moving around in his stall as an introduction to meeting the world outside at the end of a halter. Once he's comfortable about wearing the equipment, it's time to saddle him, without the stirrups, because they can slap against his flanks and make him skittery.

You wait again until a saddle has been on him often enough so he's calm under it, then you hoist a boy on the yearling's back. In '26, the year that Albert Johnson got 20 percent of the winner's purse for jockeying Bubbling Over at Churchill Downs on Derby Day, I was the boy in the saddle of Mr. Parrish's horses.

Saddling is best done in the stall, where the animal's restrained and a boy's not so likely to be damaged. "Take it easy" is one of the working rules in a well-run stable; you're allowed to move fast under only two conditions: if the horse is about to kick you or set his teeth into your hide.

There's a standard bit of instruction to give the boy: "Don't let him throw you." If that happens, it can get to be a habit with horse and rider, and it's nothing to be tolerated in either one of them.

It's natural if you're like me and it's your first time on a promising horse to want to take off and go. But a yearling may not be of the same mind. You have to learn patience before the horse has the inclination to dump you. You wait and see until he says the day has come for him to be led out of his stall into an outside walking ring, with a groom leading him with a shank.

If he's taking note of his schooling so far, he's ready to learn to trot, circling left or right and then in loops around so he can do it in both directions. I already knew how to make yearlings turn, which is by changing your weight to the side you want to steer them and pushing on the opposite side with your hand and knee.

After the trot comes the canter, but you have to bide your time about the progress. Fighting a horse because he seems stubborn is never a good idea; you have to study him to understand his ways. If the breeder has it in mind to commit his yearling to racing, there's some time in store before the horse is ready for the track.

He's taught to step up the pace from a canter to a gallop, beginning slow. He has to learn how to behave with other horses, in the lead or abreast of them; to stop and wait; to turn inside or outside the others; to back up, because that's what he may be called on to do at the starting gate.

The solution to everything, I concluded back then, was care and kindness. I've never changed my mind about that conclusion.

At the age of fifteen, I was the right size, small, and the right weight, ninety-seven pounds, to have the build people look for in a jockey. Another owner in the neighborhood, John S. Ward, who shared Everglade Stables with Fred Burton, decided I was a good prospect. He said he'd be in a better position to judge whether I'd make a rider after he paid the freight for me to travel with him and some horses as an exercise boy to Saratoga and elsewhere on the circuit.

This was February of 1929, and I was in my second year of high school. I quit and never went back. When the trip was over, Mr. Ward just stuck a contract in front of my dad and me with the advice that, as a favor to both of us, it ought to be signed without dragging our feet.

3

The Weighting Game

There are people around that tell me I still walk like a kid jockey, five miles an hour easy, light and tight in the buttocks, but I'm not entirely convinced. I feel the drive slowing down, now that you have to go back more than fifty years to the day I signed to go to work for Mr. Ward.

The contract spelling out my job as "stable boy and rider" was saved as a souvenir, pasted on the first page of the scrapbooks Lucille started keeping not long after we were married. "Terms of said service," said the paper that indentured me, "shall commence on the first day of January, 1930, and shall expire on the first day of January, 1935 . . . age of said minor sixteen years, four months and no days."

I was sworn "to faithfully, honestly, and industriously serve said employer, to keep all his secrets, and to readily obey all the lawful directions and instructions of the said employer." My first year paid twenty-five dollars a month plus "suitable and proper board, lodging and medical attendance." The second year raised me to thirty-five a month, the third to forty-five. For 1933, it was sixty a month, and for 1934, seventy-five.

I left home knowing my dad felt sure I'd make a go of it, but I left my mother grieving. My sisters remembered it as one of the saddest days that had ever happened in the family. My mother wasn't one that always shared her feelings. It was a long time afterward when she said to one of the girls, "I've always been proud of him."

Between my quitting school and then signing up with Mr. Ward, there'd been some big changes in the way the country was going. Millionaires were jumping out of windows on Wall Street because they'd been wiped out in the Crash, and millions of people were suffering the pinch of poverty.

Some place down the road, my dad would be forced out of farming and driven to work in Lexington as a construction hand making twenty-five cents an hour. The slump in tobacco prices had played a part in moving us to Midway; but for that move, I wouldn't have met Mr. Ward. Now the slump in my family's luck made it a duty to send home what I could out of my pay—five dollars a month.

I'd seen a few real races during the months I was being tested for Everglade Stables, including my first Kentucky Derby. The winning horse and the trainer both bore the same name that year of 1929—Clyde Van Dusen. The animal was a little nine-hundred-pound gelding, sired by Man o' War, not much bigger than a pony in the opinion of its rider, Linus McAtee, who hadn't set eyes on his mount until he was in the paddock.

By far the best horse on the track was Blue Larkspur, owned by Colonel E. R. Bradley, a gambling man who'd bet on anything that could run, swim, or fly. But it rained and kept on raining, to turn the track to slop. The horse should have been shod with mud calks, but the blacksmith didn't think so, and Blue Larkspur finished fourth behind Clyde Van Dusen. In the jockey room, McAtee, who'd won in '27 aboard Harry Payne Whitney's Whiskery, reckoned the gelding was the sweetest little package of horseflesh he'd ever come across.

A jockey room smelling of sweat and cigarette smoke doesn't have much in the way of luxury, but it was like a dream come to life for me the first time I put on racing silks, the Everglade colors of red stars on white, with a red cap. When the valet snapped the collar around my neck as I was getting dressed, the thought crossed my mind, "They're going to hang me!"

First time out was on a Saturday the following September at Lincoln Fields, Chicago, the second race listed in the program that sold for a dime. My mount, Dodgson, was entered in the category of three year olds and up in a claiming race with a twelve-hundred-dollar purse. In the happy hunting ground of claiming, this meant anybody with a mind to do so could buy Dodgson at that price. In a storybook I would have won. But I didn't. I had to wait until winter for that.

I was picking up new habits and making new friends, one of them being a son of the boss, Sherrill Ward, who wasn't a lot older than I, and another in his older brother John, both due to become well-known horsemen. As for habits, I took up smoking, so I wouldn't be out of place among the rest of the jocks, and joined in rolling dice and playing cards for the same reason. My hard-shell Baptist grandmother wouldn't have approved if the news had been relayed her way.

Hearing some other green apprentices tell how they'd come to the racetrack added to my notion that I'd been lucky. After they'd applied to an owner or a trainer, he had gone ahead and checked out the whole family for size, so he wouldn't waste time and money on a boy who'd likely grow too big and heavy for the job. What was wanted before hiring was small bones matched by good health and strength and ambition to work with horses. If Mr. Ward had taken account of my sister Nora, he might have had reservations about signing me.

Jocks lived like part-time gypsies, traveling from track to track and putting up in boardinghouses that specialized in catering for them. Eating and drinking, and knowing when to stop under either heading, created a problem for some.

One of the tales that got passed around had to do with two riders known as Eatable Jigs and Eatable Pat. When you ate in a boardinghouse, you ate by the week, and the women who ran them charged eight dollars a week to board you. Neither Jigs nor Pat was very big, but they ate so much the landladies refused to open the doors to feed them. They were ruled off bed and board every place along the circuit.

But the chance came to arrange a contest, an eating contest, between them. The kitchen fixed them a mountain of pork chops and a whole big chocolate pie apiece. Jigs led from the start. He'd finished his eighteenth pork chop when Pat shoved his pie across the table to him, "Go ahead, hog; you win."

There was a darker side when work as a rider depended on the scales, forcing him to watch his weight closer than a fat man on a diet. One meal a day was the rule some of them chose to follow. Others stuck a finger down their throats after they'd cleared the plate, so the food wouldn't stay with them. Another method of shedding weight fast was to sit inside a sweatbox with steam rising out your ears until you were cooked dry and fit to drop.

Before American riders such as Tod Sloan introduced new styles over there, an all-time great on the English track was Fred Archer. He set records when he rode six winners in a day, two hundred and fifty-seven of them in a year, which doesn't compare with the performance nowadays of a jockey like Bill Hartack, or Chris McCarron, who scored five hundred and forty-six victories in his apprentice year. But Archer had such talent that they used to say he rounded Tattenham corner in the Derby course at Epsom Downs with one leg over the rail. Then the pounds he carried on his frame went up, and the number of mounts went down. In the end, he killed himself, as the best way out of his trouble.

Just how important weight might be is something that can be argued about all day, provided you've got time to spare. Some owners and trainers figure an extra pound can lose them a race. On the opposite side of the coin, they doubt whether adding sixteen ounces to a thousand-pound animal can make much difference. What you can safely count on is that any day on any track you'll see lightweight horses beat heavyweight horses and heavyweights beat lights.

To my way of thinking, that puts paid to the theory that by putting a few more pounds of lead weights on a good horse than you put on a no-go, you make them more or less equal prospects, without taking into account their condition, their class, the distance, and the riders. As a trainer, though, a stopwatch in my hand has meant more to me than the reading on the scales, although weight can't be ignored entirely.

The rules make that impossible. They specify just how much poundage a horse must carry and run with—jockey, equipment, and leads in a saddlebag when called for. In a claiming race, an entry with a poor record gets a weight reduction. In an allowance race, where a horse isn't up for grabs by a new owner, the extra pounds go on the back of the contender that's earned more or won more often in the past. It's the owner's legal responsibility to make sure the total weight carried matches the prescription. His horse can be disqualified if it runs too light. And on the other hand if it runs too heavy, that raises the weight assignment when it comes to handicap racing, when the track secretary sets the figure on the basis of the records kept to date.

There's a further twist to the tale. If it's an apprentice in the saddle, the amount of lead weight in the saddle pad is cut down to make up for his lack of experience. This was the edge that helped Chris McCarron set his record of victories when he was just two years out of high school. Losing it when a jockey graduates from apprentice into journeyman is what separates the men from the boys, the riders who continue to get good horses and those that have to scratch around for a living, staying hungry to hold their weight down.

I rode a couple of other races in Chicago that first year under contract, but got nowhere. Danny McAuliffe was our first-string jock; I was second boy and not very good at it either. Sherrill Ward took over from his father at Everglade when he was only twenty years old, but the friendship between us stayed warm.

That winter, we took some horses to Hialeah, which was the only track in Miami in those days. I weighed in at one hundred and seven pounds, ten more than when I'd started and a sign of things to come. Conditions around the country in general were going from bad to awful, and in Midway the family was hanging on, no more than that.

The date was the fifteenth of January, 1931, and the sixth race of the program was next. I was in the saddle on a filly I really liked, named Directly, waiting at the tape—this was before gates arrived on the scene—to take her over a mile and seventy yards. The odds on her were $17.85 to one. The horse to beat was Rosevolt; whether the name had any connection with the man who'd be voted in as President the following year, I don't know.

Leaving the jockey room, I'd handed Dick Meade, who was the valet, twenty dollars to put down on my filly. He thought so little of her chances that he had the temptation to hold on to my money, but a change of heart led him to the window.

Twenty dollars was a big risk when thirty-five was my pay for a month. But purses and the riders' share of them were so small that you almost had to bet to survive. Jockeys bet on the horse they figured to win, whether they were riding it or not. Today, that's a crime. Putting dollars down on a mount except his own can cost a jock his license. Five years' suspension was the penalty imposed on three of them by the racing commission in Maryland one day not so long ago. An earlier hearing was postponed because one of the three had tried to shoot himself to death. Five years with no work is a terrible punishment to take.

I let the filly open up as soon as they raised the tape. She was a length in the lead at the first quarter, then another length at the half mile. Down the backstretch she was still going strong when Rosevolt challenged her. She shook him off around the far turn to get two in front again at the eighth pole.

Another entrant, June Moon, took over from Rosevolt to challenge my lead. I laid on the whip as we headed for the finish. The filly was fading under me. June Moon tackled her, but it came a second or two too late. Directly's win by a nose took the race and I broke my maiden as a rider.

The closing price paid $37.70. That was on my mind, too, when I rode into the winner's circle. At the barn, I led her around the walking ring myself to cool her out before I handed her over to the groom. I'd just made $357 out of twenty. If I kept this up, I might pile up some real money for the family and me.

Booty Taylor, who was the stable foreman, dragged me down to earth. "Get in there and rake that ring."

"But I'm a jockey now, and I won today."

"You might be a jock in Mr. Ward's book, but you're still a punk in mine."

I rode Directly again one week later, took the lead, then lost it around the eighth pole to finish second. The best of riders can't win without having a willing horse, but Directly was willing, so the blame fell on me. The chart caller at Hialeah wrote that I "was of little help to her" as we came up to the wire.

That might have put a dent in some other punk's spirit, but not in mine. I was getting to know more about horses with every ride I made, and I liked them an awful lot. I took pride in my job, and my mother and my dad had pride in me.

If it hadn't been for betting on a winner now and then, it would have been hard to make ends meet and help out a little at home, even when you bought a pack of cigarettes for a dime. On the big-time tracks, you got paid fifty dollars for a win, forty for a place, thirty for a show, twenty for a loss. In the bush leagues, you might walk away with a five in your hand if you were lucky.

A 10 percent share of a winner's purse meant less and less as the size of the purses went on shrinking, as it did through most of the thirties. There was considerable distance between the $537,000 that Swale earned at Churchill Downs and the value to the '36 winner, Bold Venture, which was $37,725.

The green boys, the journeymen, and the big-name jockeys were mostly all cut from the same bolt of cloth. None of them tipped the scale at much more than a hundred pounds, and if they weren't tough when they entered the game, they soon toughened up or else they quit. Competition had a sharp edge on it when you lived on the border of poverty.

Betting on your own mount sharpened up the competition, and the tickets a trainer bought for you as an extra incentive made it keen as a razor blade. Some of those jocks showed willing to kill to win a purse, and top riders could be as rough as anybody—maybe rougher. They wouldn't let you by without brushing, bumping, squeezing. Or under heavy pressure, they'd let one of their own kind feel the whip as well as the horse that was under them.

The famous fighting finish of 1933 between two Derby jocks was a real example of rough and tumble. Herb Fisher was one, Don Meade the other, Fisher aboard a horse called Head Play, Meade on Broker's Tip. Fisher had taken the lead on the backstretch, then swerved out to cut off a challenge from a horse close behind. Meade pushed Broker's Tip through the gap that opened up on the rail, bringing the colt alongside Head Play. Fisher nudged his horse back toward the inside, an arm's length away from Meade. The battling was about ready to start.

Meade stuck out his right arm to fend off Fisher, who he figured was aiming to put him through the rail. Fisher responded by laying hold of Broker's Tip's saddle. Meade grabbed at Fisher as the two horses ran neck and neck into the stretch.

Meade won by a nose, which drove Fisher to reach out and whip him, then raise a complaint with the stewards that he'd been fouled. When they ruled they could only penalize both the riders or neither of them, Fisher burst out crying.

Meade left the winner's circle, a Derby winner at twenty years old, and headed for the jockeys' room to take a shower and change his clothes. Fisher jumped him, swinging punches, hollering his head off until a valet dragged him clear. The tears were still falling as he slunk off to the showers.

Don Meade grew up to be a great rider, one of the best, and a big gambling man besides. He covered the bases, as he thought, by betting against himself, but he got caught at it, and he lost his license. It was proved that he'd placed a lot of illegal bets. But not one of them was on a winner.

The fighting-finish Derby of '33 was shown on the newsreels with a sound track, since talking pictures, as we called them, had been around a few years by then. But cameras at the finish line hadn't appeared as yet. That was only one of a list of changes to come.

We didn't wear goggles back in those days, and there was no

testing, before a race, of every horse's blood and urine to check for traces of drugs, with the process repeated after the finish for the two that placed first and second.

They didn't use ponies then to take you to the post. I never rode with a pony alongside to keep my horse calm. If you couldn't gallop him up to the starting barrier that was made of crisscrossed webbing, you couldn't ride him.

There were no bars serving liquor at the tracks and there was only bootleg red-eye to buy until I'd turned twenty years of age. We had some horses at Pimlico at the time, and I walked into a saloon in Baltimore to buy myself a ten-cent mug of beer. Prohibition hadn't stopped quite a few jocks from turning into drunks. They survived as best they could, touting or panhandling or selling programs and pencils, winos with no place to go but the track. I've heard tell that one of them at least—his name was Carrol Shilling—was found dead one morning under a horse van parked on Hempstead Turnpike across from Belmont Park's main gates.

The horseplayers didn't have electronic tote boards flashing to tell them how the betting was going on every entrant, the payoffs on the previous winners, and the times in fractions of a second of the race in progress. Nor did they get instructions in a ten-cent program on how to place a bet at the window. Before exactas, perfectas, and quinielas came along, the assumption was that you wouldn't be there unless you knew how to put your money down and pick up your winnings, if there were any, without the tax man taking a bite.

I didn't like to throw money away, so I didn't bet heavy, and if I ran short, the Wards would advance me on my wages, on the understanding they'd be paid back a few dollars at a time if that was a comfortable way of doing it. I follow the same practice as a trainer because it was a kindness worth repeating.

Not every jock found it that easy when he was in the red. A run of bad luck when he'd bet his last shirt could push him deep into debt. If the word spread, then his luck might get worse, because trainers wouldn't hire him to ride for fear his creditors would pressure him to throw a race to help dig himself out.

Before there was a Jockeys' Guild and various kinds of charities to give help if you fell sick, one kind of insurance was for jocks to agree ahead of time that the winning rider would split a big purse with the rest of them. This was called "saving," which the rules now say is illegal, because it can blunt the edge of competition, but it goes on just the same.

I was never a "saver," and saving didn't enter the picture in another race I ran on Directly at Hialeah. One of the other jocks, Joe Bollero, was a friend of mine, and he still is. He'd been having trouble fighting weight, and he had no more money to burn than most of us did during the Depression. But he had a good mount in a filly named Watch Girl, and the price was right where he wanted it—close to ten-to-one. He reckoned that all he had to do was beat the favorite, Directly, eight-to-five.

He bet his bottom dollar, making a total of three hundred, on Watch Girl, then came up to me in the jockeys' room with three win tickets in his hand. "Here. Take one and make yourself a little cash."

I wasn't looking for that kind of deal. I owed it to my boss to do the best I could with his horse. "Not interested, Joe, but thanks, anyway."

The tape went up, and I started rolling. From the rail on the backstretch I heard voices hollering, "Go with her, Woody! Stay with it, kiddo!" Over my shoulder I saw Joe driving hard to catch me on the turn, but he wasn't going to make it. "How much you want to give me now, Joe?" I yelled.

I won by a head from Madelon. Watch Girl was running out of kick and had faded to third. As we rose in the stirrups to slow our horses, Joe gave me a shout. "I reduced for a week to ride this son of a bitch. I don't have to worry about that no more. I don't have nothing to eat *with.*"

I liked riding with my mind clear, thinking about nothing but getting first at the wire during the minutes and moments it takes to reach it. If anything's bothering you, you'll ride below your form, and you're in trouble.

One advantage some of the green boys have is that they're not wise to the risks involved, though stricter rules and the cameras have cut down some on the rough-and-tumble today. There were more pileups on the fences when I was a jock, because the traffic was thicker. When horses were packed in close, it wasn't hard to get away scot-free with hooking a heel into somebody else's stirrup or poking an elbow into his reins.

I'd guess there used to be more broken bones and worse than that in those days, though I don't know of any figures to prove it. But you had to be on the lookout for trouble when another jock might grab his chance when your horse had all four feet off the ground flying, and the other boy would give a push to knock you sideways.

I was glad I could concentrate on riding without worrying about a burden of debts or where the next meal was coming from or whether I'd get caught betting on a different owner's horse. And I felt content that I wasn't married yet when you saw how many jocks had trouble to contend with there, and you could judge the kind of life the wives were forced to put up with.

The run against Joe Bollero was the last race I won as a jock. I kept growing taller and gaining weight, so Sherrill Ward concluded I was better suited for only galloping horses. But trainers wanted exercise boys light; there weren't many around that weighed over one hundred and twenty pounds.

One morning in Chicago, I galloped a horse as usual. On the way back, I noticed Sherrill glaring at me. When I got off, he took me by the arm and led me to the scale. I stepped on it, and it hit one hundred and thirty pounds. He never said a word—just took me to the barn and handed me a rub rag. I was down to being a groom, not an exercise boy.

I got demoted in the last year of the contract, when I was being paid nine hundred dollars for twelve months' of work. That same year, Captain Harry F. Guggenheim bought six yearlings at Saratoga to launch a stable he called Falaise. It had no bearing on my life then, but it had a lot of impact later.

For the while, I decided to be the best groom there ever was in the world, to learn more about the care of horses, about the importance of their legs and feet, than any exercise boy or jock could ever know.

Sherrill didn't give up on me. He wanted me to make it, because he'd always liked me, and I him. He could have let me go when the year ended. If he had, I don't know what might have become of me. Instead, he said, "If you have a future in racing, it's in training, not riding."

I guess the luckiest thing that ever happened was for me to get fat. I didn't think so then, though. The biggest disappointment of my life at that time was the fact that I'd lost out at being a jock.

4
Making or Breaking

It's a whole lot easier to ruin a good horse than to train him to bring out his best, and a groom makes a big contribution either way. The best of them care for the animal in their charge like a mother tending to a young child, feeding him, bathing him, always with an eye open for the first signs of a sickness. They're patient, they're gentle, and they're kind.

The meatheads among them are a different story. If a boy's mind is set on the betting money he hopes to make and not on the condition of the horses in the barn, then he's useless, and he deserves his walking papers. There's a strong possibility he'll lose his temper and turn ugly when an animal acts up, as some do by their very nature.

Then you'll see the meatheads curse and kick and pummel them, snatching their heads and abusing them every way they can think of. That brand of treatment will do such damage to a horse's disposition that he'll never forget it for the rest of his days.

As a groom, you teach yourself to put up with prima donnas when you've got one on your hands, calming them down with a gentle word and a gentle touch. There's no gain in treating a champion like a champion and a loser like a loser. To a groom, every horse has to have the potential of being a winner someplace sometime, even if it isn't fit material for big-purse racing.

One way of getting the best attention for a horse from a groom is to pay a stable bonus, a percentage of the trainer's share of the purse. It's a practice of mine—1 percent. A boy on my payroll last year picked up ten thousand dollars in the course of a month, which for him was like striking gold.

The Wards worked along the same lines, so the seventy-five a month in contract wages got sweetened a bit at Everglade Stables. One day I had the hope I might have enough put by to go looking for a girl to marry; right then, I was engaged with horses.

The hours you spend with a rub rag in your hand are a surefire way of improving your education on the subject of horses, if that's what you count on doing. Contact as close as that brings you to realize as never before just how delicate a thoroughbred is.

"Delicate" might seem out of place as a word to apply to a creature that measures roughly eight feet from poll to croup, but lay your hands on the legs and ankles, and you know it to be true.

Now, a man is born with three main joints in the bones of his arms and legs—shoulder, elbow, and wrist in one case; hip, knee, and ankle in the other. A horse has an extra set. One of the thighs in its hind leg starts in the hip joint, set close to the buttocks then sloping forward, still out of sight, to link with the stifle. A second thigh, called the gaskin, goes down from there to meet the hock, which is like a man's knee except it swings forward instead of back. From the hock comes the cannon to join up with the ankle, otherwise known as the fetlock, where a much shorter bone, the pastern, goes to the hoof.

It's much the same in the foreleg. The first arm bone runs from the point of the shoulder inside the breast, down to the forearm that's joined to the knee, where the cannon bone takes over to tie in with the fetlock, and so on.

The pounding those ankles and legs suffer when a horse is going full out on a racetrack makes them the focus of your attention when you've the ambition to be the best groom the game's ever had. The condition they're in decides his value and performance as a runner.

The key factor here is conformation, the shape and structure of the limbs and body of the animal. I learned to look for a horse's legs to fit him right. I wanted him to have nice feet and come in the right size, because I didn't like horses too big anymore then than I do now. And in his pasterns he shouldn't be too big or too straight.

I found the length of an animal's back was worth studying, too, in its effect on his running. A back that's too long puts a swing in the gait that can result in cross firing, one leg hitting another and slowing him down. A short back out of balance with long legs can produce overreaching and scalping, two other defects that cause contact and interference when a horse is on the move.

Hoofprints provide a clue to potential trouble. Pigeon toes are inherited, and the crook might start way up in the chest or as far down as the fetlock, showing up as paddling, when the feet turn out over the outside toe. This can be corrected sometimes by the right trimming of the feet in a foal and the right shoes on a yearling. But a splay-footed horse that toes out all the time is usually beyond curing, since the legs are crooked from their starting point.

Watching a horse in action tells you most everything about his condition—that was one more lesson. A sore leg on one side leads him to limp, throwing his weight on an opposite leg. If he drops his right hip, there's pain in his left hind leg. If his head nods left, he's hurting in his right foreleg. Sore knees show up in spreading the legs wide apart. And you take oats left in the feedbag as a certain sign of something going wrong.

Your eyes and your hands are your best equipment for spotting the need for treatment or for rest. When you use them to check the legs and feet, working slow and careful, your fingers can detect the smallest degree of temperature change, telling you if there's fever in a joint, which is an early warning signal.

Some of the stuff in the medicine cabinet of a barn has changed since I was with Everglade, and some of it has not.

The antibiotics you buy on a vet's prescription weren't there, because they had to wait to be discovered for the treatment of people before they were used for dosing horses. But a lot of old-time remedies I remember from back then are still on the shelf today, like colic medicine, liniments, blisters, iodine, and leg paint.

We were slower then by a long shot about bringing in a vet. The stable took care of minor hurts and ailments on its own. If you felt you were out of your depth, you asked for help from somebody with more experience. A trainer who was fifty years old by then, Preston Burch, wrote once that "when a man hangs around the race track for a few years and gets so no-account that he can't make money enough to buy himself a square meal and has the respect of nobody, everyone calls him 'Doc.'" I've known that kind, too.

I'd signed on for five years with the Wards, and then I stayed two more, long enough to get my first printed credit as a trainer. I hadn't put on any more weight; in fact, I might have lost a pound or two. So I was galloping horses again, in particular one named Deliberator. We took him to the old Latonia Race Course on Pina Pike in Covington, a factory town in Kentucky where it's linked to Cincinnati by seven bridges crossing the Ohio River. The track was never in the same class as Belmont Park—for part of the year it was given over to harness racing.

Sherrill Ward told me that my name could go on the program: "It might do you some good." It had been five years since that had happened, and then I'd been listed as a rider. But there it was again: Deliberator in the sixth, "Trainer: W. Stephens." We won by a neck over Crowning Glory, and I'd got my feet in the water, preparing to swim.

I was warming up for something else, too. I'd been going home to visit my folks in Lexington whenever I could, which was none too often when you were on the move from track to track. Living stayed hard for everybody in the family. My dad was working twelve hours a day for next to nothing. No matter how hard he worked he couldn't make any money because there was none there to make. I saw him turning old from grief and poverty.

On one such trip I was introduced to a girl who lived two streets away. Raymond Norton's family were next-door neighbors of my own folks; he and some of my sisters had gone to Henry Clay High School together, walking two miles to get there. He took me over to this girl's house one day, saying, "Lucille, I have a buddy here I want you to meet."

We made a date to go to a movie. I thought she was a real nice-looking girl, but there wasn't the time to date her again because the winter racing season was rolling around, and I had to pack and take off for Florida.

Another year went by, and I'd forgotten her name when I made another visit to Lexington. She had a job downtown now, and from the front porch of our house I saw her get off the bus at the stop on the street outside. Getting up my courage, I went down and asked her if she'd like to go out with me.

She hesitated. "I don't think my mum and dad would let me, because I haven't really started dating yet."

That was enough encouragement for me. I went over to her house on a bicycle, the only set of wheels we had in the family, to ask her father. He owned a small garage and fixed cars there. He said she could, so we got to know each other during the next three months while I was breaking more yearlings. Then I took off for Florida again, and I wouldn't be back in Lexington until one more year had gone by.

This time, it was easy to remember Lucille Easley. I came back to her in the summer of '37, and we were married that September. I'd just turned twenty-four, and she was almost twenty. I got close to her brother Ralph, who still goes to see a lot of our races in Florida, to every Kentucky Derby, and to Saratoga for a few days every August. Lucille and I stood up with Raymond Norton when he was married, but he was killed in '42, out of luck while mine held firm.

Lucille had come up with nothing, just like me. Getting married, we didn't know which way we were going. She didn't have any money; neither did I. I just kept hoping we could make it, and she backed me every mile of the road, as she always has. But the thought of what might go wrong down the road ahead of us would cover the palms of my hands with sweat so I could barely hold them together.

With a wife to support, I had to look for a way of earning a better living than I'd found so far. I'd signed on with the Wards as a boy. Now I was a man, not a boy, and that line of type in the program at Latonia, "Trainer: W. Stephens," held a powerful appeal for me. Lucille pasted it in her first scrapbook as a kind of incentive. The Wards understood why I was striking out for myself, and I was on my own, make or break, for the next three years.

Lucille had lived in Lexington since she was three and had never known life on a farm. She knew nothing about horses either, but she was eager to learn, because we had a life to share. So I started teaching her everything I'd picked up on the road I'd traveled since the time I rode my pony. My feeling about horses rubbed off on her, which was a bonus; otherwise, she never could have understood why I wouldn't throw in the towel and find something easier to do than hang in, hoping our luck might take a turn for the better.

I had to scratch around for work to do like a squirrel digging for nuts. I broke yearlings at Keeneland for men like Bull Hancock and Russell Firestone. I kept my hand in with a rub rag as a groom. I'd gallop some beat-up horse for two miles, then when I got off, the trainer would give me five dimes. But I wouldn't admit to being licked, and neither Lucille nor I had a thought that I should go back begging to the Wards.

For one thing, that would mean I'd be gone for a long stretch of the year, and she wouldn't be going with me. She didn't want that any more than I did. I was twenty-four when we were married and Lucille nineteen years old. Sticking together was important while we shared the same ambition and could prove how much we cared for each other.

I called myself a trainer, but I didn't have a thing to train until a man named Earl Horn asked me to take a few cheap horses to Latonia and see what I could make of them. This looked like a break in the clouds, and I started figuring what I might do with that 10 percent of the purses which is a trainer's due. Number one would be to put a little more money into my family's hands besides the few dollars I was contributing right now. But there wasn't a winner to saddle among Earl Horn's string. I was still stuck down there at the foot of the ladder, with every rung of it waiting to be climbed.

We tried again with a couple of no-good animals, a two year old and a ten year old for two separate customers, vanning them from one bush track to another and always seeing them beat. I remember having them at Penn National in Chicago. We'd go over at night from our lodgings to tend to them after I'd been working at other men's stables all day. I'd graze the two year old while Lucille grazed the other, which was too old to be up to anything, anyway. She'd look up at me, and in the black of night I knew she'd be smiling. "We're having a lot of fun," she'd say.

I might have made more money then as a jock, picking up twenty-five dollars for a win, ten for losing, no percentages, and ten cents on the dollar for the agent. But though I was whittled down some, I still carried too much weight to ride.

Then in 1940 I hooked up with Steve Judge, who was somewhere past sixty and looked older, wrinkled like the bark of a tree. He came from Oakland, California, where he'd been a streetcar conductor and then a betting man before he took up training horses.

He asked me to take a three year old, Our Boots, to Hot Springs, Arkansas, and train him there for next year's Kentucky Derby. He'd no need to ask twice. Steve had an arrangement with Woodvale Farm, outside of Lexington, where Royce Martin, the owner, stabled somewhere around four hundred horses. I was onto some steady money at last, and I needed it bad.

The link between Steve and Mr. Martin dated back more than thirty years, to 1909 in Juarez, Mexico, where Steve was working horses and making his barn his home, as he always did. He slept there and cooked his meals there, and one morning he was fixing breakfast when a stranger, Royce Martin, came by.

"My, that coffee smells good."

Steve growled, "Help yourself."

Martin was a Texan and a character in his own right. He'd spent some time with the Mexican national railroad before he threw in with Pancho Villa, who ran a ring of cattle rustlers and carried a government price on his head, which was an incentive for him to join the revolution that was under way, aiming to change the whole form of government. Martin taught Villa how to write his name, ran guns across the border for him, helped him stash twelve million dollars away in Cuban banks. Martin was the only man Villa had enough trust in to let himself fall asleep when they were in the same room. Otherwise, Villa went to bed alone, with the door bolted and barred.

The two men stuck with each other for seven years, with a few interruptions, like the time Villa got captured but made his getaway to Texas. He came back to take over Mexico City, then was driven out to hide up in the mountains. Martin was the only gringo he respected, which was indicated when he led four hundred men up across the border with New Mexico to set fire to a town and kill sixteen people. It was around that time that Martin split from him, and when Steve and Martin's trail had already crossed.

They'd gotten into racing horses together—Tijuana purses were bigger then than they were in this country. They had a good horse entered in a race, and Villa bet a thousand dollars to win. Martin went to him with a suggestion: maybe he should up his stake to three thousand. Villa lugged two guns out of his belt and banged them down on the table. "Okay, but he'd better win." They scratched the horse.

Steve's bed was the hay in Martin's barn when he hired me. He could barely write his own name and nobody had ever seen him wearing a necktie. But Martin, on the other hand, had hit it big, making millions as chairman of the Electric Auto-Lite Company that put out every kind of part for automobiles, from spark plugs to wiper blades.

After three months in Hot Springs, I brought Our Boots back to Kentucky. We ran him in the Blue Grass Stakes at

Keeneland, and he whipped Calumet Farm's Whirlaway in winning it, which we hoped he'd do again on Derby Day.

The Calumet colt had a habit of running to the outside rail instead of holding a straight course and heeding instructions. That was why he lost to Our Boots, and we reckoned he'd lose again at Churchill Downs. But Warren Wright, who ran the farm on money inherited from Calumet Baking Powder, had a hotshot private trainer, "Plain Ben" Jones, out of Missouri, where he'd been raised in the company of horses and cattle.

Maybe it was because the war had already started in Europe and a lot of people were wondering how much longer we'd keep out of it, that they were enjoying themselves while they could. But whatever the reason, there was a record crowd at Churchill Downs in 1941 and a record count of guests from Hollywood—Lana Turner; Tony Martin; Robert Young; Don Ameche; a Derby regular, Joe E. Brown; and I don't know who else. All of them watched another record broken: Whirlaway won by eight lengths in two minutes and one and two-fifths seconds.

Ben Jones had run him with a blinker covering his right eye and taught him to breeze straight through an opening just a few feet wide. Eddie Arcaro, his jockey, called him "the runningest son of a bitch I ever sat on." That made the first Derby win for Calumet Farm, and Mr. Wright went on to win five more.

Our Boots finished eighth. Royce Martin gave it two more tries in his lifetime, which is another story I'll save 'til later.

Steve Judge cooked beans for his supper most nights before he bedded down in his barn. If he'd had a win that day, he'd toss out the beans and put a chicken in to stew. There was nothing more than beans on his plate that Saturday night.

He was as tough and mean as they come, with owners and animals alike. He ran a colt of Martin's at Saratoga one day. The horse dumped the boy at the gate, tore off down the track, and cut his leg. Now, when Steve got mad, he'd tell the groom, "You go to the barn and fix some water to give him a bath; I'll bring him home."

That's what he said this time after they'd retrieved the colt.

He took hold of the horse and whipped him right in front of the Saratoga clubhouse. Martin wasn't there, but he turned up at the barn a couple of days later. He took a look in every stall until he found this colt.

"Steve, they tell me you worked this horse over pretty good with everybody watching you from the clubhouse."

The old man looked hard at him. "They told you, did they? If you'd been sitting up there, you'd have seen it, and they wouldn't have had to tell you." He wouldn't back off of Martin, and Martin wouldn't back off of him. But Steve could train horses to go any distance, long or short, and Martin wasn't the only owner who respected him for it.

As an independent operator picking and choosing whose horses he'd take, the old man didn't like being tied down to anybody or tethered anywhere too long. I was *his* assistant, not Mr. Martin's, so his ups and downs were mine, too. He took such little care of himself that every once in a while he'd be feeling so bad he thought he was falling apart. Then he'd drop everything and duck out for Hot Springs to soak himself in the baths there until he considered he was back in shape. When he showed up again looking for horses, he'd always found them—he was that good at the game.

But the years were piling up on him. After his latest trip to Hot Springs, with Mr. Martin picking up the tab, Steve was beginning to run out of horses. I told him it was time for me to move on; he couldn't afford to keep me. I got a glare and a growl: "I'll let you know when."

Then one afternoon he said, "Woody, you be here tomorrow and make sure you have your suit on." In those days, if you had a suit, you were lucky, but I did have one. I was wearing it and I had a tie on, though he didn't, when he walked me up to the clubhouse.

He'd heard of an opening for an assistant to Ross Higdon, who was the trainer at Woolford Farm that was owned by Herbert M. Woolf, a big gambling man out of Kansas City, where he was in the clothing business. He was also into politics, in the same school where Boss Tom Pendergast and Harry Truman had been in during their younger days.

Plain Ben Jones had worked once for Mr. Woolf when he had a colt, Lawrin, that he was heading for the 1938 Kentucky Derby provided Ben would solve the problem of the horse's sore feet. He brought in a blacksmith and a set of heavy bar plates. The shoes did the trick in the Derby trial, when Lawrin placed second. Then for the main event Ben had him reshod with lightweights as the next step in the treatment. Lawrin made it first to the wire, with Dauber second and a show for Can't Wait, owned by Myron Selznick, the Hollywood agent and brother of David, who was up to his ears making *Gone with the Wind*.

Owning a racehorse or two got to be a hobby with a lot of Hollywood people, including Fred Astaire, after Louis B. Mayer went into racing, and mixing with movie stars was one of Herbert Woolf's hobbies—he'd had a hand in getting Jean Harlow into the picture business. Ginger Rogers was sitting with him in his box when Steve led me up to be introduced.

"I understand you want an assistant to Ross Higdon," he grunted. "I recommend this man."

All Steve had to do was open his mouth and put in a good word for you, and people listened. The job was mine there and then.

Ben Jones had been gone from Woolford Farm for quite a while by now, off to a much bigger job with Warren Wright at Calumet. Like most owners, Mr. Woolf wanted to win them all. On top of that, he bred his own horses, so every foal looked good to him. He had sixty-five head in his barns in 1942, but none of them amounted to anything, in my opinion, and the blame rested on one man's shoulders—Ross Higdon's.

As a trainer, he didn't come within a mile of Ben Jones. Higdon chewed tobacco, and his ulcers plagued him more than indigestion did me. He trained every animal as a sprinter, and they couldn't get a route. They all carried as much flesh on their bones as yearlings vanned home fresh from a sale. In other words, he was what's called a Sunday trainer, too easy with his horses, making them too soft for a hard track.

A better man would have worked them harder to get the fat off them and build endurance. He'd have stretched their speed a notch at a time and brought out the tiger in them, if there was any. I said, "What the hell, I've learned more about this game than he has," but I said it to myself. He was my boss, and talking to him was like shouting down a well.

In the two years I stuck it out, Woolford Farm didn't have one decent stakes win. Somewhere along the line, I got called to take the medical that's required before you go into military service. I wasn't accepted to fight in the war because the doctors found a peptic ulcer. I could guess where it had come from —aggravation. But it was luckier than owning a suit and tie.

Mr. Woolf soured on the business as a losing proposition and decided to split the stable, sending Ross Higdon to Hialeah, me to New Orleans. I wasn't too sorry. I'd never seen eye to eye with Higdon, but I didn't blame Steve Judge for getting me the job.

In 1944 I quit Woolford Farm. I was getting nowhere, dead in the water. An offer came up from somebody named Earl Snyder, another job as an assistant, this time in Chicago. I took it, and Mr. Woolf didn't hold that against me. When Christmas came, he sent me six ties, six shirts, and a light raincoat. The same thing happened every year until he died in 1964.

I was coming home with three hundred and a quarter a month from the Snyder job, and it was as big a bust as working for Higdon had been, with not a horse on my hands worth its weight in corn. Then the sun came up. I met a man named Jule Fink, a professional horseplayer out of Cincinnati who reckoned he knew how to win with some horses of his own, so he was starting to buy.

Would I train them for him the way he wanted them? It would mean saying goodbye to Chicago, hightailing it to New York, and signing a contract for a thousand dollars a month.

"I'm your man," I said to Jule. "I'll take a shot at it."

5

The Speed Boys

The buildings on the skyline across the Hudson River looked awful tall to Lucille and me as they swung into view through the window of the train that was bringing us in across New Jersey from Chicago. We didn't have a guess in the world about what might happen to us in New York City, but we'd have to work fast, because all we had between us was four hundred dollars, and maybe the new job was too good to be true.

So it was a case of make or break, my first try at being top hand in a stable. I'd had some doubt about Jule when he told me what he had in mind. A trainer gets 10 percent of the purses. But Jule said, "I'll give you 15 percent of first money, but I don't want you telling anybody. The extra five is for you to bet with."

"I don't know whether I'll make it with him," I'd said to Lucille. "This man's a gambler."

"So what if it doesn't work out, Woody? You can always go back to what you've been doing."

But I couldn't, not if I wanted to have respect for myself. So far, I'd been only an assistant. This was 1944, and I was thirty-one years old. I figured I had a better-than-average touch with horses. What I needed was a chance to prove it.

We carried our bags out of Pennsylvania Station and checked into a cheap hotel room until we could find a place to rent, which wasn't easy when the war was going on. A few things were clear to me. I told myself, "If you come to New York and you don't hit, you'll fall flat on your face. A million people have tried, then had to get out and go back to Kentucky or New England or wherever it was they came from. But test yourself here and do well, then you will have *arrived*. You'll be in the big league, like playing for the Yankees." It was worth taking a chance with Jule.

He was a thickset little feller who stood a touch shorter than me, and he was smart as a whip. When he was twenty years old, he'd taken ten cents in carfare from his mother and parlayed it into thirty thousand dollars in a span of ten days, most of it by betting the right horses with pool-parlor bookies in his hometown. His secret was to spend hours and days studying form in the racing charts. What he went for were horses with plenty of speed.

Now, speed didn't have as much attraction for horseplayers and trainers back then as it does today. Endurance and stamina ranked higher in importance, and those were the qualities horses were bred and trained for. The distance of ground to be covered was mostly longer, too. Races lasting a mile and a half like the Belmont Stakes are a rarity now, when a majority of them are measured in furlongs, an eighth of a mile or two hundred and twenty yards, and some maidens cover only five furlongs for a purse of eighteen thousand dollars.

These distances used to be counted as no more than sprints when I was a kid warming up to start, and they were reckoned to be one reason for the shortage of good American riders at that time. A book on the subject put it this way: "The prevalence of the sprinting distances makes judgment of pace, generalship and similar qualities ineffective amid the general scrambles that ensue." The same book also blamed the fact that "the American weight scale is so low that riders of matured skill and experience become virtually outlawed from the saddle just when their skill is growing most assured, because of their excess weight."

I could say amen to that.

The average distance got shorter when the racetracks stretched their programs from six or seven to nine or ten races a day, and there may be some connection between those changes. Most everybody at present looks for a quick turnover of his money—owner, trainer, gambler, speculator, track management all alike. Put it all together, and you know where the stress on speed comes from.

The surface of the track itself is faster, too, as a general rule, though one may vary from another by a full second on your stopwatch, and there's always somebody seeking a way to make the footing faster yet. Just open up a record book and see how many of them were broken after the war ended. Then give a thought for Man o' War hauling one hundred and twenty-six pounds over eleven furlongs at Belmont Park in 1920, when I was in knee pants riding my pony. The big chestnut stallion did that in two minutes and fourteen plus one-tenth seconds. Fast tracks or not, no horse has ever matched that performance.

Jule concentrated on figures, the percentage of horses that went to the lead and stayed there without wilting. He called himself "speed-conscious," and that's what counted most in his book. He didn't give a lot of attention to the distance a horse was trained for, when that was what horsemen usually talked about.

"I'm a bettor," he told me, and he made no bones about it. "You won't win 'em all, but you've got to win some to stay in business."

I figured I'd be good for him and he'd be good for me. I'd learn the value of a horse, what made him win, what made him lose. I'd profit from the experience, while I was pulling down more money than I'd ever seen.

Lucille and I never had lost the habit of watching what we spent. We thought if we had a couple of dollars to spare to go to town and see a show, we were in pretty good shape. We didn't have children, and now I was with Jule we felt we could spread ourselves. We found an apartment in Jamaica, empty because the tenant had been drafted. We did the rounds of the sights and the shops of Manhattan, taking it all in like a couple of kids.

Handicapping was Jule's game, and by the standards of those

days he was a master at it. If there was such a thing as perfection in the matter of professional handicapping, the whole field in a race would reach the wire in a photo finish. Of course that's never happened and never will, because there are so many variations it's impossible to calculate them; so the outcome of any event can catch everybody off base except those who've backed a long shot for no valid reason.

At Belmont Park, by the grandstand lounge on the second floor, there's a spot they call Handicapper's Corner, where they post, day by day, up-to-date workouts, charts, and a sample of past performances of the entrants on the program, all this for the benefit of the players. It's some kind of help in deciding to bet or not to bet, but you need to dig a lot deeper before you come to a decision, so you can leave the racetrack with more money than you brought there.

Somebody once listed the main factors that go into smart handicapping: the distance, the pace, the track, weight and current form, the rider, the class and sex of his mount, the way the horse looks and behaves in the paddock, the stable he's out of, and who trained him.

The item on the list to pay the most attention to is the horse. The best trainer in the world can't show a consistent pattern of winning unless he has good animals, and the best jockey can't win without a good horse under him. The horse knows when he's ready to go, and the trainer has to let him tell him.

So betting on trainers is bound to empty your pockets in the long run or maybe sooner, and the same goes for betting on jockeys, though there's one simple fact to be weighed in the scales—the best trainers are likely to get the best horses, and so are the jocks who are hot in a particular string of seasons, although some of them fall out of fashion with the owners for no worthwhile reason.

Handicapping comes down to guesswork, because of the variables and uncertainties involved when you've got a big field running one against the other at close to forty miles an hour. But in the case of a sound handicapper, it isn't blind guessing. He has packed all the available facts into his head and weighed them up before he walks to the window. The smart bettor puts his money down only after he's found the right horse in the right race with the right man in the saddle. And the key word in all of this is consistency, of the animal, the trainer, and the rider.

When I went with Jule, I wasn't exactly sure how to place horses or pace them or claim them and step up their class, stretch out their speed. Claiming them was Jule's way of building Marlet Stable. I guess he paid a total of fifty thousand for them in the course of time, and he sold out for three hundred thousand in the end. Other men, like Buddy Jacobson, who led the field in winners saddled in '65, picked up the trick, but Jule was some sort of pioneer.

He was in business as what's called a halter man, which is like holding a legal license to buy horses from somebody else's barns at prices you look for in a fire sale. The rules provide that any horse in a claiming race can be bought by an accredited horseman at a preset figure.

He kept his eyes glued to the condition books that the tracks put out to specify the races coming up in the next few weeks, the purses, the weights, the distances, the age and past performance of the horses eligible, maidens, three year olds, three year olds and upward, and so on, including the closing date for entries. A typical limitation might say: "Nonwinners of two races at a mile or over since August 1 allowed three pounds; of such a race since then, five pounds"; this would be for a run early in September.

Logic tells you that if you own an animal you value at ten thousand dollars, you don't enter it in a five-thousand-dollar claimer, not even when the purse is, say, twelve thousand, because, win or lose, you're obliged to sell that horse to anybody that wants him. But you may have concluded, on his recent form, that he isn't worth the ten thousand you paid for him, so you're out to unload him for the five thousand to cut your losses.

By his study of the charts, Jule had a shrewd idea of when to move. It was my job to take the bargain he bought and work to improve its class. Then next time out, we planned to win with it. I stayed with him two years and three months. During that time, I clocked up one hundred and fifty-seven victories, including my first stakes win—Saguero in the Excelsior at Aqueduct in '44.

We were hitting at just the right moment. The war poured big money into the racetracks, and things were turning around from what they'd been in the darker days. Rosie the Riveter and everybody else who worked in a defense job finished the week with a fat pay packet, and the betting rose higher and higher. Not all the cash was earned the hard way. Shortages of what you were inclined to buy, and the rationing coupons you needed, were the foundations of a black market. A lot of those dollars came to the racetrack. The Mafia began to get a hold in the business, too, making some of the owners a cut different from what they'd been before.

Jule and all of us who followed him to the betting window got tagged with a label, the Speed Boys. Nobody could remember anything quite like us, and the New York racing crowd has the reputation of being the shrewdest in the country.

Because I'd been raised to value money, I was still putting some aside as savings, never investing it, since I knew less about investments than Lucille did about horses when the clergyman married us. But I was laying out that extra 5 percent betting money that came with the contract, and it was paying off dividends, though I doled it out more like glue than water; twenty or fifty dollars was my range of gambling. But I had no need to get down heavy when Jule's figuring indicated a horse we entered in any race had a better-than-average chance of winning.

I respected what he contributed, and he had similar regard for me. He used to say, "Woody keeps his antenna up. He's got the eye and the touch for a horse. He can feel around with his hands and find any problem straight off, then know just when to back off and when to go on."

I needed help in the stable, so I hired a boy named Eddie Neloy, who was coming up the hard way, just like me. He too had been a dropout in his second year of high school. He'd gone to work as a hot-walker, cooling horses off after they raced, then as a stable hand and a groom, paid a dollar a day.

When jobs around the barns got scarce, he washed dishes as a pearl diver in the track kitchen in Detroit. He was pulled into the service, but they let him out early—when I took him on as foreman, he was missing an eye; he'd lost it at Anzio in Italy, as a gunner facing German tanks. But there are good horses with a similar problem, and Eddie proved to be a good man, one of the very best.

Toward the end of '44 we decided, Jule and I, to ship eighteen horses out to California and race them there. When I started in the business, horses traveled for the most part in vans, and it took long days to carry them between racetracks. By now, a lot more roads had been built, but then cross-country highways laid down by the government were still few and far between; horses went by rail.

Lucille and I took the train to Los Angeles with Jule and his wife, Ethel. Our timing was off. The men in Washington concluded that too many people in defense work were putting in too much time and spending too much money at the betting windows instead of concentrating on the job to be done. Every track in the land was shut down until further notice.

So we had eighteen horses out there and nothing to do but rest them in the hope there'd be some racing again in the spring. We'd go out in those orange groves and pick grass with a taste just like celery; horses get served celery in a stable for dessert. They'd chomp on that grass while the juice dripped out of their mouths.

With no choice in the matter, we set out to take a vacation. My regular salary was still paid month by month, so we rented a place in Arcadia; saw the Rose Bowl game; watched them make movies at studios like MGM, where the boss, Louis B. Mayer, was spending millions buying high-class horses in this country and in Europe to build up his California stable. We had a lot of time to kill, and we got awful restless.

I wasn't much struck with California at that time, and I've rarely raced at Santa Anita or Hollywood Park since, which puts me in a class different from other trainers like Wayne Lukas, who flies his horses between Los Angeles and Kennedy Airport on a schedule about as regular as TWA's. There's almost always enough racing here in the East to keep me satisfied.

We left California as soon as spring came, traveling Pullman aboard the California Limited out of L.A., with two carloads of animals, destination New York. The Germans in Europe would start surrendering a few days from then, but the fighting in the Pacific, at Okinawa, was still going hot and heavy. It was slow going when troop trains heading west had the right of way. There was a change of trains to be made in Chicago. I was stretching my legs in the station when I heard the radio: Franklin Roosevelt was dead from a heart attack.

About this time, the government ban was lifted, and the tracks reopened, one or two at a time. The twenty-first of May was the day at Jamaica. In the second race, we had Tarpan, claimed for forty-five hundred dollars the previous year. He shot out of the gate and led at every pole. I don't recall exactly how much Jule had riding on him, but Jule never hesitated to get a couple of thousand dollars down on the right horse.

Eddie Neloy had already trained his first horse and saddled his first winner at Narragansett when he came to me as foreman; then he got the itch to be moving on, bitten by the same bug as I, the urge to reach the top. He lived rougher and maybe drove himself a shade harder than I, but otherwise I could see only one big difference—he'd always been too big to be a jock.

I found another man fresh out of the service to fill his shoes —my brother, Bill. I think I cinched his ambition to get into the game and make some money at it when he reached thirteen and I bought him a bicycle out of my earnings as a rider. He was a great boy, but I wanted him to have more schooling than I. I offered to help him into college like my little sister Anne, but there was no holding him back. He'd come to me first when he was sixteen and Lucille and I were living in Chicago, racing cheap horses on tracks like Homewood and Washington Park. Bill had never learned to gallop horses, but he'd been an awfully hard worker, doing a great job as a groom.

Then his draft number had come up, and he was scheduled for Fort Warren, Virginia, for basic training. Steve Judge had noticed what my brother was making of himself, and the old man's parting words to him were encouraging: "When you come back, don't ask me if I need a man. Just pull off your coat and go to work."

As a G.I. he'd been lucky enough to draw tanks—a gunner. After six months or so, they gave him a furlough to come home because he was going overseas. Then he was on a troop train, traveling, not a man on it knowing where he was headed for—the Pacific, Europe, or maybe someplace else.

When they pulled into Chicago, he had the answer. He knew the town, and he knew the racetracks there. They were coming east not west, due to fight in Europe. They were brought into New York and put on the *Mauretania*, fourteen thousand of them.

They'd go to bed, wake up, and they'd still be going no place. Then finally they sailed. He spent maybe a year in camp in England and at two o'clock one morning, the voice of Eisenhower came over the speakers: We're going to France; there'll be no turning back.

Bill went ashore in Normandy on D-day-plus-two, forty-eight hours after the first landings, to go with Patton's Third Army that was made up about twelve miles inland. He fought with them all the way through, and when it was done, he was too young to have enough points to get out.

Then that thing happened that changed the whole picture and the whole world, too. I heard about it from a groom who'd been tuned in to a radio. He came up running. "They just dropped a big potato on Japan."

So the soldiers got shipped back as fast as possible, and Bill arrived at Fort Knox, Louisville. They put him on a three o'clock bus that stopped in Lexington that Christmas morning of '45. I was in Kentucky for the first time in three years, so I drove downtown to pick him up, and we walked in through the door of the house together.

We had a lot of talking to do, and I admired what he'd done. But then I wasn't sorry the Army hadn't gotten me. A letter had come from the draft board about a year earlier: Get into defense work or you'll be in olive drab. But there'd been no answer when I sent in a doctor's certificate confirming I had an ulcer beyond any doubt. So I reckoned that had been my luck, getting the jump on some other young trainers who were just coming back from the war.

Steve Judge's offer to take on Bill as soon as he was out of uniform had run out, not because the old man had had a change of heart but because the years had finally caught up with him, and running any kind of stable was more than he could handle. So Bill was available for Marlet, and he made a first-class groom to two of our best horses, Pucka Gin and Jazz-rail, doing the job so well you'd never suspect there'd been a break in his career.

We didn't keep contract jockeys at Marlet Stable. Any good journeyman in the saddle could usually perform up to snuff when he had a horse under him whose speed had been stretched. We didn't hire duds, though, or get caught with one the way Jimmy Jones, Plain Ben's son, did one day after he'd saddled a horse at Hialeah. He took a look at the odds spelled out on the tote board. "The horse can't be that bad," he said to the jock. "It's got to be you that's sixty to one."

What we did keep ourselves in when I was at Marlet were some classy clothes. Back then, you could have a nice suit made for fifty or sixty dollars. I caught on to the idea that you left a better impression on people if you didn't dress sloppy. So Jule and I would go to a tailor, Billy Williams, and order the finest sets of threads you could buy, at a hundred and fifty a crack.

I bought fancy hats from Cavanaugh's at Forty-fourth and Park—and threw one of them away without flinching. I was running a horse, Away Away, in the Cowden at Belmont Park and not really counting on him winning. It was first time out for the Cavanaugh fedora I was wearing, and ten minutes before I saddled, the rain came down like nothing you've ever seen. I was dripping water when I got to the clubhouse to watch him run. The track was as sloppy as a pigpen. He loved it, and he won. I took off for the winner's circle. Somebody yelled, "Woody, you've ruined your hat." I whipped it off my head and skimmed it at the crowd. "I wear them only once, anyway."

That happened in 1950, when the Marlet years were over, but their effect on the whole business of racing was as permanent as though the record had been chiseled in stone.

In 1945 Jule and I had the show on the road, and we were rolling, making money hand over fist. Besides Tarpan, we had Adelphia, claimed for five thousand dollars and another steady winner once I'd stretched his speed. Timgad, His Jewel, Wise Admiral, and Herodotus. Huntsman, First Gun, White Wine, and Old Grad. Ringoes and K. Dorko. We had enough horses to keep us working our tails off to find the right slots for them and make sure they were in top condition.

The thirtieth of August at Belmont Park was the best day the Speed Boys ever had. I saddled three winners on the card: First Gun paid $16.30, Herodotus $8.50, and Huntsman $11.70. Since opening day, we'd cleaned up on twenty-eight races.

There're always a lot of sore losers around, and sore losers get suspicious. The word was spreading that at Marlet Stable the fix was in. Nobody came flat out and claimed that we were using dope to win—we could have proved that was a lie. Nobody said our jocks were using the tricks of the trade to get the horses first at the wire, which was no way true. Nobody with an ounce of brains in his head could have believed we were paying off owners or trainers or jocks, because in a field of maybe ten, you'd have to buy too many people to make sure of the result.

What the doubters and the Dismal Dans wouldn't accept was the truth that Jule was playing it a little bit smarter than most, and I was putting everything I knew into getting speed out of a horse.

After those three wins in one August afternoon, I got my first and only call in a lifetime of training from the stewards of the Jockey Club. The man facing me was Marshall Cassidy, executive secretary of the club and a brother of George Cassidy, the Belmont Park starter. He wanted to know about Huntsman, a colt we'd claimed for six thousand dollars after he'd been trained for Belair Stud by Sunny Jim Fitzsimmons. The colt had a bowed tendon, and I'd put a lot of time and thought into improving him, changing his shoes as part of the

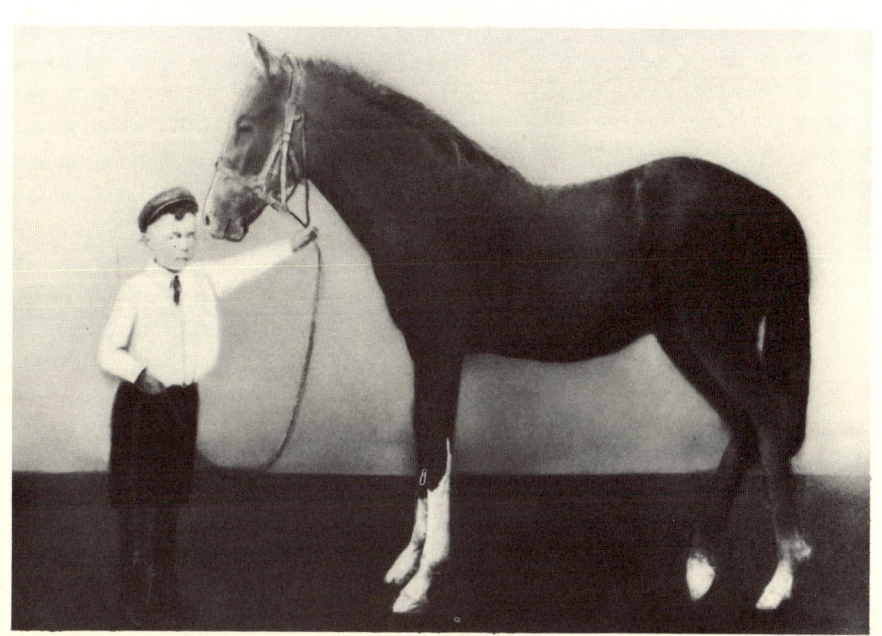

The first of them I could call my own, Bill, the pony, a present from my grandfather for my sixth birthday.

My dad and my mother, Lewis and Helen Stephens.

The Speed Boys in 1944. The other man is Jule Fink.

Hialeah, January 1930. I was sixteen years old, and I rode my first winner here.

With Lucille in New Orleans, 1942. Royce Martin's Bay Port won the Rue Royale.

Lucille and I in Lexington, 1946.

In the winners' circle, 1949, with owner Royce Martin and rider Conn McCreary. I've forgotten who the lady was.

Blue Man won the 1952 Preakness at Pimlico. Here he is, Conn McCreary aboard, with owner Arthur Abbott and his wife, who liked to feed his horses sugar cubes.

President Truman presented the trophy when Bald Eagle set a track record to win the 1960 Widener. Left to right are George Widener, the President, jockey Manuel Ycaza in front of Lord Derby and Captain Harry Guggenheim.

Bill Shoemaker on Captain Guggenheim's Never Bend after a two-lengths victory in the 1962 Futurity at Aqueduct.

The 1962 Futurity. James Cox Brady hands the trophy to Mrs. Guggenheim. The Captain and I stand by.

Here's Cannonade, covered in roses, in 1974 after Angel Cordero rode him to win my first Kentucky Derby.

Princess Margaret at the mike after Cannonade's 1974 victory at Churchill Downs. I'm with Lucille, next to Lord Snowdon, Mrs. Lynn Stone, Kentucky Governor Wendell Ford, and Lynn Stone, president of the track.

process of getting more speed out of him. He'd gone into that race at eighty-to-one, and the Speed Boys had gone down heavy and made a real killing.

"I noticed a big reversal in form in that colt today," said Mr. Cassidy. "How do you explain it?"

I wasn't looking for a long discussion. "I said, 'This isn't much horse, and I can prove it.'"

"How do you intend to do that?"

"Run him in a claimer and see what happens."

I let up on his training and waited a few days before I entered him in a claiming race at thirty-six hundred dollars, which he lost. His new owner fancied he'd picked up a real bargain. But with a bowed tendon, Huntsman never did well for him, and the Jockey Club had nothing more to say to me on the subject.

But anybody with a nose enough sharp could smell bigger trouble ahead in the wind. Not all of Jule's share in Marlet's winnings stayed with him. A friend of his who ran a restaurant in Cincinnati had always had part of Jule's play. Then the Army got him, and Jule told him before he checked in for duty, "While you're gone, you've still got 10 percent of my play whatever I do." So when the boy came back from the war, Jule felt obliged to pay him a fat bundle of cash, as a debt of honor.

He used that money to expand his restaurant, including a back room where he started booking horses, but Jule didn't see cause to break off the friendship, and a time bomb started ticking under our feet.

That winter of '45, we found some doors being shut in our faces. We applied for stall space in Miami and California. "Sorry. None available. All sold out." So we were compelled to stay on in New York without a race to run in because the season was over.

Spring blew in and we were back in business. We hung on through the summer, but the reception we were getting was cold as ice. I was at the point where I was scared to win and scared to lose. If I won, we were stealing. If I lost, we were cheating. It was a hell of a situation to be in.

There wasn't a shadow of doubt when winter was on the

way that if we aimed on heading for Florida or California again, we'd be going there as tourists. At the stables, the bars would be up to keep us out. So Jule concluded he had to sell. When he added up his profits from disposing of the horses—about a quarter of a million—plus the purses and his betting wins, he came up with a figure of around a million dollars, made in two years and three months. I'd gone in with four hundred. By Lucille's reckoning, and she's good at arithmetic, we had seventy thousand to our name now.

But I'd gotten a name for being a gambler, which I didn't deserve. People doubted I was on the up and up. I knew I had a fight on my hands to get that reputation off my back.

As things turned out, I had it easy, where Jule had it hard. The Jockey Club got after him on account of his friend who took bets in a back room in Cincinnati. Jule's license was lifted, which lost him the right to run any horse of his anywhere.

6

The Rules of the Game

The kingpins of the Jockey Club claimed the final word on everything concerned with racing in those days. They held so much power in their hands that nobody dared say boo to them.

No animal foaled in this country, Cuba, or Mexico was allowed to run on an American track unless it was listed in the American stud book under Jockey Club rules. The name of the horse needed approval by the club, too—no more than eighteen letters, no "suggestive, vulgar, or obscene meanings," and fifteen years of waiting if an owner wanted to duplicate a name that had been used before.

Everybody around the tracks—owners, trainers, jockeys, and handlers—had to have a license. The club decided who should have one, or lose it, under a law passed in Albany in 1934. If the stewards judged a man to be "undesirable," and the appeal board's decision went against him, then he had no place to go but home to look for some other line of work.

They took back Jule's license on the charge of "associating with gambling groups to the detriment of the best interests of racing." Nobody in fifty years had the gall to take the stewards to court to challenge any such ruling. Jule did, with the lawyer pushing his case, Charles H. Tuttle, who'd once run for governor of New York, the job that Thomas E. Dewey was doing then.

Jule appealed to the state's supreme court; he was turned down. He tried again in the appellate court, and he got thrown out. It wasn't until March of '51 that he won on his third try; the appeals court reached a decision that changed the ground rules of racing.

Every judge on the court agreed that the Jockey Club's power to give or withhold a license ran contrary to the Constitution of the United States. It was illegal, so it had to be dropped.

The club cried "foul." The decision, it said, would spell the end of racing in New York by letting anybody run a horse, and nobody would know whether or not it was a dirty business loaded down with crooks.

Governor Dewey and his crew found a different way of handling licenses. A state racing commission, with a licensing bureau answering to it, would take over to keep a rein on all the people involved in the racing of thoroughbreds, from those who owned them to those who mucked out the stalls. Anybody who broke the rules would lose his license and be ordered off. The Jockey Club would still keep tabs on the horses, since Constitutional rights didn't apply to them, and the door of the bureau was open for members of the club to enroll, which some of them were quick to do.

Not much was really changed by the time the dust had settled. The power of the club in itself was broken, but the licensing regulations stayed in place, with a different authority deciding who got bounced. Jule got his license back, and we stayed close, though he never did as well again as when we were the Speed Boys.

When he and I called it a day, I went to work training for a man named Frank Frankel. All during this time I couldn't help but be worrying about how I was going to clear myself of the suspicion that I was heavy into betting because of Jule. Until that was done, I could climb no higher than I'd come so far, which was a long way from the top. What I could use best would be some good, clean wins, but in this job with Frankel I couldn't get a hold of horses to do it, and I began to look around again.

Royce Martin pulled me out of the hole, remembering me from the Steve Judge days. Mr. Martin wanted me back at Woodvale Farm under a contract that called me a "conditioner," which gave me leeway in taking on other horses besides his. A friend of his mentioned something to him about me being a gambler.

"If Woody Stephens is with you and not with those players, you've got a good horseman," said the friend.

"If he is with them," said Royce Martin, "and he's not letting the horses run, I'll find out. But I don't want nobody *telling* me."

It was like getting back into the world again to have some winners in my care, for him and one or two other people. After a gap of four years, I went for the money in stakes racing, and the horses romped home—Hal's Gal, Page Boots, Sports Page, Halt, Lady Dorimer, Tall Weeds. At Jamaica, Delaware, Atlantic City, Keeneland, and Saratoga. Purses for the Miss America Handicap, the Kent Stakes, the Leonard Richards, the East View, the Ashland, the Test Stakes, and the Blue Grass, all of them in '48 and the year after. That was the end of the dead-end road. I turned myself around, and I was on my way again with Mr. Martin, hungry to bet, voting his confidence in me.

He had a two year old named Iamarelic, a name I was sure had never shown up before in the stud book because "I am a relic" didn't amount to a show of faith in his ability. This was a nice horse though that was coming around as I trained him, and I knew he was worth more than the value put on him in his previous start, a seventy-five-hundred-dollar claiming race.

He worked a half mile in forty-six seconds, and a furlong in twelve is considered good going, but the clocker must have had his eyes shut or maybe his watch was on the blink. So I entered Iamarelic in a ten-thousand-dollar claimer at Aqueduct. "To keep all his secrets" was one of the things I'd bound myself to do when I signed up at the age of sixteen with John Ward; I followed the same route for Mr. Martin. I spread the word, for the sake of protection, that the horse had tried making a lunge toward the outside fence when he should have been working on the rail. I didn't want too much attention being paid him, and the story that he bolted could be believed; on his last time out he'd broken poorly, so nobody had grabbed him at seventy-five hundred.

He needed a rider who'd get him going fast out of the gate. My choice was Ovie Scurlock, but his agent was worried by the rumor, in case his boy got hurt and put out of action. "Just how bad is this horse?"

"He gives you warning before he bolts," I said, figuring he would, provided it ever happened. The agent gave the impression that he wasn't about to risk a solitary dollar on Iamarelic.

I walked over to Ovie's trailer. "Believe me, you can ride this horse with a halter. He'll *fly*."

"Get two hundred down on him for me" was Ovie's reply.

I did that, along with fifteen hundred of my own, the biggest bet I ever made in my life, but this was the next best thing to guaranteed money. In a claiming race, horses are pretty much of the same quality, but this one had shown up special.

He broke well out of the gate, then never looked back. A length lead, then three into five to win by eight. Ovie picked up seven hundred and sixty dollars, and there was fifty-seven hundred for me. That was playing the game as it was meant to be played; a pretty fair bet for a country boy.

The best of the horses to reach the stable was a giveaway from Steve Judge, who was closing in on his eightieth birthday, old and sick. He'd bought Blue Man in Florida for nine thousand dollars after he'd run first in his first start at Hialeah, then sold him to Arthur B. Abbott, who was once a professional baseball player and at that time owned the ice-cream concessions at Playland Amusement Park on Long Island Sound in Rye, New York.

He called his stable White Oaks. It had been a hobby of his for thirty years, but not much more than a hobby. He couldn't be classed as a big owner when he had just one other horse besides Blue Man, and he'd come with his wife to feed them sugar.

Steve was running out of time as well as horses. Blue Man was all he was training. Royce Martin saw him and said, "Steve, I want you to go to Hot Springs and get yourself straightened out. You're running around here in all kinds of weather, and it's raining outside right now. Send that horse over to Woody at my barn tomorrow morning."

Steve didn't tell him yes or no, but a day later I saw him walking toward the barn in his beat-up old clothes, leading the horse with one hand, carrying his feed tub in the other. "Here. Take him. Run him anywhere you want. I don't care how cheap—claiming races, anything."

Steve was down to the point where he was getting the colt out to exercise in the dark, hiring any boy that happened to be around. Blue Man had been outrun at Jamaica at a claiming price of twelve thousand dollars, then outrun again at ten thousand. The next stop on the road would be seventy-five hundred.

I found he was washy and awful nervous. If you tried to take hold of him, he'd fight the bit, throw up his head, and it was over for the day. But I thought he might be a pretty good horse if he was treated right. I gave him a lot of time that fall to quiet down and get working. He was trained to the letter when I ran him in an allowance race at Belmont Park. I bet on him, and he paid forty-seven dollars. I ran him one more time. He won again. I felt I was making headway.

I shipped him to Florida that winter of 1950, and when the train pulled in, there was old Steve, feeling good from his soaking at Hot Springs. I put a shank on the colt and said, "Here's your horse."

"I don't want him. You're the one that saw his possibilities. You keep him."

So that's what I did.

December turned into January, but holidays don't make much change in the routine and celebrating is done short and sweet when your business keeps you at a canter every day of the week. Nineteen fifty-one was going to see some odd turns in the road for racing, most of them never expected, like the judges' finding for Jule.

For one thing, there was big labor trouble. A flood of money was pouring in, and the stable help reckoned their cut of it was too small. Some of them went on strike, some took a walk, and the rest were none too happy. In France, owners threatened to hold their horses out of racing until the purses improved; this was a new twist in the rope, but conditions over there were always different from ours.

After some riders got to discussing the idea at Santa Anita in '39, they had a union of their own at last, the Jockeys' Guild, though it fell a long way short of having 100 percent membership. It aimed at upgrading their quarters, raising their take, getting them a say in writing the regulations, and insuring them in a high-risk business, with the tracks paying the premiums.

The statistics show that twelve or thirteen people out of every thousand engaged with the game one way or another get killed in an average year, making boxing as safe as Fort Knox by comparison. In '51 there were casualties to curl your hair.

A jockey in Uruguay got shot by the owner for losing. In January a rider named Johnny Gilbert broke his neck. Later on in the year, Gordon Glisson, who'd come down in the world after being U.S. champ in '49, was aboard Little Nonnie at forty-eight-to-one in a thirty-five-hundred-dollar claiming race at Santa Anita when he took a spill that broke his back; the filly's back was broken, too, so she had to be put down. Johnny Glisson, his brother and a rider, had been killed the previous year at Del Mar.

Seventeen horses died in a barn fire in Phoenix which was set off by a stroke of lightning maybe, twenty-six more in Grove City, Ohio, when somebody with a score to settle put a match to a stable there.

A jock was suspended for coming up with a new trick, sticking phonograph needles in his boots so he could spur his mount without leaving traces. It was part of an old tradition like hiding a battery in the saddle to jolt a horse that wants to quit. Or popping some woodworking nails in your mouth to needle him with before you spat them out coming up to the finish line.

New York State counted its last year's take of pari-mutuel money, and it came to more than twenty-eight million dollars. At Epsom Downs, home of the English Derby, bookies offered odds of two-hundred-to-one on a horse that was already dead. And in Hollywood, the fad for owning thoroughbreds began to fade.

Rita Hayworth sold hers. Bill Goetz, a producer who was Louis B. Mayer's son-in-law, tried to collect a quarter of a million dollars from Lloyd's of London for a horse of his, Your Host, that he thought had to be destroyed, but the insurers paid the vets to save it to stand at stud. A bettor who'd backed the wrong horse busted into the box of Louis B. Mayer after he'd won the Santa Anita Handicap with Moonrush; he was going to blow up the whole track, said the sore loser.

Mr. Mayer was still buying, and he had brought something brand-new to the game. He had bought in France, but he didn't want his animals stowed away in the hold of any ship; he wanted to fly them over the ocean. That had never been tried before, but American Airlines was willing to give it a shot.

A supervisor there called in a man named John J. McCabe, who'd picked up a little interest in racing as a kid, going off to the track with his father. McCabe was stuck with making all the arrangements. The horses were unloaded in good shape, and he smelled the makings of a good, new business. Now, he's got about a hundred competitors to contend with, operating out of every major airport equipped to handle passengers that weigh in on four legs at half a ton apiece. During the season in New York, they arrive at Kennedy as live cargo half the days of the week—five hundred animals shipped by air every year.

I introduced a little filly, Marta, to the track in '51, a sweetheart who went on winning races all the way through to the end of '54, but the best of the crop in my judgment was still Blue Man even though he had a skittery streak in his nature, along with his speed and class.

I ran him in the Flamingo at Hialeah in '52, and it was one more win. I spotted Steve standing, shabby and frazzled, in the crowd, so I went over and brought him back with me into the winner's circle. "Here's the man you ought to be cheering," I hollered. They did just that, which was what he deserved, the old man who'd always been a friend to me.

I thought so much of Blue Man that I offered to buy him from Mr. Abbott, but he wouldn't sell. "He's the first good one I've gotten in thirty years," he said. Instead, he unloaded his only other horse for thirteen thousand dollars, which could go to paying the expenses now that we were going to enter Blue Man in the Kentucky Derby.

You had to figure in '52 that an owner spent five thousand dollars on an average entry in the final days before you got to the starting gate on Derby day, and the costs have gone sky-high since then. The train fare for shipping Blue Man from New York to Louisville came close to a thousand dollars, and that didn't include the van charges at both ends. There was the trainer to pay, the exercise boy, the groom, the watchmen. If an owner had to watch his wallet, he was best off keeping his horse in the barn and seeing the whole thing on coast-to-coast television, which he could do for the first time that year. On the little bit of a picture tube that was in style then, he might have caught a glimpse of Lyndon B. Johnson, who was sitting in the grandstand.

The horse Blue Man had to beat was the favorite, Hill Gail, trained by Plain Ben Jones of Calumet Farm, ridden by Eddie Arcaro, who'd been first at the wire in four previous Derbies. A jock as popular with the bettors as Eddie can bring down the mutual price, which makes his mount favored.

For my three year old I picked Conn McCreary, so small he was next to a midget; he'd won on Pensive in '44, then fallen on hard times, out of fashion with the owners.

Hill Gail started acting up in the paddock, but Plain Ben gave him a swipe with his open hand to teach him better. When the bell rang and the gate flew open, my horse scraped a side of the stall and couldn't quite make up for that trouble. In the last couple of furlongs, Hill Gail was running out of steam, but he held off a late try by Sub Fleet, with Blue Man following third.

The Preakness in Baltimore, Maryland, is one of the three

classics that with the Kentucky Derby and the Belmont Stakes add up to the Triple Crown. Winning a classic would be a real victory because I'd never done it before. But first I had to figure out how to cure Blue Man of the trouble he'd had on Derby Day. His only flaw was his phobia about being pushed into the starting gate and having it slammed shut behind him. If he was going to earn his salt at Pimlico, he needed help.

So every morning when he was exercised I rode alongside him on my pony, calming him down with the companionship. Now, instead of dancing, he walked, without any complaining. A pony went with him to the gate for the Preakness start. He fussed for a moment, then went in like a gentleman. When the gate sprang open, he left in the right frame of mind, not spooked but eager to win.

He ran the way he liked to, dropping far back before he surged near the first pole, to drive on from there to wear down the lead horse, Jampol, and cross the wire ahead of everybody. The President's wife, Bess Truman, out of Independence, Missouri, who had a fancy for race horses, was there that day with their daughter Margaret. She saw Blue Man win by three-and-a-half. Mr. Abbott made $86,135, and he gave me a gold money clip engraved "W.C.S." as a souvenir.

I was definitely moving up in the world, but the pressure was beginning to get to me. I called my sister Nora to tell her about the day. She knew the sort of life I was into and what it took out of me. "How can you put up with it?" she asked.

"It's what I have to do, the way it is. This is my *business*." I told myself I could handle any kind of pressure that came along and still keep going; it took a while before I was proved wrong.

Royce Martin was never invited to join the Jockey Club and neither was Arthur Abbott. There was no fit there for a man in the ice-cream business or the other, who was rich enough, but who had hoisted himself up by his own bootstraps, which wasn't any recommendation. The same applied to Louis B. Mayer and others of his kind.

One of the handicaps was that the money they had was fresh made, while the members of the club took pride in the fact that theirs was old money for the most part, handed down in the family and usually handled so well that there was even more to pass on to *their* sons and daughters.

The club was born around the time my dad was still in school. New York City was the place where most of the country's money was concentrated, and that's where August Belmont put the Jockey Club together before he got to building the old Belmont Park and breeding Man o' War, who still has the reputation of being the greatest racehorse ever seen on the tracks; he ran twenty-one races and won all but one of them.

The aim of the club was to clean up racing: set dates for meetings to put an end to conflict between the tracks; bear down on violations of the rules and rewrite those rules, too; appoint officials to be relied on for honesty; identify horses by means of the stud book to keep ringers away from the starting gate.

The Jockey Club threw a hold on thoroughbred racing that was loosened only once—by Jule Fink. Today it still rewrites the rules when the stewards see the need, then proposes the changes to the various state commissioners, who almost always accept them.

The richest horse owners in the country, fathers and sons, have followed one after the other into the club. The Vanderbilts, Whitneys, Phippses, Wideners, Mills, Belmonts keep company with the top breeders like the Hancocks and the Combses. That's where the power was from the start, and they've had no reason to let it go.

It used to be said that the door was shut to women, blacks, Italians, and Jews, but it eased open in the 1950s, and Captain Harry Guggenheim got in, the master of the Cain Hoy Stable which he set up with the six yearlings bought in '34 when he called it Falaise, not Cain Hoy.

He was looking to sign a jockey, and he took on Manuel Ycaza, a top rider but a rough one. When Ycaza turned up with his agent to put his name on the agreement, he had some doubt in his mind, and it might have shown on his face. But he went ahead, anyway, and the captain congratulated him.

"Manuel, to be a success in anything, you must put your

trust in somebody; have confidence in him. By signing this contract, you've shown you have trust in me. Is that correct?"

"Yes, sir."

His new boss threw away the paper and wrote up another, giving him better terms. "You haven't even started working for the man," said the agent, "and he's already given you a raise."

It wasn't too long before I found out for myself that the captain was just that kind of boss to have.

Lucille and I had gotten tired of living in rented places, though she was always easy to get along with and never one to complain. New York was where we wanted to be, but here we were with nowhere to live that we could call our own. We went scouting around, and there was this little brick house a man and his son had just finished building in Franklin Square, ten minutes' drive from Belmont Park, with a "for sale" sign in the yard, because the son had been called into the service.

Since there was just the two of us, we didn't need a great big place, so we bought it, and we've never left. We changed the one-car garage into a double; we put in a sprinkler system to keep the grass green, Kentucky-style; we installed burglar alarms because we had to count on being away five or six months of the year on the schedule that takes you to race in Florida from December through April, to Kentucky in May, and Saratoga in August.

It was a comfortable, convenient house, and it still is, without carrying a big tax on it. I was working too hard to be entertaining people there, but one thing we didn't foresee was the room we'd need for all the trophies that kept coming along and the amount of wall space for hanging all the paintings and photographs. Lucille says today we could use an addition: a museum. But in the more than thirty years we've been in Franklin Square, I've yet to hear a car go by the door.

If you live long enough, you've seen most things happen before, and there isn't a lot left to cause surprises. In those days, some of the stuff we now take for granted was either recent or new to the scene. The New York Racing Association, with firm ties to the Jockey Club, was put together to improve the condition of the major tracks in the state that were in sad shape from overuse and lack of repairs. The group took over Belmont Park, and it was condemned to make way for long-term rebuilding. The old Aqueduct was torn down, and the new Aqueduct went up nearby on two hundred and fifty acres of Ozone Park in Queens County. Jamaica disappeared from the face of the earth, and the architects got busy giving a face-lift to Saratoga.

Owners who couldn't make it into the Jockey Club had some other place to go after 1940, when an organization called the Horsemen's Benevolent and Protective Association (HBPA) was formed at Rockingham Park in southern New Hampshire, thirty miles or so from Boston. It was a fitting choice of a site, because the track was built in the first place to compete with Saratoga, though the effort failed from the start, and Rockingham stood empty for years on end.

The HBPA catered to ordinary people, some of them well-off, some of them depending on racing to make a living, some of them hard pushed to pay their stable bills. Breeders and trainers were welcomed, too. Nowadays this rival of sorts to the Jockey Club claims fifty thousand members, and the roll goes on growing, all interested in raising the size of the purses on offer by track management.

Two years later, in '42, the track bosses got together in Chicago with the idea of forming something they tabbed the Thoroughbred Racing Association. One immediate thought was to set up a central office to look for ways of drawing bigger crowds to the ticket windows. Another was to identify horses by means of tattooing a code number inside their mouths. And a protection bureau was organized as a kind of police force to clear out the fixers, the touts, the ringers, and the dopers.

The times were changing sure enough. Starting gates were the thing now, not the old-fashioned webbing and the risk of a jock getting hung up in it, plucked off his mount and sent sailing through the air doing a double jackknife; I know that came about at least once. The ponies are used today to take a horse and its rider to the post because by the time they've galloped there, the jock is too tired to handle him. In my day, if a horse got tough, we turned his head toward the outside fence and galloped him. He might have had half a grain of heroin on his tongue, too, and he'd get so sharp he'd run through a wall if he was pressed.

I'd come up in the world under Royce Martin, cleared my name, and pulled in good money. I stayed with him to the finish. He had his heart set on making good for Our Boots' loss of the '41 Kentucky Derby and for Halt's running fifth in '49. He thought he had the horse that could do it in '54—Goyamo, whose biggest win to date had been the Bahamas at Hialeah. I picked Eddie Arcaro to ride him.

Mr. Martin on Derby Day wasn't in Louisville but in Lexington, in a hospital bed under treatment for a heart condition, watching a TV set. A second or two after the start at Churchill Downs, he saw Goyamo caught in a traffic jam along with a little gray horse, Determine, flown in from California by John McCabe for the owner, Andy Crevolin, who was an automobile dealer.

The little gray broke out of the crush with Goyamo right behind him. That was the order they were in when they entered the stretch, and that was the order Royce Martin was expecting them to finish in, a win for Determine, a second for Goyamo. Then Royce Martin blacked out, and there was nothing the doctors could do to revive him.

Lucille and I were walking around, going back to find our car. I was paged to go to the general office, where they told me Mr. Martin had died at four forty-five that afternoon, never knowing that Goyamo had come in fourth.

In a few days the lawyers called me. All his horses had to be sold on the tenth of June. I went up to see Mr. Martin's two daughters to ask if they had any interest in staying on in the business. "There's a colt in the sale, Brother Tex, that can run real good, and nobody knows it at present but me." I figured that horse could do well for the three of us if we got together. But the ladies wanted out. So Alton Jones, president of Cities Service who'd been Royce Martin's friend for years, bought Brother Tex for me for thirty-six thousand dollars.

Another owner I'd been training for at the same time as for Mr. Martin was a man named Clifford Mooers, a flyer in the

First World War and then a breeder whose colt, Old Rockport, had finished fourth behind Ponder in the '49 Kentucky Derby. Traffic Judge was the horse of his I was working on in '54.

I had Traffic Judge ready for the Breeders' Futurity at Keeneland, and in the same race I entered Brother Tex, ridden by young Pete Anderson, a jock I was bringing up in the game.

Mr. Mooers told me, "I want my colt sent to the front as soon as he's out of the gate."

"But he pulls up short when he finds he's in the lead. You got to bear that in mind."

"That's how my colt's going to run—just the way I said."

And that's what I told the jockey to do, but I told Pete to take back with Brother Tex. When the starting bell rang, Traffic Judge shot out, took the lead after three furlongs and held it to the head of the stretch. That was where Brother Tex caught him and went on to beat him at the wire. And I knew that, horse for horse, Brother Tex had no business beating Traffic Judge doing anything.

I sold Brother Tex in '55 to Travis Kerr of Oklahoma, where his brother Bob was governor. But I was proved wrong about the colt's potential. He didn't turn out to be the horse I thought he was.

I kept some good, strong memories of Royce Martin and Steve Judge, backed up in Steve's case by the gold stopwatch of his he gave me before he went the same route as Mr. Martin. I used it until a year ago when a jeweler in Lexington found it wasn't running right on account of one of the jewels being cracked, though it was one of the finest timepieces he'd ever opened. I sent it to Switzerland to be fixed no matter what it cost, so I could have it back in working order, a souvenir of Steve that's a hundred years old.

7

The Captain's Stable

I guess that when you're on the way up in any business, you come across a handful of men who rate above the rest. Steve Judge was one of them, and Eddie Neloy was another. I'd hired Eddie as a stable hand, but he'd driven himself hard like me, and now he was enjoying much the same kind of luck.

Up to now, we'd both been private trainers, which usually meant drawing a salary and expenses—my arrangement with Jule Fink had been something out of the ordinary, to say the least.

In the year Royce Martin died, 1954, Eddie had joined up at Maine Chance Farm as trainer for Elizabeth Arden Graham, who used the first two of those names to run beauty parlors and sell a line of makeup for ladies. She had a habit of hiring and firing a man quicker than a turn on a Ferris wheel, which might have been why her wins at the racetrack were so few and far between.

The '47 Kentucky Derby was one of the few, and she was lucky that her horse, Jet Pilot, was alive to be entered; twenty-three of his stablemates had died in a barn fire a year earlier. But Mrs. Graham went on paying six-figure prices for more stock and getting rid of trainers—one of them, Al Scott, because he had the gall to talk to her with a wad of gum in his cheek.

Eddie was number forty-six to go with her when she set her hopes on winning another Derby with a horse named Black Metal. Every year before the big day there's an event known as the Derby Trainers Dinner, where Eddie was introduced that evening as the man from Maine Chance—"at least he was at seven o'clock when we got started," said the M.C.

Eddie stood up to take a bow. He said, "I've just called New York, and as of eight forty-five, I'm still her trainer." After Black Metal finished thirteenth, Eddie got the bounce.

There were a few more names besides Eddie's on my admiration list. Sunny Jim Fitzsimmons, who trained for William Woodward at Belair Stud, was on it. So was Plain Ben Jones of Calumet. Both of them worked for just one boss, in the private end of the business.

Sunny Jim won three Kentucky Derbies—with Gallant Fox, Omaha, and Johnstown—but he didn't see any one of them finish. His back was so bent he couldn't get a sight of anything over the heads of the people who jumped up in front of him. If any horseman started worrying whether his health would stand up to the pace, he could think about Jim Fitzsimmons, who was advised to quit or risk a heart attack as a young man and then lived on until he was well past eighty.

Plain Ben, who trained five Derby winners, was bringing up his son Jimmy as a conditioner and assistant to take over at Calumet. There wasn't either a son or a daughter to follow me, and my dad was dead at the age of seventy-three; my mother carried on alone as a widow in the house I'd bought for them in Lexington.

Max Hirsch is the final name on my list of greats, a spare-framed, hollow-cheeked man, tense in his manner and slow to smile. He took a King Ranch colt, Assault, that had a permanent limp in his right foreleg from stepping on a nail or a shard of glass, then trained him so he could win the Triple Crown.

We were just racetrack friends with Fitzsimmons and Ben Jones, but with Max it was something more, close and personal. We went to all the parties together and did the rounds of New York restaurants—Gallagher's, Luchow's, Dinty Moore's. On the Belmont Park backstreet, we were next-door neighbors, Max in Barns 1 and 2, me in 3 and 4.

His track cottage was where he lived, and in his last years, when he got real sick, I made a point of stopping by to see him most every night. If I skipped one, he would call me. "Woody, why didn't you come by? I was waiting for you."

When winter put an end to the season in New York, we'd go together to Columbia, South Carolina, to get the young horses ready for racing in the spring and give the older horses a rest. That gave us a little rest, too, and the chance to go hunting or fishing. We also played a lot of cards, as part of the good times we shared.

Poker, stud or draw, was his only game, but he was always saying, "I can't beat Lucille." One night he drew four jacks and thought he had it made. But he was wrong: she had four aces.

He taught his daughter Mary everything he knew, to make her the first trainer of her sex in the record of racing. In my judgment, there was nobody better than Max Hirsch, and he was different from the others who stood high in my estimation: he ran a public stable, tied to no single owner, which is what I planned on doing. I'd given it a lot of thought. Private was maybe safer, and public was risky. But going it alone could be a quicker route to the top, which was where I wanted to be, and I'd lose respect for myself if I didn't take chances. So I plowed ahead, as happy as when I rode my first winner as a jock.

A public trainer, instead of drawing a salary, bills the owners of his horses on a per diem basis and as standard practice gets 10 percent of their earnings. The charges cover his work on the horses, feed, stall space, and routine care, but not the services of vets or blacksmiths.

The daily rates vary, according to the location of the barn, higher at the major tracks, cheaper at the lower ones, with the New York barns in the top rank. In 1954, when I got started, an owner paid maybe ten dollars a day for each of his horses.

Today, it will cost him six times as much in New York and about forty dollars at other tracks.

The owners are called on to provide their own tack, blankets, and silks in their registered colors. The trainer expects a percentage of every horse sold.

In the 1960s anybody setting out to keep a thoroughbred in training without any surprise calls on his wallet had to reckon it would cost him anything up from ten thousand a year. Today, the average horse must earn twenty thousand a year to break even, but that same average horse brings home only about five thousand in purses. There's a lot of red ink in the racing game.

The best of trainers counts on one win in every five entries. The lesson was as clear in '56 as it always was and always will be: you can't hope to come out ahead unless you've got good horses to work with.

I was standing on pretty firm ground when, after Mr. Martin died, I opened a public stable in New York. I was lucky again. If you get to the point in the racing game where you have to ask someone for something, you're in trouble. The help might be there, but you've lost a lot of prestige. Some good animals were walked into my barn without the need to go begging for them. I was brought horses owned by Mildred Woolwine, Raymond Guest, Mrs. Thomas Dunne.

Alton Jones, president of Cities Service, was part owner of Goyamo, which was enough to persuade him to hand over his own horses to me. John A. Morris, an investment banker on Wall Street, showed the same kind of trust and something else, too: he showed me where to put money, although I'd never invested anything before in my life, because I never wanted to. Lucille dove in first and bought a few stocks, then she really had to go to work to talk me into it. Mr. Morris helped me do the shopping just the way he helped three jockeys I knew. Almost everything he steered me to turned out well. I was grateful; it gave me something to look forward to if I happened to fall on my face.

All you had to do was take a look at the condition books to know where the kind of money was that I was bent on making for everybody concerned. Not in claiming races nor in allowance races, but in stakes, in the Grade One classics, where the purses were already by far the biggest and getting bigger season after season, although if you'd forecast the day when a million-dollar bonus would be added to a purse at Belmont Park, you'd have qualified for the happy farm. Yet that's what Slew o' Gold pulled off all three of the big stakes races in the fall of '84, when the racing association threw in an extra million as a sweetener to promote the programs in New York.

The Carter Handicap, the Suburban, the Widener, the Beldame, the Gotham, the Travers, the Wood Memorial, the Futurity—these were the kind of targets I was drawing a bead on for my horses to hit. When I ran them would be my decision, not the owners'. If I didn't consider them fit, they'd stay in their stalls. I wouldn't tolerate some feller who couldn't think straight pressuring me into running a sure loser into the ground just so he could see his colors on the track.

There was plenty of money around for us to get a decent, honest cut of it. The first jock to earn a million dollars in a single year had been Ted Atkinson—they called him the Slasher; that came about when I was with Royce Martin. Ten years later, in '56, that figure was doubled by Bill Hartack, who didn't hesitate about getting off a mount in the paddock if he doubted its condition to run. To make that much in earnings, he was in the saddle for thirteen hundred races and first at the wire in three hundred and forty-seven of them. A trainer couldn't expect a killing on the same scale, but a few of them had passed the half-million mark.

My stable got off to a good start. Marta added the Vagrancy at Belmont Park to her string of firsts. Mr. Morris's Missile took the Flash at Saratoga. Brother Tex won the Sanford, also at Saratoga, and the Breeders' Futurity at Keeneland. At Hialeah, Goyamo captured the Bahamas Stakes. The word was spreading that maybe I knew something about horses.

Lucille took care of the bookkeeping. After she closed the ledger at the end of '54, things were looking rosy. I said to her, "Would you like a nice present—a ring or a mink coat?"

"No," she said. "I want a horse, a yearling."

Now the breeders put out sales catalogs listing the animals coming up for bids. Those printed pages weren't as fancy as they are these days, but Lucille went through them as carefully as if they'd arrived in the mail from Neiman-Marcus.

She spotted what she was after, and I took myself off to the sales in Kentucky to pay eight thousand dollars for a filly she named Lucky Mistake. As a two year old, she won her first start, she won again at Saratoga, and she lost the Matron Handicap at Arlington Park by a head. Lucille was as happy as if she'd been personally introduced to Santa Claus.

But Lucky Mistake performed every bit as well as a brood mare after we retired her. Her first foal was a filly, Lucky Tune, that Sherrill Ward trained for Lucille before we sold Lucky Tune for sixty-five thousand and she won eight of eleven starts. Her mother had her best years ahead—a mare's in her prime at the age of twelve—and she was ours. We still own some of her family today. But keeping her and some of her offspring caused us trouble down the road after I'd spent nine years working for a man who could be stubborn as a mule: Capt. Harry Guggenheim.

The horses in that public stable of mine made '55 as good as '54 had been. Clifford Mooers's Traffic Judge was the best of them, coming home with everything in sight—the Jerome, the Ohio Derby, the Withers, and the Woodward, with the Laurel Turf Cup his to grab the following year.

Captain Guggenheim had approached me two or three different times after I opened the stable, sounding me out about his horses. At Jamaica one afternoon, he walked into the stall and watched me saddle one of mine, Blessed Bull.

"Woody, I'm going to bet a hundred dollars on Goulash."

I said, "Captain, bet two hundred on this one I'm running."

Blessed Bull broke the track record in the Queen's Handicap that afternoon and paid sixteen dollars. Then the captain said, "Woody, would you drop by my stable after the races? There's something I want to discuss."

When I walked into his office, he explained. "Lloyd Gentry is training my horses. Nothing wrong, except he wants to go back to Kentucky, and he's going to leave me. I should like to change trainers once more in my life. You."

"Well, right now I'm tied up to where I just can't take the job."

I judged that the captain wasn't used to turndowns, but we stayed on speaking terms. He had another man lined up for the job a few months later, but before he hired him, he called me in Miami. "I want to talk to you one more time about all of this."

"I just can't leave right now."

He let a year go by before he tried a new slant in the fall of 1955. "Now I'm going to make you a proposition. You can take horses for me in two different ways: have so many in your public stable, or give it up and work for me."

"I'll try to make room for some of your horses," I said.

He called me again. "The proposition I made still goes, but I'll tell you what I'm prepared to do, Woody. If you see your way clear to work for me as a private job, you name the terms."

I said, "Captain, if I was to go to work for you, all I'd want is as good a job as there is in New York. No less, no better. You name the figure."

He said he'd get back to me. Lucille and I chewed it over for a couple of days. Working for Captain Guggenheim would give me a leg up into a class I was a stranger to so far. The load on my shoulders might be eased up (but I was wrong about that). And provided I was left to decide where, when, and how his horses ran, I was certain I'd have winners.

I called him. "What's your offer?"

"Fifty thousand a year, 20 percent of all profits, no share in purses."

"What's the cost of running your stable, Captain?"

"Roughly $450,000 a year."

I did some fast thinking. Percentage of profits was an inducement. But he had the reputation of changing trainers like he changed his shirts. What if I had to quit? I could always do what Lucille said: "Go back to what you've been doing." She was right. Start over again in public—I knew I could do that. So when you came down to it, I didn't really *need* the job.

"It's a deal," I told him.

"I will give you until the first of April to get all those other horses out of your stable. Mine can come in now. You'll have mine and the others for the present, but by the first of April the others will have to go." That gave me six months to get ready.

One way or the other, I learned a lot about him during the nine years I stayed with him. He was sixty-six years old when I went with him, and he was in the Jockey Club, which was something new for a Guggenheim.

He was the great-grandson of the original American Guggenheim, a tailor who had come from Switzerland to settle in Philadelphia. The family business, with its fortune made from mining copper, was now in the hands of the Guggenheim Brothers, with offices on Broadway, and there was a string of Guggenheim foundations helping in such things as aviation, summer concerts in New York parks, prize money for artists, and the new museum on Fifth Avenue that was named for his Uncle Solomon, with the ground broken the year I joined him.

He had put in four years as ambassador to Cuba, starting in 1929 before Batista took over as dictator, which triggered some young Cuban riders into coming to this country to find work and then score high on our tracks because they were good as well as small. In those days the trains hauled horsecars all the way to Key West to be loaded on a boat for the crossing to Havana, where the Sunday purses were fatter than anything on offer in Florida. But the '39 hurricane wiped out the railroad tracks, and that was the end of that. Planes took over to fly the horses out of Miami.

The Cubans who rode for twenty years in America stashed away most every dollar they made, to take back home for investment. Then Castro moved in on Batista's heels, and those jocks were washed away like the railroads. You can see some of them in Miami now, doing anything they can lay a hand to.

Harry Guggenheim had served in Europe with the flying navy in the First World War and came out of it a lieutenant commander. He was called back in for the second one, to take command over Mercer Field, New Jersey, where they commissioned combat planes for aircraft carriers. He was aboard one of them, the *Nehenta Bay*, for the invasion of Okinawa, and that was how he got promoted to a captain, the title he wanted used when you had anything to say to him.

His Cain Hoy Stable had won one Kentucky Derby already, in 1953 with Dark Star, when the trainer there was Eddie Hayward. Only the captain had thought his entry, Dark Star, was the best horse in the Derby field. The firm favorite, at seventy cents to the dollar, was Native Dancer, the gray flash, owned by another ex-Navy man, Alfred Gwynne Vanderbilt, Jr., who was also on the rolls of the Jockey Club and one of its stewards, too.

With more and more people buying TV sets, Native Dancer was the star of the show on Saturday afternoons just the way Ed Sullivan was on Saturday nights, though one appearance was over in a matter of minutes, while the other lasted an hour. As a two year old, the gray colt romped home in all nine of his starts and was named Horse of the Year before he went to Louisville in '53 with an eleven-for-eleven record. He ran with a style of his own, laying back in the field, staying off the pace until it was time for him to extend himself in the stretch. Dark Star couldn't be considered in the same class; he started in the Derby as a longshot—a two-dollar bet would pay $51.80. But he broke fast out of the gate and led by a length at the clubhouse turn. Native Dancer, running eighth in the pack, was beginning his move when he was bumped and shut off by a horse named Money Broker; intentional or not, nobody ever decided, and even Mr. Vanderbilt was in two minds about that.

With six furlongs left, the big gray picked up momentum again and lay fourth at the far turn. His rider, Eric Guerin, dropped him onto the rail into third, while Dark Star was winging away fifteen feet out, two lengths ahead. His jock, Hank Moreno, pulled him closer inside, and Native Dancer had to move out to start his run all over again at the sixteenth pole. Moreno took a peek over his shoulder, and it scared the daylights out of him. But he held on, to win by a head.

Both the horses were entered in the Preakness at Pimlico three weeks later. In less than two minutes that afternoon,

Dark Star had run his last race. He sailed out ahead just as he had done at Churchill Downs, but in the stretch he broke down with a bowed tendon and was sent off to retirement. Native Dancer went on to win the Belmont as well.

So now Captain Guggenheim was eager to have another Kentucky Derby winner and on top of that a victory at Epsom Downs, in the English Derby. He was willing, however, to bide his time. "I don't expect anything for three or four years" was what he told me.

It was just as well, it seemed to me, when we'd have to come up the hard way; Cain Hoy was short of a big three year old in the barn when it's the top three year olds that earn the most money as a general rule.

He was a demanding, opinionated man, and if I hadn't stood up to him, I'd have been dead. He had me run a horse, Victory Morn, one day though I told him, "I don't think this one's quite ready." We got beat by a head because I wouldn't abuse that animal, and that was the instruction I gave the rider.

Next morning, the captain came to the barn. I didn't dream anything was wrong when we walked through together. "Come over to the office," he said. "I want to talk to you."

We sat down there, and he said, "That horse should have won yesterday."

"He probably would have if I'd told the rider to sit right down and really kill him. But next Saturday's the Dwyer Handicap, a hundred thousand dollars, and I think that's a lot more important. This horse came out of yesterday's race well, and he should have a good chance at Aqueduct."

He took a hard look at me. "Woody, are you happy on this job?"

"Captain, let's put it this way: I'm happy as long as you are. But the moment you're not, you tell me so, and I can leave here before it gets dark."

He stuck out his hand. "I'm happy." Next Saturday, I won the Dwyer with Victory Morn.

In the first full year at Cain Hoy, I didn't make expenses, the almost half a million dollars it cost to run the place. The same held true for the second year, 1958. The captain sat tight, waiting to see what was coming next. He was a good loser. When his horses weren't getting anyplace, he took off to go fishing or shooting. But when you started winning and doing well, he was on top of you, wanting more.

The idea of winning the Derby on both sides of the ocean stuck in his mind, and he decided to send a couple of horses, Bald Eagle and Red God, over to train on the other side to see if they would work their way into doing that for him. His choice was to go first-class with everything—everything kept neat and spick-and-span, and half a dozen new sets of white-and-blue block racing silks bought every spring. So the job in England was to be done by nobody except Captain Cecil Boyd-Rochfort, forty years in the business and trainer for Queen Elizabeth.

At that time there were no jets taking horses overseas; in a propeller plane it was a thirteen-hour ride. I was the only one with a passport among the stable crew, so I was going across with the animals. I'd have liked Lucille to come with me, but she was worried about flying in the month of December. She'd rather have gone by ship, and then only in fair weather.

I flew over under instruction from the captain for me to report my opinion about everything I saw. I met and ate dinner with the Queen's trainer, who stood a head taller than me, with a back as stiff as a poker. A Kentucky boy and an English blue blood had some trouble understanding what the other was saying, but we had a bond between us in the subject of training blood horses.

I went to Epsom Downs for a look at Tattenham Corner, where a lot of horses have come to grief running the Epsom Derby. This was the racecourse that had sparked the interest of Americans more than a hundred years back, when they set about renting land south of Louisville from two brothers, Henry and John Churchill, whose name stuck to the track where the Kentucky Derby has been run every May without a break since 1875.

I paid a visit to Newmarket, the headquarters of English racing from the very beginning, long before accurate records were kept. That's where that country's Jockey Club first saw the light of day, another hundred years before its American counterpart was put together in New York.

I was looking to see what the rules were here; what kind of shoes a horse should be shod with when plates with toes on them weren't allowed on these grass courses; what kind of animal would make the best fit when a speed horse was out of the question because he'd never run the distance, a mile and a half.

One way or another, I picked up a bit of history, and I reached some firm conclusions. Captain Guggenheim had it in his head that I could train an entry for Epsom Downs back home in America, then fly him over and win. Everything I'd seen convinced me that was impossible.

The next stop was France, Chantilly racecourse, twenty-five or so miles north of Paris, where the French Jockey Club holds its annual events and the stables were built thirty or forty years before the English club was ever founded. It was the same story there as I'd read at Epsom. Too much difference. I wasn't going to try training the captain's horses to race here, because it would never work out right.

I'd been away for ten days when I got back and went in to report to him. It's been a principle of mine to tell any owner the truth about everything. If you have a problem, you don't hide it. So I told him straight, "There's no way I can train horses over here to win over there."

With a touch of the South you could hear in his voice, he said, "Tell me what makes you decide that."

It took hours on end to spell out the reasons for him. English racing is done on grass and most American on dirt, which provides a very different footing. They run their races in the same direction the hands of a clock go around; we run them backward, as the English reckon. Distances are longer there, so the speed is usually higher here, the horses have a shorter career, and the purses are way bigger. There it's still the "sport of kings"; here it's more of an industry. The climate's different, which affects the quality of the fodder you can buy, and it takes a while for a horse to get acclimated. The whole scene's so different, I told him, there were days when I felt I was adrift without a compass.

I had an awful time convincing him his idea of winning at Epsom Downs with an imported horse hadn't a Chinaman's chance of working. But what he heard from me persuaded him that we should bring Bald Eagle home.

Captain Boyd-Rochfort had reached the point where he hated what he called "that cursed horse." I hadn't seen him run yet, though the captain had owned him before I joined Cain Hoy. The bay had Nasrullah blood, a tough, funny breed. He'd been bought with the name of Nasser, but Captain Guggenheim soon changed that after another Nasser, the President of Egypt, grabbed the Suez Canal and laid into the United States for telling "lies" about the Egyptians.

Captain Harry liked the reputation of being a horseman, but he'd have you thinking that horses were more of a hobby for him than a major interest in his life. "I've always believed," he used to say, "that racing should be a man's outlet, even though it sometimes grows into big business. But in my own case I wouldn't want it to be my sole or even my chief concern."

It took the best part of a year to get him steamed up over Bald Eagle. The horse came to me with a cloud hanging over his head. Nobody believed I could do anything with him. He was tough to handle, and I wondered whether Boyd-Rochfort had gotten too old for the job. I used to get on my lead pony and take Bald Eagle out with blinkers on him. I noticed how on tight turns he loved to be tucked in and let the dirt of the track relax him. Then we'd slice him out and let him come.

I got to thinking that over on the other side, training him on the downs and those big, wide open heaths, he would have gotten lost. As for the straightaway courses up to a mile long, he didn't take to them at all. He'd been intended for the English Derby; he might not have had the constitution to take it.

I got him as a three year old in 1958, but I didn't do any good with him for almost twelve months. And then he started to fly for real. The captain started calling him "the most exciting horse I ever owned." Getting him into shape had called for a lot of patience and caring, and I'd come close to having a nervous breakdown.

8

The Nature of the Business

The ulcer that had kept me out of the service stuck with me, calm if I stayed calm, acting up when the pressure of the job got to me and I felt I was rowing for shore against the tide. That feeling hit me most every day of the week.

I watched what I ate, but my stomach still growled at me, and it kept me from doing much drinking. I should have been smoking less instead of more, but I was in deep now at three packs a day, and sometimes it was a struggle to get air into my lungs.

Two people had to be satisfied with the job I was doing, the captain and me, and I was the one applying most of the pressure on myself. He'd given me up to four years to turn Cain Hoy around. I wanted to do it quicker than that.

In the spring of 1959 we had a barnful of fast horses, including three year olds, whereas when we'd started we'd been without a solid colt to go after the prizes in that age group. There was Heavenly Body and Hidden Talent among the fillies, Make Sail, One-Eyed King and, best of all, Bald Eagle.

Some eighteen young horses were down in Columbia, South Carolina, and I flew there to check them out, counting on a return flight to Miami that was scheduled to take off at seven in the evening. I drove the rental car to the airport, built as an improvement over an open field at the fair grounds that I was familiar with from previous trips. The counter clerk said my flight would be four hours late.

I took the car back downtown to kill some time in a restaurant, then turned it in at the airport ready for the eleven o'clock takeoff. The plane stopped at New Brunswick, Jacksonville, and everyplace else along the way. I fell asleep and woke up with the sports coat I was wearing soaked with sweat. A storm was blowing over Miami, so we were out over the ocean, and now I was cold, listening to the propellers turn—the jets came in for the first time a few months later. I got a blanket down off the rack to wrap myself in.

It was still raining when we landed at six o'clock in the morning, but I went straight to the stable to work the horse called One-Eyed King, because I thought he was going to do well for us. When I reached home, I told Lucille about how I was feeling, and she called a doctor. He found my temperature was up, and he gave me some medicine.

There was no improvement showing a few days later, so he sent me to the hospital to get checked out. They gave me the full GI, and he said, "Woody, you should stay here for a while." But after two days, I left for Lexington, Kentucky, where I'd shipped some horses.

Next morning, I was up real early. I was staying with my mother, who was living alone, getting on to seventy years old. There was snow on the ground, which you don't often see in April in Fayette County. Two or three more days passed, and I went on working. Then I woke up during the night and found I'd gone through those same sweats as I had on the plane, followed by the same feeling cold. I got out of bed and turned up the thermostat as high as I could before I wrapped myself in a blanket to lie down on the couch in the living room.

In the morning I checked myself into Central Baptist Hospital; it was sixteen days before they let me out. The doctors said it was some kind of virus, but I knew that what I was really going through was a bad case of tension; I was pushing myself too hard.

Bald Eagle was at Keeneland, ready to run his first race on dirt, along with eight more of the captain's horses. All I could do to keep up the training was make phone calls to Bill Flynn, who'd been stable foreman for thirteen years.

But I wanted to quit, wanted it bad. I couldn't go on the way I was going, because if I did, I wouldn't be going on much longer. I called Captain Guggenheim, and he came to see me there in bed. I told him I wanted out.

"You can't leave," he said. "I tell you this, though: if you'll get up and go see my doctor and he says you need six months' rest, I'll turn these horses away."

"You can't do that, Captain. They're too good." Nothing was settled one way or the other.

Sunday came, and Lucille took me out, over to my mother's, where we stayed for three or four days before we flew to New York for the checkup by the captain's doctors. The results were pretty much what I guessed they'd be. In simple terms, my foot was too heavy on the gas, and I was revving my engine too high. Taking time out might help some, but only I could cure myself.

They said, "What do you want to do?"

"Keep working."

On the following Thursday, I took a plane to Louisville, where Hidden Talent was running in the Kentucky Oaks next afternoon. I had some doubt about going to a hotel in case I got sick again, so I went to visit some friends of mine in that city. On Friday I saddled the filly, and she won. That night I was off to Baltimore; tomorrow at Pimlico I'd be saddling One-Eyed King for the Dixie Handicap, and winning that, too.

In between times, I began to figure out what had to be done to avoid having a nervous breakdown. I was pretty good at training horses to get more speed out of them. Now I had to learn to train myself how to slow down some, to walk a little slower, because I was middle-aged and no longer a kid with the itch to make a go of it. The last few weeks had been the toughest I'd ever known. But I'd survived. Things would probably get tough again sooner or later, but I knew I could come through in one piece, maybe without pushing myself into another hospital bed, where a dozen phone calls are worth less than a single feel of an animal with your hands.

And since the captain had stuck by me with his offer to turn away his horses if I was in need of some long-term rest, I'd stick by him, regardless of what it cost in terms of health.

I really had more concern for the condition of the horses than for my own, and there was a kind of sixth sense that signaled trouble. A plane bringing me back to New York landed about nine o'clock one night, and I got the feeling I should go to the stable. I found my night watchman getting ready to give One-Eyed King some colic medicine, thinking he had nothing worse than a bellyache. I looked at him in his stall and knew without a second look it was something more than that. He was in bad shape, losing all of his fluids.

I got hold of a doctor, who stayed with him through the night, pumping glucose into him through a needle stuck in a blood vessel to replace those fluids. There was improvement by morning, and the colt lived, but his coat turned the color of bark on a tree. That season he'd taken the Donn at Gulfstream Park and the Lincoln Downs Handicap, as well as the Dixie at Pimlico. But I let twelve months go by, without a word of argument from the captain, before I ran One-Eyed King again. In his second start in 1960, he won the Arlington Handicap for a hundred thousand dollars.

In that year of 1959, I put Cain Hoy where I wanted the stable to be, over the top as the biggest money-maker in the country with a total of $742,081 in purses. The horse that won the Gallant Fox at Aqueduct, the Suburban at Belmont Park, and the Washington, D.C., International at Laurel brought in $278,357 of it—Bald Eagle.

Now the captain was steamed up about doing it all over again next year. The fire was blazing in the boiler, and the pressure was up as high as it would go. Captain Guggenheim sent his chauffeur to deliver a smoked turkey to the front door in Franklin Square, along with a check for seventy-five thousand dollars and a card that said, "We've had a good year, but we don't rest on our laurels."

Money wasn't the most important entry in Lucille's accounts. She kept the same friends she had when she was a girl in school. She'd look them up when we were in Kentucky, and wherever we were she'd give anyone of them a call if she'd heard that friend was sick. Nothing ever changes with Lucille. She has the same gentle nature today as when we were dirt-poor and just married. When owners on my list met her over the years, it seemed they always liked her, and that helped me a lot, too. But Captain Guggenheim didn't care to have too many people around him, and he didn't ask many to his box at the track.

His wife, the third of them, who was born Alicia Patterson, was different; she was outright friendly. It might have been because she was raised to work on the newspapers her family owned and published, the Chicago *Tribune* and the New York *Daily News*. She had an aunt, Eleanor, who ran the Washington *Times-Herald* before she died in '48 and it was sold.

Mrs. Guggenheim could ride a horse and fly a plane, too, as a result of encouragement from her father, Joe Patterson, who was another man who liked to be called "Captain." As a reporter, she'd worked on assignments as a theater cashier, a store detective, and a door-to-door seller of subscriptions to magazines.

She was a little bit of a woman, not much more than five feet tall, who liked to go fishing and shooting. She also had the ambition to own a newspaper, but she got no encouragement from her family. She had to wait for that to come about until she was married the third time—to Captain Guggenheim.

They'd been man and wife just a few months when, in 1939, he bought the printing press and machinery, set up in a garage in Hempstead, Long Island, that had been used to bring out a newspaper that had died after nine days. He found a new home for the operation and over the next six years pumped in $750,000 before *Newsday* showed a profit. Before I went with Cain Hoy, Mrs. Guggenheim steered the paper to looking into graft at the New York trotting tracks; as a result William DeKoning was found guilty and sentenced for a shakedown at Roosevelt Raceway in Westbury.

The day came when the captain and his wife were due to go

somewhere in Maryland, and so were Lucille and I. He had his own private plane; he'd had one since he bought a flying boat in the First World War so he could learn to fly. The invitation to go along with them was from Mrs. Guggenheim, who called Lucille.

Things kind of opened up after that. As the hostess, she had us to dinner a few times at the house on Long Island that was called Falaise, the first name he'd given to his stable when he started with six yearlings.

He built Falaise on property bordering the estate of his father, Daniel, on the headland of Sands Point in the days when the North Shore was the Gold Coast of the island. He told us about Daniel going off in his yacht most mornings and being served breakfast on board before they tied up at the foot of Broadway, close by his office.

We'd drive up from Elmont to Port Washington, then out on Middle Neck Road to make the turn through the gates and wind our way along the road, between stands of oak trees in a forest that was almost two hundred years old, with dogwood, viburnum, and spicebush in bloom, depending on the season.

The house itself looked like something you might see in France, in the country around Chantilly. The rooms inside told you where the captain's interests lay—aviation, horse racing, pioneering in the kinds of rockets the Germans worked on to develop into the V-2s they fired in the Second World War. He showed us the room where Colonel Charles Lindbergh stayed as a guest after he'd flown the ocean in the *Spirit of St. Louis*, writing a book about the flight. The captain knew the value of the pictures that hung on his walls, but we didn't, so we could only guess at just how many millions of dollars they were worth.

Outside, there was a private golf course and some of the fanciest stables I ever hoped to see. In the stalls where his father had kept his carriage horses, Captain Guggenheim had some of his thoroughbreds, working them in fields that stretched on over acres and acres of fenced-in parkland. I had a stable hand who came here day by day, doing double duty and getting double pay, because the captain was never tight with his money.

I reckoned I'd met and worked for some high-class people before I threw in with Cain Hoy, but all of this was something new—Falaise was *elegant*, and a bit like a museum.

The captain was also the master of a much bigger place, twenty-seven thousand acres about thirty miles from Charleston, North Carolina—Cain Hoy Plantation, which he took for the name of his stable. He asked me down there in the wintertime to go bird shooting with him—I still have the guns at home.

We'd drive in five miles through a sandy road to the hunting lodge he'd built. He'd invite a few guests at a time and not a woman among them, because that was his rule. He enjoyed the company of the top brass in the services, so General Eisenhower came there. So did Jimmy Doolittle, who'd been a colleague of the captain's in operating La Guardia Field and Kennedy Airport when it was known as Idlewild, and Dick Merrill, who was big at Eastern Airlines.

I got a real kick out of working our way through the pine forests, bagging quail and doves and wild turkeys. At the end of the day, we'd come in, have a couple of drinks by the log fire and settle down to swap stories before we ate dinner.

Doolittle came up with a story, about being in command in North Africa in 1942, where they were sending off bombers to make drops on the Germans and taking heavy damage from antiaircraft fire. He would walk out on the field when they got back, he said, to see for himself the shape they were in. He saw a plane one day with its tail almost shot away, and he asked the sergeant who was standing by it, "Were you aboard?"

"Yes, sir."

As he turned away, Doolittle heard the sergeant mutter to another crewman, "Where did the little bald-headed son of a bitch think I was at—in Brooklyn selling peanuts?"

Walking through the pine forests, you came across whole stands of trees daubed with red paint, and sections where all the timber had been cleared and there were only saplings, growing by the thousand. On one of the last times I was at the plantation, I asked Captain Guggenheim about this.

"I take a hundred thousand dollars' worth of timber out every year."

"How long can that go on, Captain?"

"Until the end of time. Forever."

I concluded that he was a man with a lot of confidence, and so far as his horses were concerned it wasn't out of place, because they went on winning. In March of 1960, Bald Eagle grabbed the Widener at Hialeah, and Harry Truman was there with Bess to present the cup. "If you're ever in Independence, look me up," he said, wearing a grin, to me. The captain put in a word or two after that. "He tells that to everybody," he said, without a smile.

That same month, with Ycaza in the saddle, the colt rallied from fourth place at the quarter pole to grab a hundred-and-twelve-thousand-dollar purse by three quarters of a length in the Gulfstream Park Handicap. Then Make Sail won the Kentucky Oaks, and in November it was Bald Eagle's turn to take his second Washington, D.C., International at Laurel, Maryland; no horse had done that ever before.

The international entries came in from all over the world, and the race was run hot from the start. It was the year an American U-2 spy plane was shot down by the Russians and Khrushchev canceled his appearance at the Big Four Paris conference because Eisenhower wouldn't apologize. The rider of the Russian horse finished with blood pouring out of his nose, the jocks from Australia and Venezuela both lost their mounts in a scrimmage. Ycaza didn't complain, since he beat the French favorite, Tudor Era, by two-and-a-half lengths, but Eddie Arcaro reckoned it was the roughest ride of his career, and he was one of the handful of jocks taking home a million dollars and more every year.

Our horse came out of it undamaged and ready for retirement with a total of $692,922 to his credit, not counting future stud fees. For the second year, back to back, Cain Hoy sat on top of the heap at earning money.

After Bald Eagle left to stand at stud, we had a thinner year in 1961. Then in 1962, Never Bend took over to lead the nation his first year out by making $402,969, a record no two year old had ever matched. He won his maiden at Belmont Park by eight lengths. Running him in the Futurity brought in something close to ninety-five thousand, the Champagne almost one hundred and thirty-five thousand, and at Hialeah in the Flamingo, he galloped to the wire five lengths ahead of his challenger.

Captain Guggenheim thought that with this one he had a good chance in the '63 Kentucky Derby, and I had no cause to disagree. As we got into May, he played his cards close, as he always did. The horse was "masterfully trained," he told one reporter, but "I would not like to predict the outcome. If Never Bend is beaten, it will be by a better horse." Nobody would argue with that.

The field for that run for the roses included four horses that had never been beat. Never Bend was one. Another was a big chestnut colt, Candy Spots, owned by Rex Ellsworth, who didn't qualify for the Jockey Club; he'd been an Arizona cowhand, and now he gave 10 percent of his purses to the Mormon Church.

The bettors' favorite was Candy Spots, with a Green Stables entrant, No Robbery, as second choice, and Never Bend their third. All three horses had always finished first, and the value of a win this time around was $108,900.

I boosted Ycaza into Never Bend's saddle, and horse and jock took a fast lead at the start, with No Robbery and Candy Spots lying close behind. They stuck to that order—one, two, three—until they reached the upper stretch. Then a horse named Chateaugay, who started way behind, came pounding down the center to pull ahead at the last turn and take it by a length and a quarter, with Braulio Baeza, out of Panama, standing high in the stirrups, and Never Bend placing second. If Chateaugay was the "better horse" the captain had talked about, it hadn't shown up in his career earnings, which up until then had totaled only $38,457. But he'd never been beat before, either.

It's a practice among good owners to give a trainer the right, once every season, to have a mare of his covered by an owner's stallion, which is like a cash bonus worth a mint of money in some cases. That's how Lucky Mistake, bought as a gift for Lucille in place of a mink coat or a diamond ring, foaled a daughter by the captain's Dark Star, winner of the 1953 Kentucky Derby; Lucille named her Star Luck. Then it was Bald Eagle's turn to sire a filly for us, Lucky Flight, with another to follow, Lucky Eagle.

Like the rest of Lucille's horses, they went to Sherrill Ward for their training, and I heard no objections from Captain Guggenheim about that, anymore than I did when I was added to the long, long list of Kentucky colonels by the governor at the time, Bert Thomas Combs, whose name is on the mountain highway that runs now through the Daniel Boone Forest and on past Stanton, my birthplace, changing the scenery every mile of the way.

Since he said nothing to me, one way or the other, about her fillies, I concluded that Lucille, like me, was just what the names she chose for them said: lucky. As things turned out, we were dead wrong, but the proof of that remained to be seen.

"Iron Pig" was the handle they'd given in England to the big, dark bay animal the captain brought over that summer after Never Bend failed him at Churchill Downs. Iron Peg, as he was registered, looked like a loser. He'd been out five times on English tracks, including Epsom Downs, and done nothing. The idea was to unload him—sell him for what he'd bring, because the prices were better here than they were in Europe. Captain Guggenheim figured he might pick up twenty thousand dollars for him when he went under the auctioneer's hammer at Keeneland or Saratoga.

He was a sound, good-looking horse with a sweet disposition, and when I checked him out, I could find nothing wrong with him, so I recommended that for the time being he shouldn't be put up for selling. Instead, I took him to Columbia to start his training there and find out why he hadn't performed in England, but I still came up blank.

One morning, I called Captain Guggenheim. "Captain, according to his record, this colt has got a hole in him as big as this barn, but I can't find any hole. He can't be far wrong. I think he's a good racehorse, maybe as good as Bald Eagle."

The captain didn't want to hear it. He turned to talking about something else, but I went on working Iron Peg, training him slow, though he'd been in this country long enough by now to settle in and get activated.

The Columbia track was deep with cuppy sand, and this was a big animal. I clocked him at three quarters of a mile on it in one minute and one sixteenth of a second, which put him right up there in the class of champions. That got me thinking: maybe the reason he hadn't run well for the captain in England was because they race on grass there and this colt liked dirt better.

The following May, on the twelfth, he made his first start, his maiden in America, and he won it. Sixty days later, I ran him in the ten furlong Suburban Handicap at Belmont Park for one hundred and ten thousand dollars. He left the gate at thirty-to-one and held the lead all the way after the first quarter. I put him in one more race, and he took that—three victories, back to back.

Then he was out for exercise one day at Belmont when the track was very dry and cuppy, needing water to keep the surface smoother. He put a foot down in the wrong place, and a hairline crack showed up in a bone in the leg; it can happen to any horse under those conditions.

A crack of that kind can often be fixed, which I would have liked to have done, so I could send him up to New England and run him there. But the captain decided Iron Peg was out of business, and he went to stud. As a stallion, he didn't do much better than he had when he was running on English turf. The ups and downs of that four year old's performance on and off the track were a mystery to me, though nothing on the same scale as Swale's death.

Cain Hoy was into a slow year in 1965 after Iron Peg's retirement, but Lucille's little string was doing much better than pay for its keep, thanks to two additions, Lucky Eagle and Lucky Flight, both daughters of Lucky Mistake and trained by

Sherrill Ward. Newspaper stories about them filled some pages in Lucille's expanding collection of scrapbooks.

She and I had something else to celebrate that summer: Eddie Neloy's latest job, a long way up from dish washing. Now he was hired as trainer at Wheatley Stable, where Sunny Jim Fitzsimmons had trained the horses of Gladys Mills for thirty-eight years before he quit at the age of eighty-eight. Her son Ogden was one partner, and he'd just been made chairman of the Jockey Club. The other partner was her grandson, Ogden Mills Phipps, a member of the club like his father.

There wasn't a finer stable anywhere in the world. The family was rolling in money from investment banking, oil, and trusts. Wheatley had a two year old, Buckpasser, that looked as if he was going to walk away with every race he entered. Ogden Mills didn't take his trainer bird shooting; they went out playing golf, with a ten-dollar bet on who'd win. By some accounts, Eddie didn't mind throwing every game so he could hold on to train Buckpasser.

In August that same year, I got the impression that the New York Racing Association was wondering whether I might be tempted to throw some races like Eddie was prepared to throw a round of golf. A call came for me to show up at the stewards' office in Saratoga.

The steward I faced was Mr. Francis Dunne, who wasn't a stranger to me. We used to kid about the fact that he and Lucille were born on the same day, October 13, though he'd beaten her to it by about twenty years.

We exchanged a few words about the weather and so forth before he got to the point. "As you well know, Woody, no man in your position can own a horse with another trainer. It would create a conflict of interest."

"I don't own any horses. They're my wife's, trained by Sherrill Ward."

"But that's too close a relationship. The stewards have decided you've only one choice: to send those horses out of New York or take them over and train them yourself."

"Let me think about it."

I took the problem to Captain Guggenheim and we hashed it

over at breakfast the following morning. He said he'd go talk with the stewards himself, which he did.

When he came back, he told me they'd been watching the situation for a couple of years, counting Lucille's wins but holding off from doing anything about it. He'd said he was convinced I'd never run her horses against his, yet Mr. Dunne was left worried.

I went in for another session in the stewards' office. The discussion was the same, about "conflict of interest." I said, "But I'd never let that happen." We went around in circles without getting anywhere, and there was no change in the choice I had to make.

I had no mind to ask Lucille to give up her horses; we wanted to keep them for breeding. So I reckoned that nine years of working at Cain Hoy had earned me the right to ask the captain if I could move the two fillies into his barn, still concentrating on his horses, because in the training game you're bound to pay most attention to the best you've got, and his were better than Lucille's.

The look he gave me when I did the asking was as cold as an icebox. "I've got a policy," he said. "Nobody but me puts his horses in my stable." If I was going to keep them, we'd have to go our separate routes. So after nine years with him—and nobody else had stayed longer than two or three—I told him I was ready to quit. There was no telling whether he was glad or mad about it; he sat there with his face like stone.

"If your mind is made up, I see no point in discussing it. But you'll stay on to make the necessary arrangements, I trust."

"Yes, sir."

This was July of '65. I won nine more races for Cain Hoy before it was time to leave him in October. Meantime, he'd asked me to pick my successor; "I don't want an old man or a fat man," he said. But I hadn't anybody to recommend.

Then he called me one day to say would I meet him in the trustees' room at Aqueduct to say hello to his new trainer. Roger Laurin was the son of Lucien Laurin, who'd come up the hard way as a jock on the bush tracks of Canada before he made his score as a trainer for Bull Hancock and then for Penny Tweedy's Meadow Farm.

"Woody," said the captain, "I'm happy you weren't in a hurry to leave, but now I'd appreciate it if you'll stay on two more weeks to show him the way around the barn." I said I'd be glad to, and he paid me for the time.

My intention was to go back to keeping a public stable after Lucille and I took the first real vacation we'd had since we hit New York. I wanted to start small, so I'd be able to pick up a good horse or two if the opportunity came along, which can happen when you least expect it, like getting Blue Man because Steve Judge fell sick in 1951.

I finally parted from the captain in November and took off for Florida, knowing I could count on getting five yearlings to train from James Cox Brady of the Jockey Club, who had followed his father as owner and breeder at Hamilton Farm. The next summer when I was in Saratoga, I spotted the captain watching me from his car that was parked under the shade trees by my barn, and I wondered why.

Roger Laurin lasted at Cain Hoy about as long as he should have expected if he'd known what he was getting into with a boss who demanded a lot from every man. Captain Guggenheim turned to another Stephens to fill the slot—my brother, Bill.

After Royce Martin died, Bill had left me to be full-time trainer for Frank Rand. My brother did well, in particular with Clem, a horse named for Clem McCarthy, the sports announcer, that beat his opposition three times within thirty days at a hundred thousand a crack. But during that time, his wife died, thirty-six years old, and he took the blow real hard.

He was into his second marriage when Captain Guggenheim invited him to have dinner with him and listen to a proposition. Bill came back and told me he'd decided to take up the captain's offer. "When you do," I told him, "you'll find he's an opinionated man. Everything has to be straight and aboveboard. Otherwise, you'll be in for trouble."

After about eight months, however, the captain became restless again and decided to make a change. He let Bill go and started hiring new trainers, one and then one more.

I still ran into the captain once in a while. We'd exchange a word or two about something or other, but we were never close. He was winning races but losing interest in the game. In 1969 he sold off all his horses, more than a hundred of them, for $4,751,000. They could have brought a whole lot more, but they weren't in the best of shape. He got in touch with me to ask if I'd help in the dispersal, and he kept urging me to buy one of his colts, Never Bow, sired by Never Bend, foaled by Anchors Away. The asking price was thirty-five thousand dollars. I had a strong suspicion that all the captain wanted me to do was say yes, and he'd have given me that colt for free, as a kind of souvenir. But I said no; I didn't want him. So Never Bow was sold elsewhere.

He was being walked up the loading ramp for a flight out of Kennedy when he shied and fell off in a spill that killed him. His market value at the time was half a million dollars. All I could think of when I heard about it was that luck can take some funny turns.

In January of 1970, when the captain died, eighty years old, at Falaise on Long Island, Cain Hoy Stable was only a name in the record books.

I flew up from Miami for the funeral, and that night I sat down to dinner with Jimmy Doolittle. Over a couple of drinks, he told me something that explained what had been on the captain's mind when he sat watching from his parked car at Saratoga the summer after I left him. He had shared his thought with Jimmy, on condition I wasn't to hear it until the captain was dead and gone. "I made one mistake in the racing business," said Harry Guggenheim, "letting Woody get away."

9

The Horse Has the Right of Way

I opened up a public stable again in the spring of 1966 on the backstretch at Belmont Park. There was only a number painted on the barns, no name, because in my business you leave it to the owners and breeders to come up with fancy labels like Hideaway and Red Oaks and Restless Wind. Everybody who knew me knew where to find me, and that was good enough.

There were two barns with a cottage set between them, all rent free, but the landlord, the New York Racing Commission, has a rule that says unless you run an active stable, with plenty of action on the track, your time is up and you're out on your ear.

The front door of the cottage opened into a little office, and that door swung on its hinges a dozen times an hour as the parade of people stopped by—assistants, jocks and their agents, grooms, vets, blacksmiths, ticket agents, friends in the same line of work, and an occasional owner.

Off to one side was a dining room and back of that a kitchen where a girl who lived upstairs did the cooking; there was an ice machine in a corner to supply cubes for the tubs you stand a horse in to treat him for sore legs. Behind the office you walked into a sitting room that Lucille furnished with stuff moved out of our house—a couch, a coffee table, some chairs, a TV, a bookcase. A back door led to the yard, where the horses were walked to cool off, get a bath, or just chomp grass.

A different entrance took you up to the floor where the stable help was quartered. An army barracks would have provided more comforts, and the grooms had to walk over to another cottage if they wanted to get under a shower.

Something like seventy-five hundred people held licenses to train racing thoroughbreds in America at that time, some of them with no more talent than it takes to peddle tip sheets, others so green they'd have had trouble housebreaking a kitten. Only a couple of dozen of them stood out in the crowd for consistency in winning, which you might say was one out of every five or six starts.

That went for the men who worked for a single owner as well as for those who trained for more than one at a time, though there was more money to be made going public than there was staying private. Howard Jacobson, known as "Buddy," was proof of that, if you were looking for any. For three years, back to back, he had saddled more winners than anybody else in the world and cleaned up a total of $2,396,000, which still left him trailing way behind the number one rider, Baeza, who in the past twelve months had beat that figure by nearly two hundred thousand dollars.

Buddy Jacobson from Brooklyn reckoned everybody in the business was there only for the bucks—breeders, owners, trainers, riders, as well as the players at the windows. That didn't fit with my way of thinking, though he started a public stable, too.

I'd never switched from believing that to do any good as a trainer you had to have affection and respect for the animals in your barn. If you had that, along with the experience to tell you how to treat them right, then the money would come your way sooner or later, provided your luck didn't change.

I needed good horses, because I couldn't win without them, and good horses came to me from good owners, people who shared my point of view and would listen to what I told them, not try to call every shot themselves.

A lot of those seventy-five hundred licenses were in the hands of men who didn't deserve them because they were greedy, or weak in standing up for their opinions, or maybe both. Under pressure from owners who wanted to see their colors out on the track no matter what happened, and under pressure to make a buck, some trainers were ready to run their horses into the ground, breaking them down by overracing so they suffered avoidable damage. And this applied to high-priced, high-class stock the same as it did to cheap animals without a hope of winning.

I didn't plan on changing my ways and my methods for anybody. I'd stick to my guns, as I'd learned to do, and let every owner know the truth about everything just as I saw it. If there was a problem, I wouldn't hide it. I'd respect them, and they'd respect me; back me up on my decisions.

If you get to the point in the racing game where you're low on horses and really need more in your stable, it's hard to get them. If you don't need them, it's easy, and you can turn them away. Ask someone for help as a matter of necessity, and you're in trouble; you might get it, but you have lost a lot of prestige.

Some of the owners came to me as a result of contacts I'd made when I was with Captain Guggenheim; John W. Gaines of the Jockey Club was one of them. Louis Lee Haggin, another Jockey Club man, had three two year olds with me, and three more on the way. John Morris, the banker, was back on my list. John Olin, board chairman of Olin-Mathieson in St. Louis, got aboard, and J. J. Mullion sent me Florescence, an English-bred colt that won four out of seven starts over five furlongs that first season, making up for the disappointment I'd had when Captain Guggenheim sold Mr. Mullion a horse named Ragusa that went on after the sale to be a champion.

I soon had a couple of dozen thoroughbreds in training. It wasn't the rest treatment I'd been expecting, but I felt better in myself than I had for a long, long time. Provided I could round up enough crew to lift some of the weight off my back, next year would see me with a first-class, smooth-running stable.

I thought the horse with the biggest potential in the string was Bold Bidder, who'd had a roller-coaster career before he arrived at my door.

He was foaled at Claiborne, with Bold Ruler his sire and his dam High Bid, who'd been barren for a year before Bold Bidder was delivered. Gladys Phipps of Wheatley Stable owned both the parents. Her trainer, Bill Winfrey, found the colt slow in maturing as a two year old, and he kept him off any track until he won his maiden at Hialeah.

After that, he had a mixed career, losing his first stakes, winning an allowance, then out of the money in another. For his next start, the Belmont, he was chosen by Winfrey as the pace horse, to wing his way before he was dropped back to leave the road clear for another Wheatley entry, Dapper Dan.

The strategy didn't work. Dapper Dan faded in the stretch and finished fourth. Bold Bidder did what was asked of him and led for a mile, but he was last in the field at the final pole. Mrs. Phipps was open to offers. A Florida horseman, Paul Falkenstein, and a trainer out of California, Randy Sechrest, walked over the hill and bought her horse for forty-five thousand dollars.

He did well for them as a three year old, with wins in the Jerome, the Hawthorne Diamond Jubilee, and the Ben Franklin Stakes. Well enough for them to make a clear profit of better than half a million when they sold him to a partnership—John Olin, John Hanes, and John Gaines. They kept Sechrest on as his trainer.

Some days he'd make them happy, some days not. He ran fourth one afternoon in the Malibu, then third in the San Fernando. Two weeks later, in the Strub Stakes at Santa Anita, he set a track record for a mile and a quarter with a six-lengths win over a field of a dozen other horses. On the same course for the Santa Anita Handicap, he crept home ninth.

John Gaines took him back to Gainesway Farm in the Bluegrass to turn him out and test him as a stallion with four mares, resulting in a crop of three babies.

He was brought to me as a four year old in the spring of '66. As soon as I saw him work out, I knew there was a lot of speed in him; what he lacked was consistency. I'd have to gear him up so he'd put his heart into it and obey instruction every time the gate went up, not pick and choose how he was going to run.

He seemed to have been raised obstinate, not caring much whether he won or lost, and that was a habit he had to be rid of, which wouldn't be easy at his age. He had to get feeling pleased with himself when he beat out the field, and he had the class to do it if I tried. So what I did most of was to pay him attention, fuss over him, beef up his responses.

It worked when he took the Monmouth Handicap at Asbury Park, New Jersey, and it pushed Randy Sechrest into needling me every time we ate breakfast together in the track kitchen at Belmont Park; he always left me to pick up the tab.

"It's going to take an awful lot of them, Woody, to make up for the commissions you're taking away from me."

I rode with the gag until I got tired of it. "Do you really think I've submarined you?"

"Figure it out for yourself."

"If that's what you think, you ain't seen nothing yet."

My contract rider was Pete Anderson, and I thought he was a pretty good horseman. According to all I heard, he held a similar opinion of me, saying "Woody's the best damn trainer in the business." I guess that was why I spoiled him some, even when he complained, "You're working me too hard."

He was a flashy dresser, who claimed he had twenty-six sports coats hanging in his closet, and a man who counted on spending his money before he collected it. He sat in a TV studio one day watching a playback of a race he'd just won aboard a horse of John Morris's named Missile Belle, who shot into the lead at the eighth pole. "I expect you knew you had it made about here," said the interviewer. "Won?" said Pete. "I'd already spent half the money."

He didn't do so well on Bold Bidder in the Aqueduct Stakes. In the paddock I told him, "If you draw post eleven at a mile and an eighth, you either scratch or you take back and cut for the rail."

"Okay. But suppose I can't get inside some of the slow runners?"

"Then maybe you should send him early, outrun the field, and then take hold."

That's what he tried, but it didn't work. He lost a lot of early ground and had to keep driving all the way. It was one of Bold Bidder's best races, but not one of Pete's. The colt was still a good second in the stretch, but he was beat by three lengths, and it wasn't his fault—it was Pete's.

Otherwise, the year was Bold Bidder's. He captured the Charles Bidwell Memorial by twelve lengths in Cicero, Illinois, and the Hawthorne Gold Cup by four on the same track. At Monmouth Park, he captured the Amory Haskell. He set a new record for the fastest mile and two furlongs. He was timed over the second fastest mile in racing history—one minute thirty-two and four fifths seconds, only a fifth of a second behind Wheatley Stable's Buckpasser, trained by my pal Eddie Neloy. Bold Bidder, with earnings of three hundred and sixty thousand, was voted champion handicap horse of 1966.

I shipped him to Florida to keep up his training there. In his only start at Hialeah, he showed third, and then I found an inflammation in his legs that spelled an end to his racing. John Gaines negotiated to sell four-year breeding rights to him for thirty-four thousand apiece. I got a turn for free for Lucille's mare, Lucky Mistake, which is how we came to own Lucky Bidder, sired by Bold Bidder.

Then Mr. Gaines followed the road that leads to bigger money—syndication. The total price of a share added up to ninety-nine thousand, and there were forty of them. At stud, the horse carried a value of $3,900,000, a pretty fair price in those days before the market went flying through the roof.

When Lucille closed the books at the end of our first year, she was satisfied, and so was I. We weren't in the same league as Eddie at Wheatley, who'd saddled ninety-three winners and earned a record of nearly two and a half million. But he was pushing himself too hard, where I convinced myself I had plenty of slack left to draw on. Next year would be easier, I thought, now that I knew every rule and most of the ropes of the game.

The way they were written, the rules were strict, as they still are, although there's some leeway in making them stick. A trainer is held responsible for notifying the racing association every time he hires or fires, and everybody on his payroll gets a badge to wear when he's working.

According to regulations, it's an offense to "annoy, create a nuisance, or in any way interfere with the well-being" of a horse, and "horses being led or ridden shall be given the right of way at all times." Dogs don't have it that easy: they "must be tied up or leashed at all times," and they have to be registered with track security.

Fire is a terrible threat when a single animal might be valued at thirty, forty, fifty million, and the barns are full of other stock worth their weight in gold. So the book says no smoking, no storing of paint or flammable fluids; no storing of hay, straw, or bedding unless it's within eighteen inches of a sprinkler pipe head; no plug-in adapters to overload a power socket.

It's. No to drugs, and anybody caught with them gets thrown out, along with everybody else who might be in the same dormitory room, which is open to inspection at any time by the Pinkertons. No changing a lock on a door; no alterations without the association's okay; no heaters until the association has inspected and tagged them; no visitors unless they're other workers on the backstretch, and then only before ten o'clock at night and after six in the morning; no boarders, male or female, under the age of eighteen; no pets; no dice games; no guns.

Today, the rule books are handed out in two languages, with *Reglamentos y Regulaciónes* printed on the back cover. Immigration officers come by now and again to catch any wetbacks who've found a hole in the system. After those roundups, a lot of barns are left kind of shorthanded.

My day began in darkness long before six o'clock, just the way it did on my dad's farm. I'd see the horses moving in and out of the shadows thrown by the lights on the dirt roads and the shade trees, where even the sparrows are still dozing. It can be raw and nasty that time of day wherever you are, including Florida, where I've been colder than in New York. I just couldn't get warm, so I'd hunch down in my jacket and keep the collar up. At Belmont Park, you might hear a rooster crow from someplace, you didn't know where.

Inside the barns, the boys would be mucking out the stalls, boys of all ages from green kids to old blacks, whites, or Hispanics spending a lifetime doing chores around the tracks for a few dollars a day.

The horses would already have had their first feed by then—mine got breakfast from the night watchman at three o'clock, lunch at ten-thirty, dinner at three: forty-five horses, all of them fed the same, big or small, and the same meals every day. We served the babies eight quarts of white oats, the stake horses nine, and both got two quarts of sweet feed on top of that—cracked corn, flaxseed, molasses, bran.

In the old days, every stable kept a big iron cooker for preparing the mash that was part of the diet, especially in winter. But mash made a horse soft and fleshy. So we turned to 707, a diet supplement that perks up appetite and goes into the feed for young foals at the time of weaning. Dessert was also on the menu—sweet corn and carrots.

At six o'clock, I'd arrived from the house with my copy of the New York *News* and some hot Sanka in a thermos, wearing working gear—cap, sports jacket, corduroys, mud boots. I'd sit on the wood chair at the little beat-up office desk, thumbing through the paper and swallowing coffee before I walked down to the shedrow to say good morning to the help and take a look at the blackboard, checking out the makeup of the three sets of horses that were to go out, one following the other, during the time allotted on the track for exercising them.

The rider of every horse to be worked that day got his instructions: whether he'd to be galloped or breezed, how far and how fast he had to go. I used to ride a pony out through the chute that takes you to the course, but I gave that up after I broke some ribs in a fall at home.

There were some other things to do before we left. Look into any problem that someone had brought up, and there was usually something or other when you had an organization with over thirty people on the payroll. Make sure every horse was eating what he should, bearing in mind that an animal in training gets worked up and loses the edge of his appetite, while a pony will gorge himself until he's sick if you give him the opportunity. But a feed tub left full is a sure sign of something wrong.

If I was racing that afternoon, I might remind the foreman about the equipment he should send to the paddock with the entrant, including the little bottle of antiseptic that's used to dab on cuts to guard against infection. The horse might need blinkers to get him faster out of the starting gate. Or a shadow roll, caulked shoes, or a change of bits in his mouth. The rules call for any difference in equipment to be notified to the track officials in advance. Without their permission, you can find your horse disqualified.

In the shedrow, I wanted to know that the saddles, bridles, and everything else in the nature of tack was in first-class shape, because a flaw in a rein or in stirrup webbing can cause a bad spill for both the horse and his rider. An exercise boy who's careless with the stuff he's responsible for has had and has no place in a barn like mine.

The same goes for the grooms, who handle three horses apiece. Are their stalls clean and smelling good? What's the condition of their rubbing rags, scrapers, and brushes? Were the leg bandages wrapped on right? How about the cribber—there's one in every barn—who'll chew on anything in his reach, not forgetting a loose length of electric cable?

I might see the need to call in the blacksmith to trim some feet and change the shoes, which is a regular routine, or the vet to treat a sickness. I might order a rack of hay hung by a stall door for a horse to nibble on and calm him, which was something I would do for Sabin when his time came.

All of this was done in the course of the day, because it was necessary for the reputation of a smooth-running operation. Once the first go-around was done with, it was time to go out to the track with set number one, with my eyes peeled to watch the performance and a stopwatch in one hand and the other in my coat pocket, keeping warm.

Watches were one thing I was never short of. I had Steve Judge's, and Mr. Olin gave me two more, both of them jewelled, gold-cased, and engraved for this country boy.

Your workouts go in any every kind of weather, hot or cold, wet or dry, because your knowledge of a horse comes from watching him in action—walking, galloping, breezing, which is a brisker pace than a gallop. Some do best in mud, specially when they're sore and finding comfort in a softer surface. Some like to run in slop, when the track is firm underneath with water on top of it. Others hate having mud kicked up in their faces and can perform only when the going is hard and fast. Where these personal preferences come from, nobody can do better than guess.

Watching them some mornings used to take my mind back to the early days when I'd been a rider myself. I remembered hunching up well forward over the withers of horses long since dead, head down low to cut down resistance, holding still so I didn't disturb the pace, feeling the wind blowing in my face and the ripple of the mount's muscles under my knees, listening to him pull air into his lungs and the drumming of his feet on the track, maybe saying a word or two to encourage him. I'll never forget being a jock even though I didn't make it.

When the workout was over, the horses were taken back in to cool out. There's no water or feed for them until that's been done. On a hot day, they get a bath in water at body temperature, then they're walked with a blanket over their backs round and around the ring, outside in good weather, inside if it's chilly, taking a drink of water every now and then. It may be an hour before they're ready for their stalls.

The second set is being worked meantime, and after that, the third. Around ten o'clock I was back in the office for another swallow of Sanka and to tackle another side of the business, reading the *Racing Form*, studying up on what the competition was doing, figuring where to place my horses and who was going to ride them, thinking about track conditions and the weather and how the race should be run if I was entered on that day's program.

The brightest hope of winning is based on calculating the combination of horse, rider, track, distance, size, and nature of the field that's been entered. Since no two horses are identical, and the same applies to everything else on the list, it's a job where experience counts for a lot, where a trainer with some long years behind him has the edge over the green ones. If he's got an owner breathing down his neck wanting to overmatch an animal or run it before it's good and ready, the odds against winning are a million to one.

The next hour or so would bring a burst of activity, the front door swinging as the callers walked in and out, the phone ringing itself off the hook, the pressure building. I was lucky that there wasn't a load of mail—training is a business mostly done by phone—and what there was, Lucille attended to at home on the typewriter, sometimes with a little nudge from me.

On the road outside during the season, the traffic would pick up early. Water trucks hosing down the dust. Vets and blacksmiths out on their rounds. Pinkerton cars on patrol. Lunch wagons coming by, licensed like everything else by the association that charges a vendor a hundred dollars a year as the price of admission. Flatbeds and pickups delivering fresh feed and straw. Trash and manure pits emptied as the pigeons that freeload off them took a break on the roofs of the barns.

By eleven o'clock it was time for a break for me, too, to stretch out on the couch in the house in Franklin Square, where Lucille would answer the phone. When I was running a horse, I'd be at the barn again an hour before post time to make certain everything was in good order in advance of saddling. Up in the rafters today, there's a stuffed owl to scare off the pigeons that used to mess up the place and steal so much feed we had to keep it covered.

Twenty minutes before the start, the announcer's voice would come out over the speaker, "Attention, horsemen, get your horses ready" for whichever event on the card they were running in. It was important to stick to schedule, because you can be fined or disqualified if you're late. The second call comes ten minutes later, "Attention, horsemen, bring your horses to the paddock . . ."

My barn was only a stone's throw from the chute, so we held off taking the horses through, timing it to get them there without much hanging around, which can make them nervous, the two year olds in particular.

The paddock's the spot where you look for signs of trouble—a sore horse, a lame one, an animal that's stale from overwork. Tension shows up when they twitch their ears or dance around tossing their heads, as well as in the clear-cut cases where they're fighting their grooms, although that can be due to lack of good manners taught by the trainer.

It's a mistake for a horseplayer to believe he'll gain much by trying to listen in on what a trainer says to a jock as he boosts him onto the mount's back. By then, the strategy for the race has usually been decided if you know what you're doing. The advice may be nothing more than "Bring him home safe" or "Don't abuse him—save him for next week."

Unless it was a "dark" day, which is how it's marked up on the calendar for Tuesdays when the Belmont Park track is closed, sometimes I'd put on a suit and tie and eat lunch in the trustees' room, where the walls are panelled in wood, the carpeting is thick, the table linen fresh, and you can watch the racing through the plate-glass windows or on closed-circuit TV. I might decide to bet a few dollars, or I might not, but there never was or is a shortage of friendly faces. Some of them are gone now, like the horses I rode as a kid, but plenty of other people have come along to wave a hand and say, "Hi, Woody."

I made a point of getting out to go to the barn when the feed tubs go in at dinnertime. The difference between the place you've left and the place you're in can pull you up short, and it's only a few minutes' drive between them. The clubhouse is a showpiece, like the grandstand with its escalators and elevators serving crowds of seventy or eighty thousand. The trees are kept trimmed, the flowers in bloom, and a water cannon keeps the grass of the infield as green as fresh paint. The backstretch didn't and doesn't live up to the same standards. That's where the work gets done, and it would look better with a coat of green brushed on the shingles.

Six o'clock, and it was time to call it a day, one more of them out of the three hundred and sixty-five. Some evenings, it was hard to squeeze in a full meal because the phone kept ringing. Otherwise, I'd like to sit with Lucille, listening to the radio before we turned in not much later than when the clock strikes nine.

That's pretty much how it was in the sixties, and that's how it is today. I had some good horses back then, but nowhere near as many as Eddie Neloy had at Wheatley Stable and nothing in quite the same class as Buckpasser. His colt was a champion two year old, then voted Horse of the Year in '66. At four, he had lost only six of his thirty-one career starts, earned nearly a million and a half dollars and a place in the Hall of Fame at Saratoga. But Ogden Phipps made more out of him than that. Syndication was coming into style at the prompting of Bull Hancock. Buckpasser went for $4,800,000.

Eddie broke records by saddling ninety-three winners for purses of $2,456,250 within a period of twelve months, and by capturing forty stakes victories in the same amount of time, which is a figure I'm still trying to match up to. But he worked himself to death doing it.

One day at Belmont Park he complained about pains in an arm and in his chest. Dr. John McKenna was in the first aid room examining him when Eddie's heart kicked out. He was fifty years old, and I was going to be fifty-eight next birthday.

On the newspaper clipping she pasted in the scrapbook, Lucille scribbled, "Woody beware; slow down."

10

All in the Blood

I knew something more than the ulcer was wrong with me when I found I couldn't do all the walking I was used to doing or any exercise that set me breathing hard. But I went on inhaling those three packs a day until a doctor friend of mine came by the cottage one afternoon to have a drink with us, mine very light because drinking made me sick.

Lucille said, "Doctor Murphy, take Woody back with you and check him over. He's been coughing a lot, and his chest's bothering him."

So he did, and the next day he sent me off for X rays. Emphysema is an awful tough thing that does permanent damage to the lungs before it can be detected. He was over at the cottage again when he told me. Then he said, "Give me those cigarettes," and he fixed me a big drink of scotch.

It took me two years to forget cigarettes, but now I could drink without getting sick. Another friend of mine brought me a big sack of little licorices wrapped in pink paper. You could follow me around anywhere I went by tracking where I'd dropped those wrappers.

Finally, the thought of smoking left my mind, and I didn't want the candy anymore. If I hadn't quit, I'd never have been able to go on. I still got short of breath if the air was heavy and the humidity was high. If I carried a bag or ran up steps, I'd pay for it. I still hadn't learned to pace myself and walk slow then, and there's still room left for improvement today.

But that ulcer stopped acting up when I quit smoking and found I could enjoy a drink. When that subject comes up, I remember a party I was at, where Joe E. Lewis was the entertainer. He walked over to one of our tables, picked up a bottle of scotch, and poured himself half a glassful, neat. "My doctor told me if I wanted to live to a ripe old age I had to give up drinking," he said, "but when I look around this crowd, I see more old drunks than I see old doctors."

My brother, Bill, held a similar point of view, and he wasn't inclined to change it. After things didn't work out for him with Captain Guggenheim, he took some other jobs, but they didn't last, and then he came back with me as my assistant. I brought him in because he could maybe do with me what he couldn't do on his own, and he was still a real good horseman.

It was important to me to keep a team together, family and old friends and good workers all falling under the same heading. John Ward, Jr., was breaking my yearlings and patching up the cripples down in Keeneland just as he had at the start. If little Conn McCreary, who'd won the 1944 Kentucky Derby aboard Pensive, hadn't decided to call it a day, I'd still have been giving him a leg up into a saddle.

I'd seen Pete Anderson develop from a kid rider into a professional like Bill Shoemaker, who weighed in well fed at a hundred and three pounds. But the Shoe was smart at getting along with people, whereas Pete didn't have the same talent. He blamed ice cream for his trouble in fighting off the weight. "When I fall asleep," he'd say, "I dream about falling into a vat of strawberry."

There were times when it was mighty tempting to sell his contract, which I did once, to Walter Chrysler. But Pete came back to me a year later when Mr. Chrysler sold all his horses, and I put up with Pete again for quite a while after that.

Owners were a different story. I'd reached the stage where I wouldn't listen to any of them hand out the orders, no matter who he might be. One man came with a horse from France and asked me to take him. I talked with Lester Piggott, the English jock who'd ridden him while he was over there, and he said this was a good animal. I got the horse one day in April. The owner told me flat, "I'm going to run him in the Preakness," which meant Pimlico for a hundred and fifty thousand.

"He won't be ready."

"I bought him to run in that race."

"You might find some other trainer to run him, but I won't."

"I'll decide that. Who in hell do you think you are?"

I cut him short. "I need that stall. Get your horse out of here." He was gone within twenty-four hours.

The more class horses you're given to train, the more you'll get offered if you're staying on top of the job, and the same applies to the owners. Once you've built a reputation, you're under pressure to take on more business than you can handle, and you're forced to draw up a waiting list. But I always made room for a few of my own and raced them whenever they were ready to run, because a horse must earn that twenty thousand dollars a year for the owner to break even.

In the late sixties there were more than forty-seven thousand horses entered in about fifty-five thousand races every year, and each runner made average earnings of thirty-eight hundred dollars, with less than half of 1 percent of them taking home a hundred thousand and up. The earnings of 92 percent fell below the break-even point. During the next ten years, the purses more than doubled, but a lot more horses went out on the tracks, so that half of them finished up with twenty-five hundred dollars or less for a year of racing.

I'd have had no claim to calling myself a horseman if I couldn't do way better than that. One of the good earners in the barn was Lucille's homebred colt Lucky Bidder, Bold Bidder's son. The colt won some solid races in his class before I took him to Suffolk Downs in Boston, the biggest track in New England, for the twenty-five thousand Macomber Memorial Handicap.

At the finish line, he had an eight-lengths lead. He was easing up when we watched him stumble and go down. I left Lucille on her feet, with tears in her eyes, and I went running.

Lucky Bidder had broken a leg, and there was only one thing to be done about it.

It's never a nice sight to see any animal destroyed, although it's an experience that comes sooner or later to everybody in the game when you've been in it long enough. Your heart skips a beat every time it happens when you care about them the way I do. And then when it's finished, you tell yourself, "You win some, you lose more, and when the day's over, you go home."

If I'd made Bold Bidder the horse he proved to be, he played a big part in adding prestige to my stable. John Olin was the man responsible for it. His first interest had been in breeding hunting dogs until his wife got to listening to John Hanes, who served in Washington as under secretary of the treasury under Franklin Roosevelt before he was called in by Mr. Olin to work out the Olin-Mathieson merger.

John Hanes was in the Jockey Club and big on the subject of horses. A friend of his was Leslie Combs, who left the insurance business behind to set himself up breeding thoroughbreds at Spendthrift Farm which covers six thousand acres of the Bluegrass outside Lexington, Kentucky, a twenty-four-carat operation that's got no equal anywhere in the world.

The two of them kept talking to Mrs. Olin to the point where her husband felt he had to buy a horse so he could join in the conversation. He struck out the first time he went to bat, when he bought a Spendthrift yearling at the Keeneland summer sale for seventy-five thousand, the top price that year, and the colt had earned less than eight thousand when Mr. Olin gave him away.

His next try was at Keeneland again for another Combs yearling and another record figure—a hundred and thirty thousand for a son of Swaps out of the mare Obedient. Swapson didn't do a whole lot better than John Olin's first horse—he had twenty-one thousand to his credit before he was sold to an owner in Latin America.

Mr. Olin started to get an idea of what he was doing wrong. "When I went to those auctions and saw all those beautiful horses, I would get too enthusiastic—not want anybody to outbid me. I probably spent too much on yearlings."

But it's a habit that's hard to break. Back at Keeneland again, he paid seventy-five thousand for one more son of Swaps, this time consigned by the owner of the brood mare, John Gaines, who was following his father in the breeding business. Buying Father's Image was a bet that paid off. As a two year old, he finished second in the Futurity at Arlington to Buckpasser, Eddie Neloy's horse; he placed in the Cowdin; he placed in the Pimlico Futurity, where he ran first but was disqualified.

Mr. Gaines didn't waste any time in putting together a million-dollar deal to syndicate Father's Image as a stallion, and he bought in for two thirds from Mr. Olin. The colt did well as a three year old, stood at stud in Kentucky, and was finally sold in '73 to a Japanese for half a million dollars.

After this experience, Mr. Olin was happy enough to pay one hundred and forty thousand for a half-sister of Father's Image from John Gaines at Keeneland. He named her Royal Match, but she never raced, and since Mr. Olin didn't want to know about breeding horses, he gave her away. That didn't slow him down, though, in throwing three hundred and sixty thousand into the pot when he got together with Hanes and Gaines to buy Bold Bidder for a total of six hundred thousand.

After six years of trying, John Olin got out of the red and into the black with the colt's earnings and then with the syndication fees. As a mark of appreciation, he turned all the horses he owned over to me, and he wanted more of them, because now he was hooked on the business.

He found them again at Gainesway Farm, named by the father of John Gaines who set up the place on the profits from a brand of dog food. Mr. Olin bought wholesale and in private: eight yearlings, the whole consignment. He still wasn't satisfied. He sent me to buy him more young horses at Keeneland, Kentucky, where some of the finest thoroughbred stock available anywhere goes on sale under the auctioneer's hammer, spring, summer, fall, and winter. I had a firm tie with the place apart from the fact I came from the Bluegrass myself: Louis Lee Haggin, whose horses were in my stable, was chairman of the board and a trustee of the Keeneland Association that ran the show, although that didn't give me any edge.

You don't find much in common between a Keeneland auction and trading horses at a country fair. Keeneland has bright lights, comfort for the customers, a tote board carrying the prices bid, and identity numbers of the horses. You can examine the merchandise ahead of time when you take a walk around the barns at Keeneland course, where little cups of sherbet are handed out to cool you off under the July sun, though you don't have to look too hard to find something stronger.

The grooms from the various farms take turns at leading out the stock you'll be seeing in the auction ring later. That's when you have a chance to lay a hand on the animals to check out how sound they are. You hear some whispering in the crowd and some speculation about how much a particular horse is likely to bring, but if there's one you like, you don't say much about it because that could raise the ceiling when the selling starts.

The rules governing an auction are as tight as you'll find anywhere in the business of racing horses. The top bidder owns the horse at the knock of the hammer, and he's got thirty minutes to settle up. If he's a stranger, an unknown quantity, he pays in cash, by certified check, or with a bank's letter of credit. The horse is sold pretty much "as is" with a limit on guarantees. If you've made a mistake, it isn't easy to get your money back.

The seller can set a reserve price as the lowest he's prepared to accept, so he won't see his animal go for less than he thinks it's worth. Some auctioneers, like Fasig-Tipton, where the sales figures are generally a shade lower than Keeneland's, don't include in their year-end arithmetic the money that might have been made if all the reserves had been met. Keeneland has a different method: if a horse doesn't fetch the reserve price, it's listed as though it did, but the new "owner" is only a name used for the occasion.

The horses are led into the ring with no name at all as yearlings, but with a number printed on a square of paper stuck to their hips—the hip number, in the terms of the trade. They've been curried and brushed and braided until their coats shine like silk before they're brought out one by one as the numbers light up on the tote board.

The sight of a nice horse will stir any auction crowd, which will be made up of as many types of people as there are keys to a piano. Rich men and women dressed as sloppy as grooms, others that you reckon have got most of their spending money invested in the clothes on their backs. Owners, breeders, agents, trainers, shills. Buyers in from England, Ireland, France. Latins, Arabs, Greeks, Japanese. And every man or woman out to get the best possible horse at the best possible price, afford it or not.

J. B. Faulconer used to be the Keeneland announcer; I'd listen to him kid about his job by saying the most important part of it was letting the consignor hear his name sound out loud and clear over the speaker system. The buyer has something else to pay attention to: the man at the mike recommends the audience to study the terms and conditions of sale printed in the front of the catalog; read them or not, they're binding on both parties.

The announcer gets about thirty seconds to say his piece, and when he's dealing with the updates, it pays to tune in to him. These are the changes from what you can see in print. The sire or dam of a horse may have increased its earnings; an animal may have shown signs of trouble that can't be concealed.

Then the auctioneer takes over the mike. At Keeneland that used to be George Swinebroad, who looked like a simple country boy and knew just how to drive up the bidding, rattling along at a mile a minute like selling leaf tobacco.

"I've got fifty do I hear fifty-five I got fifty-five over there will you go to sixty I'm bid sixty now let's hear seventy here's seventy and seventy-five try for a hundred it's right there do I have twenty-five more give me a hundred and twenty-five will you make it a hundred and fifty it's there let's go for two up to two do I hear twenty-five more two twenty-five you sir two twenty-five no that's it." The hammer goes down, and the horse has gone to somebody who'll maybe cool off sooner or later and hope he had kept his head on his shoulders, and that the breeder wasn't there to unload his culls.

The bid spotters have been out in front of the crowd, each of them with a section of his own to cover, working for a flat fee —no commission for them, although the house takes 5 percent. The spotters recognize who the regulars with money to spend are, so they're on the lookout for signals—raise a finger, flick a catalog, wink an eye—that they relay to the auctioneer.

There's a man working buttons to keep the bidding reported on the tote board abreast of the action, and there's a tape recorder rolling to help settle any dispute. The pace is so fast you might conclude it's clocked with a stopwatch. That's not true, yet the bidding lasts about a minute from start to finish even when the prices are going up in jumps of fifty thousand to the millions.

George Swinebroad was a speed merchant who could sell forty animals an hour, breezing along and, when he was hearing raises of, say, five thousand, ignoring anything smaller, because otherwise he'd fall behind his timetable. He'd have blown a fuse if he'd been at the mike one day in the summer of '84 when the Keeneland officials called a halt to the bidding on a Northern Dancer colt when it reached the four-and-a-half-million mark.

They'd forgotten to announce he was a cribber with a habit of chewing on the wood of his stall and sucking air, which is a common fault with some horses. So they started over again, with the crowd figuring they'd heard the last of four and a half million. They were dead wrong. An Arab sheik, Mohammed ibn Rashid al-Maktoum from the little dot on the Persian Gulf called Dubai, added two million six hundred thousand to make the final bid for a horse that set a new record: for time spent in the ring.

The auction business has a saying: "It doesn't matter where you start a horse; it's where you stop that counts." None of John Olin's bank account got thrown away at Keeneland, because I knew just where to stop. I left with eight or nine yearlings, the best of them bought for a hundred and thirty thousand from the Hurstland Farm consignment, another colt sired by Northern Dancer.

He was registered as Northfields, and the Louisiana Derby was only one of the stakes he won the following year, which was 1971. After he'd earned $195,071, he sold as a stallion for half a million. So five seasons after Mr. Olin turned over all his horses to my stable, he could say, "I've been in the black every year since Bold Bidder."

When I went shopping for horses, I was more concerned with the conformation and feel of the animal than with its pedigree, although pedigrees are the bible of the breeding farms. A horse had to have the right balance in its build, so the weight was distributed for speed and endurance. It's like a man carrying water: he'll do better with two buckets to keep him on an even keel instead of walking lopsided with one.

Bull Hancock used to give a lot of attention to an animal's knees before he made his judgments. The legs and their fit at the shoulder and hip come high on the list with me. I let other people concentrate on bloodlines, because I've known plenty of horses that failed although they were bred from winners and stakes-placed parents. And there have been plenty of others that succeeded with nothing much in the way of sire or dam.

A farm's reputation depends for the most part on the performance at stud of the stallions, the quality of their sons and daughters, then on through the generations as they come. John Gaines calls them his "kings" and houses them and treats them like royalty on four legs at Gainesway, where he stables fifty of them.

A stallion with the power of Northern Dancer, who stands at E. P. Taylor's Windfields Farm in Chesapeake City, Maryland, can serve for twenty years or more; his name on a pedigree is a guarantee of a big-selling price, as you can tell by the fact that nine of the eleven priciest yearlings ever led into the ring were sired by him, and Northern Dancer is still covering mares by appointment only.

Potency is the key. The autopsy report on Swale mentioned there was nothing lacking in him there, which might have softened the blow for the investors in the Raceland Stable syndicate, but it riled Seth Hancock to find anybody had brought up the subject when it was too late to count for anything.

The star of the show at Claiborne today is Secretariat, who's been in his paddock there since the end of '73, when he arrived as the first colt in twenty-five years to win the Triple Crown. He lives in the same quarters that his sire, Bold Ruler, was stabled in, in the stallion barn that holds twenty-eight more of his kind. He's the horse the visitors want to see first, but breeding is a risky game—so far, he hasn't sired a foal of his special high class.

A stablemate, Alydar, who was beat by Affirmed in every race for the Triple Crown, leaves Secretariat out in the cold as a father, and the result shows up in the sales ring. An Alydar yearling will fetch an average price of half a million, where one by Secretariat averages around two hundred thousand. And Affirmed is a washout as a sire.

It stands to reason that you can no more be sure that the qualities of a horse will be passed on generation by generation than you can count on that for a man or woman. My sister Nora stood taller and outdid me in strength and weight, for one example. Ron Turcotte from French Canada, who rode Secretariat, was five feet tall, and one of his brothers topped him by ten inches and outweighed him by eighty pounds.

But bloodlines are the foundation of the breeding farms, and when it's a business of supply and demand, a powerful stallion means a guaranteed bankroll.

The fee for covering a mare ranges up to a couple of hundred thousand dollars, the mare being vanned in for service, the date and time noted in the appointment book kept by the farm. The breeding season is short—four months of the year, when the mare is in heat, which starts in the spring. The Japanese tried using artificial light in the barns in winter to fool the females, which some breeders thought was the greatest thing since the wheel, but it didn't work out.

The general rule used to be that a stallion was booked about thirty times a season for a job that lasted maybe ten or fifteen minutes. The number of bookings started going up, keeping step with the fees, until it's reached sixty or more in some cases, with the stallion given a few hours rest between trips to the breeding shed, where a muzzle is put on him so he doesn't bite and it's a public event, with the foreman and some helpers standing by.

The stud records get close study as a guard against inbreeding, matings between cousins that can result as often as not in flawed foals. When Mr. Olin was looking to have his mare Queen Sucree covered at Gainesway by Bold Bidder, there was no problem of that nature with bloodlines.

Queen Sucree had disappointed us as a filly; in four starts, she won only once, and she earned less than four thousand dollars. I shipped her to the farm for examination. The vets found she was equipped with only a single ovary. "She'll never have twins" was how John Gaines reported back to Mr. Olin.

But they bred her to Bold Bidder, anyway. The first year, she turned out barren. The next year, they tried again, because Mr. Gaines thought a combination of the sire's heavy muscle and the dam's nice medium size and staying power could produce a good horse.

The bay colt she foaled in the spring of '71 was small but feisty. Queen Sucree ran short of milk, so he was raised using another mare as his wet nurse. As a weanling, he was a real cutup, so he was quartered with a standardbred, a trotter named Way to Reason.

Mr. Olin registered his bay colt as Cannonade; he was a horse with a lot of promise.

11

The Sweet Scent of Roses

My brother, Bill, shipped Cannonade up to me from Kentucky along with a bunch of other young horses in the spring of 1973. The colt had inherited enough Nasrullah blood from his sire to make him as tricky to handle as Bold Bidder had been in his day. He wasn't really strong-made around the shoulders, but he had good hind quarters and a big, solid girth.

As a two year old, he picked up a trick of hooking a forefoot over his shank to pull it out of a groom's hand and get loose. He was off and running half a dozen times before we took care of that and knew we had to watch him every minute he was out of his stall. He'd bite and kick—not viciously but kind of rough—but it was clear he had the makings of a winner, provided he was trained right.

I sent him out for the first time at Belmont Park in May with Jorge Velasquez riding him instead of Pete Anderson, who was putting on weight again overdosing on ice cream. Cannonade got very little attention and finished fifth. Tom Wallis was in the irons for the colt's next outings. In June he ran a second, then toward the end of the month he broke his maiden at Aqueduct, leading the field most of the way home.

Earl Scheib wanted to buy him on the spot. This California

owner, who made his money spraying automobiles, offered me a hundred thousand, but I turned him down; Cannonade was going to be worth a whole lot more than that to John Olin. I recalled the first stakes I ever won with Jule Fink's Saguero in the Excelsior at Jamaica. A man tried then to buy the horse as a pacemaker for another animal he owned. I wouldn't part with him, and I entered him in the same race; the other horse never came close to catching him.

I had a free rein with Mr. Olin for every one of his thoroughbreds. "Woody will decide what's best," he would say. There was never a better owner to work for. Whatever was done for him, he appreciated. He'd have me down to his plantation in Georgia for a day or so while Bill took over at the stable. Olin Corporation headquarters were in St. Louis, Missouri, which was where the chairman lived, so our business was mostly done by phone; he was eighty years old, and we never saw him in the barn at Belmont Park. His company piled up a billion dollars a year selling everything from guns and ammunition to paper and plastics. The purses won by racing meant no more to him than a measure of how we were doing with his horses.

We were making out all right for him and the other owners, too, with earnings of more than seven hundred thousand a year, running in big-money stakes. For John Olin, I won with Eaglesham and Gunite, as well as with Northfields and Cannonade. For Louis Lee Haggin, I did the same with Summit Joy and Cohasset Tribe.

I'd trained Missile for John Morris, and now I had his Missile Belle and his wife's Proudest Roman. Mr. and Mrs. Taylor Hardin's Kittiwake and Mrs. Peterkin were on the list, and so were James Cox Brady's Hibernian, Meritus, Jungle Cove, Top Count, and Dancealot. North Broadway was a filly owned by a Japanese, Tadao Tamashima, who paid his bills on the dot but showed up just three times in the two years I trained for him, when she won four hundred thousand in stakes races. Whenever he stopped by, he'd invite me to Japan, which was the filly's final destination. I was tempted, but I could never pull myself away.

Neither Lucille nor I kept close count of the score—we relied on the sports pages of the newspapers for that—but we figured the number of stakes winners I'd saddled was somewhere above one hundred and fifty, which left only Charlie Whittingham ahead of me in that aspect of the training game.

Sometimes I sold a horse for an owner and we were both sorry about it afterward. In 1973 three of the Brady family's colts went for three hundred thousand to Sigmund Sommer, who built his stable on the proceeds from the construction business. That was the year Sham, a Sommer colt, broke a Churchill Downs speed record and placed second to Secretariat after a rough start that cost Sham two of his teeth when he banged his head against the starting gate.

One of the colts sold for the Bradys was Accipter and another was Rube the Great, who was rated by their new trainer, Pancho Martin, to be in the same class as Sham, and he was preparing to run both of them in the Kentucky Derby next year. I said to the Bradys, "There's always a risk in selling good horses before you've learned much about them." But I'd got a fair price for them, and Pancho was a decent man who wouldn't abuse them.

But back to Cannonade. Mr. Olin had faith in me, and I had faith in his horse. Cannonade came out of every race as a two year old fighting fit and ready for the next, so I kept him running. He was fourth three times in a row, then fifth the time after that. I took him to Saratoga in August, and with Pete Anderson in the saddle, he finished second. Pete stayed with him for twelve more races.

It seemed to me that the colt had enough kick in him to perform better than he did in his following three outings: there were always two other horses in front of him at the wire. His performance just wasn't consistent. One day he'd lay up near the pace; another day he'd pick it up and come up from way behind. Mr. Olin wasn't pressing for explanations, and I didn't offer any. Nor did either one of us have any regret about turning down Earl Scheib's hundred thousand dollars.

Patience paid off again after a three months' wait. In the last week of September at Belmont Park, Cannonade beat

L'Amour Rullah by five and a half lengths. After this show of his class, I entered him in his first major stakes, the Champagne. He moved up second in the stretch, but Protagonist had it over him by a length and a quarter at the finish.

Early in October, I ran him in an allowance on the grass, still testing to see what he was best suited for. He was in charge most of the way, but he faded to fifth before he was home. On Halloween he won his first stakes, the Great American at Aqueduct, in one minute thirty-four and three fifths seconds for the mile. Our hopes for him were on the rise again.

In November, I shipped him to Churchill Downs for race number fifteen in his career, the Kentucky Jockey Club Stakes. The track there is the color of mild pipe tobacco, and he took to it like a chain-smoker to nicotine with a roaring win of two and a half over the mile, against ten other horses. John Olin wasn't there to watch: the great old man had to take things easy after a heart attack, and his doctors advised him to remain home in St. Louis.

For the colt's next appearance, I brought him up to Liberty Bell to stretch him from a mile to a mile-and-one-furlong in the Heritage Stakes; he ran third. Four days after Christmas, over the same distance, he carried off the Aqueduct Handicap, with a weight assignment of one hundred twenty-six pounds.

The official birth date of every racehorse is the first day of the year he was foaled, which is why the breeders prefer an early mating for their brood mares, who carry the foal an average of three hundred and thirty-six days. Since every race is classified by the age of the horses, those that are born in the early months of the year have an edge in strength and experience over those that arrive later. Seventy-two hours after his win at Aqueduct, Cannonade was a three year old and therefore qualified in the matter of age for the Kentucky Derby.

As a juvenile, he already had seventeen races and five wins to his credit, and in forty-four years there'd been only one winner of the run for the roses with more campaigning behind him—Carry Back, who'd been out twenty-one times before he won in 1961.

Mr. Olin had never stood tall and happy in the winner's

circle with its ring of flowers at Churchill Downs, but I reckoned Cannonade might give him that chance, even if his owner's health kept him out of the picture. And I'd never been there myself on a Derby day in spite of previous tries with seven starters dating back to Royce Martin's Our Boots. It was time a Kentucky boy took one more shot at Kentucky's biggest race.

As things turned out, the gun had double barrels; I got not one shot but two. Bull Hancock's will was designed to take his sons out of racing and concentrate on breeding and selling. But in the '72 auction of Claiborne stock at Belmont Park, young Seth bought back from the estate for ninety thousand dollars a colt named Judger, sired by Damascus.

Seth didn't plan on giving up the track. "I've always liked the racing end of it more than the selling," he would say. With Judger carrying Claiborne's orange silks, he hoped to pull off what his father had dreamed of doing: win the Derby. This would be the first step on a long road leading to converting the farm into a full-time racing operation.

He figured on producing one champion every five years as the way to stay ahead, without the need to sell a horse. It was sure to be a risky undertaking, because the sales ring was the safest route to putting money in the bank, so he had a lot riding on Judger. He gave me the colt to train at the same time with Cannonade. Whether Cannonade or Judger was the better horse would remain to be decided when they made their debuts as three year olds after I shipped them to Florida.

On the twentieth of February, I brought both of them out on the same program at Gulfstream Park in Hallandale, where you can see the Atlantic Ocean from the backstretch, a lake in the infield, and palm trees wherever you're looking. Over a mile and a sixteenth in the Fountain of Youth Stakes, Cannonade finished ninth, beat by as many lengths. Judger in his own race burst out like a rocket in the stretch and ran second.

Less than two weeks later, I saddled them both at Gulfstream again to test them, one against the other this time, over nine furlongs for a hundred thousand dollars in the Florida Derby. Cannonade got into his stride within just a few furlongs and went from twelfth into the lead. He was first by four lengths in the stretch when Judger rallied to cook his goose by almost a length.

I ran them together one more time for the same size purse in the Flamingo at Hialeah over the same distance. The race was named for the trademark of the track, the infield flock of birds bred there from the originals brought in from Cuba when I was still a jock.

Judger was third that day in March. Cannonade showed his speed again before he ended up seventh, nine lengths behind. I faulted his rider, Pete Anderson for that, for not listening to what I'd told him: "Save him; don't let him out too soon."

Cannonade had shown up uneven as a two year old, when the good ones are about as reliable as any thoroughbred going at full tilt in a sprint of under a mile. This year, so far, he'd lost three out of three. I heard some speculation that it was going to be downhill for him all the way from here on in. John Olin didn't believe that.

He remembered how Bold Bidder improved between the ages of three and four: "I'm hoping Cannonade might get better as he gets older, too." I felt the same, but it would have to come about in a matter of weeks, not months, to get him ready for the first Saturday in May.

I sent him and Judger to Kentucky to graze, relax, and work. I didn't accept the opinion of some people that Cannonade was a poor second best, nor that the Bold Bidder-Queen Sucree mating raised some questions about bloodlines.

This was the year the bombing of Cambodia was stopped, the Vietnam War was winding down, young men were fighting the draft, and the Watergate situation was getting unraveled. The whole country seemed in a mood to celebrate. There were two hundred and ninety Derby nominations, and when the cancellations were counted it still left a whole heap of starters: twenty-three horses would join in the post parade.

Mr. Olin was willing to scratch his colt to save him from getting hurt. He called from St. Louis: "I hate that big a field, Woody. If you want to pull him out, it's all right with me." I told him we'd take good care of Cannonade, and Pete wouldn't be his rider.

I prepped Judger in the Blue Grass Stakes, and he took it away from a California horse, Agitate, up to then the favorite in the early Derby betting after he'd won the seventy-five thousand added California Derby two weeks before at Golden Gate Fields, San Francisco. His trainer, Jimmy Jiminez, still reckoned he had the best.

For Cannonade's major prep, I held him out of the Blue Grass, where he would have been carrying one hundred twenty-six pounds. He'd come out of Florida fit and fighting, and he didn't need another route race. I didn't want him to run out of kick over the mile and a quarter at Churchill Downs. So I entered him there on the tobacco brown track he had a fondness for, in the Stepping Stone—seven furlongs.

The jock I boosted onto his back was Angelo Cordero, out of Puerto Rico, where he'd been an apprentice at the age of sixteen. Pete Anderson had been around me for twenty years, and I'd carried him ten years longer than I should have. He'd gotten overweight again, and at forty years old or more he was riding maybe three races a week, which was no way to stay in condition as a jock. When I told him that, he got mad at me, and then I knew the party was over.

He showed up a while later at the Belmont Park breakfast they give for the trainers. He was asked to say a few words about the Belmont Stakes, but he went on to give his opinions about the Kentucky Derby and Cannonade, egging me on. When he was through, I walked over to the table where he was sitting with a couple of other jocks.

"Pete, I'll bet you a thousand dollars you don't ride five more winners the rest of your life." He didn't take me on, but I can remember only one more win for him, on a Cain Hoy horse, after I stopped using him. All the same, he was and is a good horseman. He went on to train for John Brunetti, the president at Hialeah Park, and I wished him well then, as I do today.

The Stepping Stone was Cordero's first ride on Cannonade, and I didn't want him to fight the horse and leave him rank for the Derby. In the paddock, the advice for him was simple: "See if you can get him to relax. If you're last on the backstretch, it's okay with me."

The colt didn't take to the crowd that was watching him, but he ran exactly to schedule. They came out of the gate, Cordero dropped his hands, and his mount settled down. The chart showed them eleventh at the start, then laying near the last of a spread-out field down the backstretch until we asked him to come. He made a rush down the rail, wove through the traffic, and put in a punch at the five-sixteenths pole to go to the lead and win by two.

My two Derby entries were completely different types: Cannonade rough-tempered, tossing his head, lifting a hind leg, striking out at his groom, Manuel Sauriz; Judger sweet-natured and so loose and relaxed you could bring him out of his stall, drop his head, and he wouldn't move if you walked away. At times, he traveled a bit arthritic and tight in a gallop, so we dosed him once or twice with a medication just approved under a new Kentucky law that set a time limit of twenty-four hours on its use before a race. The rule had originally been written a lot looser: any horse whose urine and saliva tests turned out positive for bute "shall not participate in the purse distribution."

That cost Peter Fuller, a Cadillac dealer from Boston, $122,600 after his entry, Dancer's Image, trained by Lou Cavalaris, won the 1968 Derby. A lab technician noticed a color change in the urine sample he was testing during the evening when Mr. Fuller and his crew were celebrating the victory. Dancer's Image had bute in his system, so the purse was awarded to Calumet Farm, owners of Forward Pass, who'd finished second.

The rules controlling bute and every other drug injected into horses vary from one state to another. In New York, for instance, there's an ironclad ban on any and every form of drugging performed within forty-eight hours of race time, and "no horse will be permitted to start who has received medication for any reason after being entered in a race."

But a few trainers at Belmont Park and Aqueduct were customers of a Florida man who smuggled in Circulon, which dilates the blood vessels in the hooves with the aim of improving the horse's speed. It's sold over the counter in Canada, but it's illegal here by federal regulation. For selling this "Dr. Kaye Horse Care" product, the importer faced up to twenty-three years of cooling off.

The list of drugs shot into horses is as long as your arm. A popular one is furosemide, sold under the brand name of Lasix and given as treatment for a bleeder, an animal with ruptures in the tiny arteries of its lungs that show in blood running from its mouth and nose.

It affects maybe half the horses on the tracks, although there's some debate about how the figure's arrived at. Where Lasix is allowed for prerace dosing, some nonbleeders get served with it, too, since it seems to step up their performance. It does something else: by diluting any other traces of drugs in the urine tests, it makes detection of them that much more difficult.

The worst of the drugs is something called M-99, known as "elephant juice," because one drop of it can be a killer when it revs up the circulation so high that it brings on a heart attack. Anybody who's looking for it can find it by shopping around New Mexico, where they test an average of not much more than one horse in every race, and there are five tracks in operation. The story goes that one trainer told about losing six of his string "before I got the dose down right."

The bottom line is that medications are designed with two aims in mind. One is to treat the ailments an otherwise sound animal may suffer from now and then or maybe be born with. The other is to deaden the pain inflicted on an unsound animal as it hits the track. Then it can be kept running until it breaks down. Some owners don't give a damn about that.

The dividing line between these two categories of drugs is very fine, because their side effects can be surprising, even to the chemists in the racing labs at New Bolton Center at the University of Pennsylvania, and in those other states that have testing laws. But any good horseman has a pretty fair idea of where that line lies and which side of it he chooses to work on.

When the fix is in by using drugs, it isn't only the horse that suffers. So do the horseplayers.

The argument has gone on for years over how to clamp down on fixing. The National Association of Racing Commissioners has a set of guidelines without power to enforce them. That's left up to the individual states where racing is legal according to local law, and not all of them are willing to comply, for fear it would cause problems at local tracks.

From time to time, a move's made to make illegal drugging a federal offense, which raises objections from those owners who are strong on states' rights and eager to race as often as they see fit when your average horse already earns only a fraction of the cost of keeping it in training.

Whether they're sold on a vet's prescription or bought under the counter, all the drugs have the same purpose: to keep a horse racing when he deserves a rest. It's an unhappy fact that no other racing country outside of America allows animals to run juiced with medication to the extent it's permitted here, remembering that we have more races with more horses entered in them than the rest of the world put together.

And another thing is certain about the present mishmash of regulations: the dice are loaded in a trainer's favor. If the drug tests show up positive, he can be found guilty only of failing to guard his horse against fixing; the penalty might be loss of the purse and thirty days' suspension. When a court finds a jock did the fixing, he does time in jail.

For my part, I favor aspirin over almost everything that can be legally prescribed. Cannonade had been dosed with nothing for his Derby run, and bute for Judger was used as the law allowed. I never liked to race with it. It takes the pain away from sore legs, but a horse treated with it will put a leg down where he otherwise would not, and that can cause serious damage.

I had enough on my mind that Derby week to leave no time for worrying about a horse getting hurt through no fault of his own making. Red Smith of the *Herald-Tribune* put it this way: "If there ever was another trainer who could come out of his barn and see both the Blue Grass and Stepping Stone winners, history has lost his name. It can do more for a trainer's ulcers than Mylanta."

I couldn't help remembering the times I'd been here before, going back to the year I was fifteen years old, watching Clyde Van Dusen win in the slop. Then there was '41 and Our Boots eighth behind Whirlaway. The horses I'd saddled myself at the Downs had all done better than that: Woodvale Farm's Halt, fifth in '49; Arthur Abbott's Blue Man, third in '52; Royce Martin's Goyamo, fourth in '54; Cain Hoy's Never Bend, second eleven years ago. Nothing since then, and my sixty-first birthday was coming up in September.

But I wasn't letting myself get excited. You had to have more than the best horse; you had to be lucky as well. I'd done the best I could. I had two fine colts, and I'd gotten both of them this far along the road, when most trainers went a lifetime without getting a chance at the Kentucky Derby. Whatever happened would happen. I'd try not to lose any rest over it, but Friday brought one of those nights when I got no more than an hour of sleep.

Judger didn't get a whole lot more sleep in his stall in Barn 42. He was behaving out of character, restless with excitement, fit to be tied. Next door to him, Cannonade was calmer, taking it easy, stretched out on the hay. It was just starting to get light when I climbed out of bed to ride my pony out to inspect the track.

The sun had baked it hard for the first part of the week before the rain had come down on Thursday. I rode at a walk on the inside and felt the going deep on the rail. Cordero would have to bring Cannonade out of it as soon as he could at post time, four-thirty that afternoon.

There wasn't a cloud in the sky when the traffic began to build up on the streets outside. By midmorning, they were clogged with cars and buses and taxis, with hawkers waving them into parking spots and peddlers shouting for customers to buy soft drinks, ice cream, two-bit candy bars, rabbits' feet, and I don't know what else.

In the clubhouse they'd already shaken the little numbered pills out of the leather bottle in the draw to decide post positions. Cannonade would be number two, which was bad news, because he'd come out close to the rail. He'd also be kept waiting for a while until they'd loaded in the rest of the twenty-three horses, and he was a fussy animal.

A total of 163,628 people paid admission to the track that Saturday, roughly twenty thousand more than the previous record set the year before. The crowd was thick as molasses every place you turned, from the Sky Terrace dining section to the clubhouse boxes on the third floor under a roof where it was standing room only. It was a mob scene around the brick pavilions in back of the grandstand, and up in there they squeezed in elbow to elbow and knee to knee, with the twin spires that are the trademark of the Downs out of sight behind them.

The tunnel leading through to the infield was like rush hour on the New York subway, belly to belly and progress made an inch or two at a time. Nearly a hundred thousand of them jammed their way through just the same, and there was no chance in the world of keeping them in rein. Most of them were kids in their teens or young twenties, some of the boys with hair as long as a horse's tail hanging down their backs.

Half of them were topless, so that center field looked like a pasture of sunburned skin. A few went bottomless, too, though it was hard to spot the streakers until one ran mother-naked across the open lawn in front of the main tote board and another shinnied up the infield flagpole to get out of his jeans and wave a greeting.

Kentucky has a reputation for horses and bourbon, but it's mint juleps that get priority on Derby day. Elbows went up, and the liquor went down, except where there was a breakout of bumping and the drinkers set in sloshing each other. From the faint smell in the air and the wisps of smoke, you'd conclude there were reefers in circulation.

It used to be that the infield crowd could push up so close to the rail that a jock got his whip snatched from his hand as he rode by. Now fences were up to prevent that happening, but with twenty thousand more people packed behind them than there ever had been before, there was no guaranteeing they'd hold up. The police were out and so were some National Guardsmen, but from a distance it was impossible to tell whether they were helpless or just plain scared. So I had another thing to think about: Cannonade hadn't liked the crowd at the Stepping Stone, and it might be the same today.

But the horseplayers among them liked him and Judger, and the size of the handle set one more record: $7,868,734. The tote board showed the two colts as equal favorites at five-dollar payoffs if either was the winner. In the past two years, Riva Ridge and Secretariat had run at the same odds, and that was encouraging for me, but not to Jimmy Jiminez. He thought Agitate should have been the horse attracting the biggest share of the betting.

The telephones, the typewriters, the miles of cables had been installed, and the TV interviewers and the turf writers bore down on us in the backstretch, which was quiet that year compared with what it had been once when some potshots were fired between the barn doors. At a time like this, every trainer tries to get in a good word for his horse.

Skip Shapoff, back in his hometown of Louisville, said they hadn't been paying attention to Hudson County, owned by Robert Cohen, who was a distributor of newspapers and magazines. In eight starts, the little colt had never run out of the money. "He has a little more quality than anybody wants to give him credit for," said Shapoff, who trained him.

Tony Bardaro blamed the poor performance of Buck's Bid in his latest outings on nothing more than bad luck and laid his hope in the fact that his horse would have a jump on the rest of the field because he had drawn the outside post position, number twenty-three.

His next-door neighbor was going to be Judger, which was fine by me, because he was a come-from-behind horse that wouldn't start to drive much before he reached the half-mile pole.

A young Englishman, Charlie Milbank, had a good-looking horse in Sir Tristram, flown in by his owner, Raymond Guest, who had once been a customer of mine. Cannonade had beat him in the Stepping Stone, but he had a first-class rider, Bill Hartack, who'd won five previous Kentucky Derbies.

Two of the colts I'd sold to Sigmund Sommer last year were included in the field, Accipter and Rube the Great, and so was a horse that had outrun Cannonade just once—Flip Sal, Kentucky-bred and a Wood Memorial winner who was trained by Steve DiMauro.

Somebody asked which was the better of my two colts. I couldn't find a straight answer; only the finish line could decide that. So I said, "I train them for different owners, and I do the best I can for both men. Cannonade and Judger are both fit. They haven't missed a day of training, and when you're prepping for the Derby, you can't miss a day and hope to catch up."

Seth said he was looking forward to being in the victory box and not up on the third row in Claiborne's, but I had a suspicion he might be in for a disappointment.

I got out of my work clothes and into a decent suit, blue shirt, and a polka-dot tie, on the theory that you ought to dress according to the company you're in. Mr. Olin had sent word he couldn't be there. His stepdaughter, Mrs. Eugene Williams, would stand in for him, while he sat at home in front of a TV set.

Just after two o'clock, a red carpet was rolled out across the dust of the track, ready for the number one guest, Princess Margaret, and her husband at the time, Lord Snowdon. They walked between two lines of National Guardsmen to take their seats on top of the pagoda in the infield at the finish line. It was easy to spot her in a little hat and dress splashed in the colors of a rainbow. The kids in the crowd hoisted a sign: "Hey, Meg —Had Any Winners Lately?"

Angel Cordero had his usual big smile on his dark face when I went in to talk with him about Cannonade in the jockeys' room. "Remember the Stepping Stone when he acted funny about people. Warm him up on the backstretch. Let him go out and look at them." The thought of that mob in the infield was getting to me.

I asked Angel to take him farther down the backstretch than any other rider during the warm-up to give him a good look at the crowd. This jock, who's called the Thief because he has a habit of stealing races, had his heart set on winning that day to make up for the three other Derbies he had ridden in and lost. He had a "savings" deal struck with two other riders: Miguel Rivera on Rube the Great, and Laffit Pincay, twice voted Jockey of the Year, who'd be aboard Judger. They'd agreed that the winner among them would give each of his pals three thousand dollars.

Angel came back happy from the long clockwise warm-up: "He seemed to like the people. I figure we can take a shot and go through with him."

The arrival of the princess had set off a real hullabaloo, swamping her with cameras and attention from the bluebloods of Louisville's high society. But she and her husband weren't the only attractions as they took their seats on top of a tote board that hadn't been invaded up to now by the crowd. Bob Hope was there; Fess Parker, who was Hollywood's Daniel Boone; and Eric Severeid of CBS.

Cannonade was the thirteenth horse led from the backstretch to the paddock for saddling, but that meant nothing unless you were superstitious and had faith in a rabbit's foot. I hadn't much to say to Angel: "Sit off the pace but stay out of trouble. Save as much ground on the inside as you can until he can make his move, then try to have a place to go." To Laffit I said, "The track's a little cuppy. Bring him home safe."

The band started playing "God Save the Queen," and the crowd quieted down some and stood in respect. The lull in the storm lasted through "The Star-Spangled Banner," but "My Old Kentucky Home" set them going again. A rush by a swarm of youngsters drove the guardsmen into retreat and cleared the way for the invasion to take over a roof next to the one where the princess and her party were perched.

There, they danced and yelled and seemed likely to drop their pants for a quick display of skin. On the infield, another charge of bodies pushed down the twelve-foot-tall steel barriers, and people went pouring through to the rail. Up on the roof, they were chanting, "Hey, hey, hey, hey . . ."

The horses were loaded into the gate, and I guess we were all wondering whether there'd be any more surprises on the program when the track announcer, Chic Anderson, said over the mike that everything was set to go. The starter, Tom Wagoner, got the field on its way eight minutes late. I wasn't expecting any speed records broken; there were too many horses, and the track was kind of slow.

Cannonade got bumped a little in the break, though it was cleaner than I anticipated with twenty-three animals busting out in a matter of seconds. Angel tucked him along the rail for a while, but not for long. Judger, out on the far side, was laying back not far from last, which looked okay for the moment.

Triple Crown, in from California, had broken fast into the lead, with little Hudson County tailing him and Sir Tristram third as the field passed the grandstand and under the wire the first time around. Cannonade was halfway back, still along the rail and taking not a bit of notice of the throng pressed up against it hollering like Comanches.

Judger was already having trouble getting hold of the track when, just ahead of him, Eddie Maple's mount, Flip Sal, broke down with fractures in an ankle that threatened to spell the end for him, but the horse survived. Pincay had no choice but to take up, then look for a hole to open up in the pack that was so tight they were bumping and clipping heels.

Angel made up ground between the five-eighths and the three-eighths pole, picking a path inside, between and around, swinging into fifth, while Judger was trapped back at twenty-first. Cannonade was really rolling, but the Claiborne colt wasn't throwing in a big run, and I knew he wasn't going to make it.

Hudson County, not much in breeding or in size, picked off Triple Crown, who was fading at the far turn. Coming up to the quarter pole, Angel angled the Olin colt out and went into full drive to lead the parade. At the top of the stretch, Cannonade's head went up as he spotted the gate. Angel gave him a lick of the whip on his right flank to hold him in the lead, four lengths ahead at the eighth pole.

Agitate, who'd been hung up and jostled in the traffic, got out of it to make his try. Hudson County, supposed to be a sprinter, dug in to shorten the space between him and my lead horse. Angel kept driving him with three more licks from his right hand, four from his left. Hudson County made up almost two lengths in the final furlong, but Cannonade had it made by two and a quarter.

Agitate, third, was no kind of threat. The colts I'd sold to Sigmund Sommer were both out of the money: Rube the Great tenth, just ahead of Sir Tristram, and Accipter eighteenth, just behind Triple Crown. Judger never found room to run, but he came in eighth. Laffit said, "I needed some luck; I didn't get it." Neither did Eddie Maple, who'd been rattled by his spill off Flip Sal, but he impressed me as a stylish rider that I intended to use when the right opportunity came along.

At the moment, time was too short to consider anything except getting to the winner's circle to see Cannonade and Cordero smothered under a blanket of roses, then make it at a canter across the track to the balcony that Princess Margaret had moved down to. "Well done; a lovely race," she said as we shook hands. Below her, in the infield, a girl had cooled off by stripping down and dunking herself in the fountain.

"We are so pleased to be here on the occasion of this Kentucky *Darby*," said the princess with her English accent. "Irrespective of pronunciation, the Kentucky Derby is as important to you as the English *Darby* is to us."

She handed a silver bowl, a five-thousand-dollar English antique, to Mr. Olin's stepdaughter; her father's share of the record-breaking purse was $274,000. Lynn Stone, president of the Downs, took the track's gold trophy from the hands of Governor Wendall Ford on behalf of the absent owner.

After a stop at the press box, the next appointment was up in the directors room, where champagne was on tap. Mr. Stone turned to the princess, who was saying she'd had "a lovely day of racing in the country."

"Princess, may I introduce Woody Stephens?"

She gave a smile. "We met at the big moment."

Before the day was over, I got in a few words with Seth Hancock without the chance to dig into details. No blaming anybody and no change in his plans for Claiborne, because men as good as Seth know that you lose more often than you win.

Agitate's trainer was something else. If the sportswriters got it right, he said, "I'm not a sportsman, I'm a businessman. How can I be happy with third? . . . I say, 'Yes, we had bad racing luck.'"

I called Mr. Olin in St. Louis. "I watched it on television," he said, "but the phone started ringing right after he crossed the finish, and I didn't get to see the replay. Was it something to see? Oh God, yes. It was unbelievable. Like the feller said on his tombstone, 'I expected this, but not so soon.'"

And then I went to bed, as you do, win or lose, but it had been quite a day.

12

How Much Makes Too Many?

Now that I'd made my mark at the Downs with Cannonade, I began to give some thought to retiring. It was on my mind when I said to a friend of mine one day, "Joe, I wonder how many horses I've saddled in my time." The only answer he came up with was "Too many, too many."

Lucille calculated that with all the hours I put in, I worked an eight-day week. "Half the time you're home to have lunch, you don't have a minute to eat a thing, because the phone's ringing," she said, and I couldn't argue with that. "You ought to ease up, so we can do more together than we've been doing." She was right.

"We could try to fit in a little time to go bowling again," she said—she was in a class above me when it came to making spares and strikes and turkeys. "You could get in some fishing, too"—I'd been doing that on and off since I was a kid tossing a hook and line into the streams that run through the Bluegrass.

It was tempting, but I figured I'd let it wait for another year or two. I kept getting lucky, and good horses kept coming my way. Ascetic, Bravest Roman, Gull's Cry, and Harbor Springs gave me eight stakes wins in '75. The following year, the score went up to fourteen with nine new horses contributing, from Bold Royal to Mrs. Warren, including our own Lucky Bidder walking off with the John Macomber Stakes at Suffolk Downs.

I had quite an organization going, and nobody to hand it over to. The payroll covered a foreman, two watchmen, six exercise riders, six grooms, six hot-walkers, plus three vets, a dentist, a blacksmith, and my brother as assistant. The monthly bills sent out to the owners were designed to bring in just the costs of running the operation, to break even. Profits were made out of the purses, which was the incentive to keep winning or trying to.

Maintaining the records was a job in itself. The trainer is responsible for notifying the track every time he hires or fires a stable hand, making sure the tally is up to date and the help is covered for pension benefits, health insurance, and so forth.

An accountant, Jim Hilt, with his office in the Frenchman's Kitchen at Belmont Park, took care of the figures and the end-of-the-month statements, as well as the Friday paychecks, which was some job when grooms and hot-walkers come and go sometimes like drifters in and out of a flophouse. Today, Jim Hilt supplies a computer printout so we can keep on top of the situation.

One dark spot in the picture was my brother, Bill. It was getting to the point where I couldn't depend on him, and I must have told him so a hundred times. I felt it was such a shame, because he was a fine horseman, better than I, in some people's opinion. Our sisters thought he had a problem living in somebody else's shadow. I wasn't sure about that, but I knew he had a tough road to follow.

I sent him with a horse to run at Keystone Racetrack at a time I was too busy to go myself. The horse lost his race, and that was as much as I heard about it from Bill. A couple of days later, the owner called me to lodge a complaint. "Who was it saddled my horse?"

"You know, my brother, Bill."

"No, he didn't. He got somebody else to do it for him."

That wasn't the kind of reputation you were looking for when you had a stable with more than its share of class animals owned by some high-class people. The thought crossed my mind that the day might arrive when I'd have to let go of him, but when I didn't see much change in myself over the years, I didn't like changing things around me. Filling the hole left by Pete Anderson's departure had been quite enough to take care of for the time being.

That year of Cannonade's Derby win, 1974, had seen Eddie Maple, who was pitched off of Flip Sal, offered a bribe by another jock to throw a race at Saratoga. Eddie refused. When the whole thing came out in the open, the racing and wagering board slapped a year's suspension on the other rider, who appealed it all the way up to the New York State Supreme Court. It still stuck. So Eddie was honest, which was another strong recommendation the way I saw it. He was a man I wanted to ride for me.

He came out of Ohio, and he'd been five years in the game. When I met him, I thought he had a nice way of getting along with people, a calm disposition, and respect for his mounts. Times had changed since the first thing you did with a promising jock was put him under contract. There was no formal arrangement between us, but I hoped my horses were going to make Eddie one of the top riders in the country. He didn't talk in those terms. "I'd like people to say, 'He was a pretty fair horseman'" was how he put it.

A rider's like a trainer in that neither of them can look forward to winning unless he's got good horses. Nothing can make up for the lack of them, no matter what your talent might be. But I was in a position now where so many were offered, I had to turn some away, and the idea of retirement got pushed on to sometime in the future. I didn't see why nor how I should quit.

Believe It, Quadratic, Sensational, and again Mrs. Warren took the big stakes for me in 1977. Next season was better yet—sixteen stakes victories, with Mrs. Warren, Quadratic, and Believe It still contributing and new arrivals in my stalls like Smarten, Terpsichorist, Too Many Sweets, and White Star Line doing the rest. Eddie, with two sons in his family, got his turn at a lot of races. By 1983 his mounts had earned a shade under six million dollars, and he took 10 percent of it. My horses made half that total for him. When Devil's Bag came down the line, I knew who was going to ride him.

Eddie was climbing up into the big league, where the living was getting to be awful rich. Lafitt Pincay in '73 had been the first of them to win races worth four or more million in a year of riding, which put four hundred thousand in his pocket.

Angel Cordero, whose mother had hopes of his being a doctor, topped that mark three seasons later, when he made four hundred and seventy thousand to push into his bank account. I thought Eddie was more consistent in the saddle than Angel, but it was Angel who broke through the sound barrier in '83 as the first rider in all history to earn a million for himself in a single year. He'd ridden his first race in Puerto Rico at the age of eighteen. In the following twenty-three years, he'd picked up eight million dollars, and he was talking about the time he saw coming when a jock would get two or three hundred thousand for pulling off a single race.

The day I read about that in the morning paper, I found myself remembering how things had been when I was in his line of business and a win brought you twenty-five dollars. Most of the boys in the jockeys' rooms were little runts who came from families worse off than mine with never enough to eat, and they were white Americans.

I never saw a black jock, although on the plantations in the South, slave boys used to be bred small to be pilots of the owners' horses. Isaac Murphy, born a slave in Lexington, Kentucky, was the first black rider to win three Kentucky Derbies. Another, Jimmy Winkfield, rode two more winners back to back and brought the score for black jockeys to fifteen out of the first twenty-eight runs for the roses. Isaac Murphy died broke, but he did receive some recognition in the end. His casket lies buried in Man o' War Park in the city he was born in.

When this country started listening to advice from doctors about "swat that fly" and "eat some salad" in the 1920s, the kids got bigger than they had been. If they wanted to be jockeys, weight was a problem they had to fight as a condition of holding down the job.

The reason for this was simple arithmetic: the number of pounds the handicapper sets for a racehorse to carry includes the weight of everything on its back, equipment, leads, and rider. There isn't a jock on the active list who tips the scale above one hundred and thirteen pounds, which just happens to be the weight Eddie Maple and Angel Cordero both carry.

So it was the fact that American families were eating better and weighing more that opened up opportunities for hard kids to move in from countries where the living was poorer and they grew up small. They'd had their start as apprentice jockeys in Puerto Rico, Brazil, Mexico, and similar places before they arrived here, looking to make it in the big time.

They came over with a lot in common: size and the ambition to win. Some of them stayed tough as nails, like Manuel Ycaza and Jorge Velasquez. Some got a name for acting like gentlemen, like Cordero, who's been known to get off his mount when he's already been loaded into the gate and go over to a shaky young rider with advice on how to take a firm hold on his reins.

On the day I got to hashing over the way things used to be, Bill Shoemaker came to mind, still a youngster by my reckoning, though he'd been riding for thirty-five years and was still at a hundred and three pounds, with push-ups and sit-ups holding him in shape to take on three or four mounts a day.

He went back to the days when twelve hundred dollars was a sizable purse and five thousand the prize in a big stakes race. Yet in a career of more than eight thousand victories, he'd been able to earn a million dollars. A leg broken on the track had kept him out of the action for one year, but he didn't take to the idea of leaving it all behind. He'd been considering making the switch from jockey to trainer, but if he'd have asked for my opinion, I'd have told him the going would be tougher than it was when I took that route.

When the years are catching up with him, or he's losing the fight with his weight, a rider's often tempted to try his hand as a trainer, but it's not a change to be made overnight. I'd started learning my trade when Sherrill Ward shoved a rub rag in my hand, and nineteen years went by before I hooked up with Steve Judge in 1940, when I began to consider myself a qualified horseman. Nobody on the tracks today could duplicate that kind of experience and tuck it under his belt.

A trainer has to steer his whole life so he lives for his horses, getting to know their personalities on a day-to-day basis, learning what they can or can't do as he tries to stretch their performances. A jock may be meeting up with his mount for the first time in the paddock, or he may have had a brief fill-in from the trainer before the horse is saddled. The exercise boy usually knows a lot more about the animal than the man who in the next few minutes has to head him for the wire.

One of the greatest jocks I ever came across took a crack at making the switch, Earl Sande from Idaho, who was fifteen years older than I. In '24 he took a bad fall at Saratoga, when he'd already scored his first Kentucky Derby win on Zev. They nursed him back to health, and he won again, with a horse called Flying Ebony. He was thirty years old when he decided to quit and take a shot at training. He couldn't make a go of it, so after two years, he was back to riding, one horse being Gallant Fox that made Earl Sande the first man since Isaac Murphy to ride three Kentucky Derby winners. Lucille has a picture of Earl stuck in one of the scrapbooks.

A million-dollar jock in the class of Bill Shoemaker, with over eight thousand wins to his credit, has likely learned how to handle himself like a businessman, whether or not he's a gentleman, or else his agent has set him straight. It's common practice nowadays for the top riders to invest their money, whereas it was something out of the ordinary when John Morris talked me into buying a few shares of stock. And the Shoemakers and Eddie Maples know how to dress and how to behave in the company of owners with more cash coming into the bank in a month than the jock will earn from a year in the saddle. On the major tracks, the roughneck days I used to know have faded clear away.

To make those big killings, the riders have to find as many as a couple of thousand mounts a year and ride about 20 percent of them as winners. This means putting in flying hours between tracks on a schedule like an airline pilot's; the Red-Eye Special between the Los Angeles and Kennedy airports brings them in by the drove. When a jockey's hot, he can't miss any chances, because next season he might find his reputation cooling off.

Since I hadn't by then counted California as a lucky place to race in, most of my plane time was spent between New York, Florida, and the Eastern tracks, not on the Red-Eye. Aqueduct, Belmont Park, Arlington Park, and Sportsman Park in Illinois, Keystone in Pennsylvania, Meadowlands in New Jersey, Saratoga, Bowie, Laurel, Thistledown in Ohio—these were the places I flew to for the score I made in '78. Fifteen stakes victories, and retirement was a subject I'd given up thinking about.

Smarten and Terpsichorist were still hitting high. Bends Me Mind and Poppycock were newcomers, and I had a great horse in Smart Angle, who ran off with six of those fifteen wins.

The only way to keep on scoring was to fly the horses there and back, vanning them to and from the nearest available airport. Ticketing them, myself, and the stable crew turned my office into the next best thing to a travel agency some mornings.

Depending on the plane and the company, you can pay as high as three thousand dollars to fly a horse between New York and Miami as live cargo, with his groom traveling for free. But if you shop around and there are more horses booked for the flight, you might knock a few hundred off the price.

When you fly them, you wrap ankle bandages on all four legs so they don't clip themselves, and thick sheepskin pads around their bridles. Some other stables add knee pads, shin guards, padded collars, and leather headgear to protect them from bumping, but I didn't go for all that. And some of the animals are shot so full of tranquilizers they don't know where they are. Since I'm not a believer in drugging, mine fly wide-awake.

They're loaded into horse boxes bolted together for the purpose in the belly of the plane, fit in tight to restrain them. They go in backward, tails toward the cockpit, because the anatomy of a horse makes it impossible for him to brace himself the other way around at the takeoff.

Takeoff is the hardest part of the trip for them, when they really fuss and try to kick, but there's no room for kicking, which frets them even more. But the old prescription will usually work if they've been brought up on it: gentle them and give them a few kind words.

Once they're up and in level flight, things begin to settle down. They'll maybe doze or nibble hay, with the grooms ready to calm them again if they start acting up, or fix them with another dose of tranquilizer. They travel a lot smoother over a long distance than they ever did when they were vanned every mile of the way, bouncing along the highways in the middle of all kinds of traffic.

For all the flying they do, the top jocks have an edge over their mounts that follow the same routes track to track. If a rider should take a drink too many and get out of hand as a passenger, the pilot has no legal right to shoot him. If a horse gets beyond control and there's no other choice if the plane's to be saved, the pilot can shoot to kill. I'm grateful no horse of mine has gone that way.

Without the horse flights, American racing never could have developed as it has today, and this is another major difference between here and Europe. Flying animals across the Atlantic Ocean isn't unusual—the Aga Khan brought Lashkari that way along with his rider, Yves Saint-Martin, as a fifty-three-to-one winner in the first of the Breeders' Cup series in 1984. But with the tracks and the countries so close to each other in Europe, there's less flying of animals on that side of the water, where they stick closer to old methods than we do.

I'd had one or two British visitors at my barn and heard them say that what American trainers had the most of in their stalls was a bunch of sprinters when there were programs here where every race was over no more than six furlongs, which you wouldn't find anywhere in Europe.

People from overseas also seemed surprised to see how much we relied on a stopwatch to check what a horse's limits were when you pushed him in a workout. Over there, I concluded, he was more likely to get easy exercise, and it was only when you raced him that you could tell what he was capable of doing.

I got an update on the British side of the business after I hired a new assistant, an Englishman, with the thought I'd need one in case my brother couldn't turn himself around.

Phil Gleaves, born in Liverpool, was seven years old when he got down his first bet, two bits each way at an honest ten-to-one on a horse called Team Spirit in the '64 Grand National. "I won," he told me, "and that's when I thought I was a genius in this game."

He was a twenty-year-old rider when he landed in this country to gallop horses in New York. Toward the end of his first year at that, I took him on to do the same job for me. I liked the way he handled it, so I marked him down for promotion.

I found that we spoke the same language, more or less, because anywhere you go as a horseman the talk isn't much different when trainers get together with the stable crew and the jocks.

We all use *I* a lot when we win or reckon we've got a chance to. "I beat him by a neck," we say, and never mind the horse. It's the same with lawyers and fight managers: "I tried the case," and never mind the judge; "I decked him in the first round," and never mind the fighter.

The Miami *Herald* got me on record once to make the point when I was thinking about the licking Cain Hoy Stable took in the '63 Derby with Manuel Ycaza aboard Never Bend: "I'm going to win with Never Bend, but No Robbery costs me the race. I tell Manuel Ycaza if Never Bend breaks running, to go on . . . But No Robbery is hugging me the first three-quarters of a mile, forcing the issue. I go the three-quarters in a minute and ten seconds, which is the fastest time in eighty-nine Derbies until then. Never Bend is cooked at the end of a mile, and I get beat a length and a quarter by Chateaugay."

From what Phil told me, I gathered in England a lot of things went on in much the same way they'd been going when I was there for Captain Guggenheim. On both sides of the Atlantic, operating a stable is sometimes a family business passed on from father to son. But it's easier for a Buddy Jacobson from Brooklyn to break in over here. In England the bloodlines of the people involved count for maybe as much as the bloodlines of the horses.

One big change had come about, said Phil. Gambling over there was wide open like in Vegas, with everything on tap from roulette to one-armed bandits. The betting parlors were draining off money from horse racing by keeping customers away from the tracks, and the big-time bookmakers pour the profits into gambling casinos instead of plowing them back into the sport they came from. In this country, a whole slew of organizations—commissioners, stewards, owners, breeders, and trainers, to name a few—work to make sure the same thing won't happen here, and the tracks get a fairer shake of the action.

Smart Angle went on adding to his earnings in 1980, and his new stablemates were bringing home good purses, too, especially the fillies like Heavenly Cause in the Frizette at Belmont Park and the Selima at Laurel, Dame Mysterieuse in the Holly at Meadowlands, and De La Rose in the Treetop and the Remsen. In the course of the action that year and next, I did some buying on behalf of the owners and attended any number of sales.

I noticed the crowds growing thicker, the bidding getting pricier and more British buyers appearing on the scene. Once, it had been British breeders who sold to the Americans and the French. Now the tables were turned, and the marketplace became this country, with the hub of it in Kentucky, where 80 percent of all the Derby winners have been born and bred in the Bluegrass.

There were always a lot of familiar faces at Keeneland and a lot of "Hi, Woody!" Robert Sangster was one of the regulars, a king of sorts in his own right, sitting on top of the British soccer pools industry and splashing money around like water. His Irish trainer, Vincent O'Brien, who plunged in first by training jumpers, was part of the team that took back home the bloodlines of some of the British thoroughbreds shipped over

Belmont Park, 1976. Lucille's Sail to Rome took the Cowdin, ridden by Jorge Velasquez, trained by guess who.

With John Morris and his wife, Edna. John was one of the very best I ever trained for.

Henryk leads his Conquistador Cielo into the winners' circle at Belmont Park after the colt took the 1982 Dwyer. Eddie Maple sits in the saddle. Lucille and I are feeling good, too.

It's the Eclipse Awards banquet at the Waldorf-Astoria, January 1984.

And at that Eclipse Awards evening, Lucille has a word with John Forsythe, actor and racing buff.

Devil's Bag and Eddie Maple win the 1983 Champagne, a record-breaking run and the colt's fourth straight victory.

Swale in the homestretch, ready to give me my third Belmont Stakes victory back to back.

Spring 1985 Today's Promise, Tomorrow's Hopes

My barn at Belmont Park. This is Soli, one of the current crop of stakes-winning three-year-old fillies.

Again at Belmont Park's backstretch. Two-year-old Canadian Winter is a half-brother of Caveat.

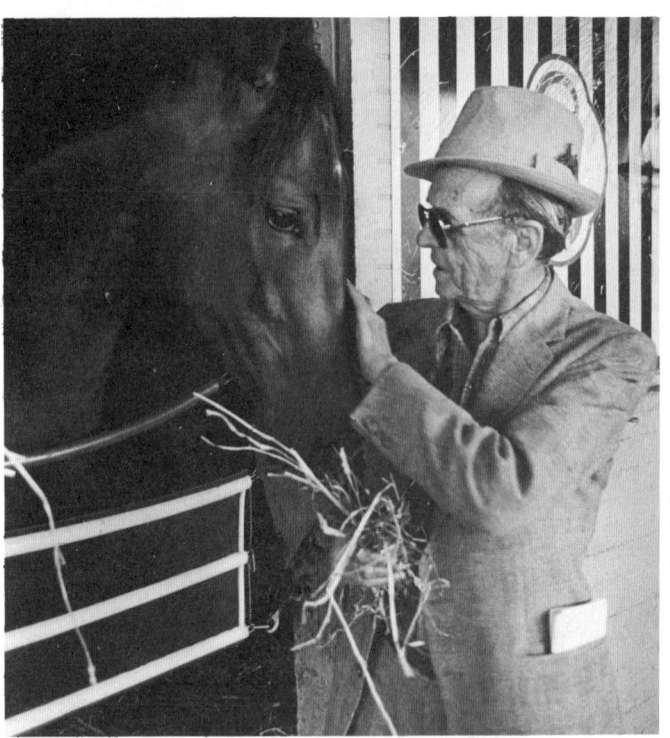

Contredance, another three-year-old filly, deserves a pat on her pretty head as a stakes winner.

My one-two sweep of the 1985 Belmont. The spunky little bay gelding Creme Fraiche, with Eddie Maple in the saddle, crossing the finish line a half a length ahead of his stablemate Stephan's Odyssey.

here after the war. Sangster didn't blink an eye when he spent nearly eighteen million dollars at one summer sale.

He told me one day, "You're the Vincent O'Brien of America." I didn't think to say that maybe Vince was Ireland's Woody Stephens.

I'd spot Nelson Bunker Hunt of Bluegrass Farm, a billionaire who pulled off the trick that Harry Guggenheim failed at: winning two Derbies, English and French, within four days of each other in '76. John Gaines might stop by to talk as we'd done more often than I can remember in the course of forty years. Or E. P. Taylor, who had the reputation of being the richest man in Canada with his fortune built on beer and newsprint; it was at his place, Windfields Farm in Maryland, that Devil's Bag was sired and foaled.

Some Japanese showed up for a while, but they didn't stay on for long. Greeks like Stavros Niarchos, who owns a fleet of oil tankers, did keep coming around to give the Arab buyers a run for their money, with a little help from Robert Sangster and his British Bloodstock Agency. Anybody who liked to hear money talk could listen to Sangster and a Niarchos agent drive up the prices and then drop out after a group like Sheik Mohammed's Aston Upthorpe Stud had been maneuvered out of an extra couple of million for a colt or a filly to ship out to race in Europe.

And anybody who treated the stud book like a bible could give a little thought to the fact that it was Arab stallions that got English breeders started three hundred years ago, and now the horses bought at Keeneland still carry those Arab bloodlines.

Seth Hancock made the rounds at Keeneland and Belmont Park, bringing in his yearlings and colts for sale, a lot of them the cream of the crop, but the prices he got often hurt his pride. He objected to the common breeders' practice of fattening them up for auction to give the look that appeals to a majority of buyers. One night he saw a couple of other colts sell for more than three million apiece, which raised his hopes that a really good yearling of his would bring him at least two million. He felt he'd been done when he got only eight hundred thousand for the horse that, named Caerleon later on, became the champion three year old of France.

He had well over a hundred brood mares at Claiborne, about half of them his, the rest boarded there by other owners. He was choosy about the stallions he wanted to serve his females, and he turned down a lot that their owners offered him. He was choosy, too, about where the foals went and where they were sold as yearlings. What he was looking for was one to hold on to for himself, a horse that would carry Claiborne silks and set the world on fire.

13

August in Saratoga

If you're willing to stay up half the night at a party before you get out of bed at five o'clock for the morning check of the stable, then August is the time to be at Saratoga, the old queen of the racetracks. So it's pick up and pack up every year for Lucille and me to drive up there for the races that start at one-thirty every afternoon for twenty-four days except the dark ones on Tuesday, almost all of them stakes, which are a trainer's target.

Governor Mario Cuomo of New York was up there to hand out the trophies when he asked, "Are you the only one who ever wins here, Woody?" It was nice to hear, but nobody wins more than he loses, and you hope the proportion will stay about one to five.

August brings out most of the sporting bloods in the East to the oldest racecourse in America—the black-tie set of Whitneys, Phippses, and Vanderbilts, the polo players and the horseplayers, the new-money people, and a crowd of players and railbirds from Aqueduct and Belmont Park, all looking for a better turn of luck, a day or so of vacation, and maybe a dose of the local water to treat their indigestion.

There's something on hand for everybody with an eye for a good horse. It's here that they run the Travers, one of the oldest stakes in America, named for a founder of the track. The Flash is another and the Alabama a third. You can take a walk through the Racing Museum and the Hall of Fame to see the history of racing spelled out in jockey caps and silks, walls hung with pictures of winners, bronze horses, and cases filled chockablock with trophies, silver and gold.

Talking about horses starts at breakfast, on the lawn at the track, where you can watch the morning workouts while you drink your coffee. It goes on through lunch—at the Reading Room Club, if you're invited—and on past dinner, for eighteen or twenty hours every day.

Even the privet hedges are clipped in the shapes of horses. Restaurant menus list an item called "Saratoga trotters," which have never seen harness—they're baked chicken legs. The visitors' guide is the *Daily Racing Form*, and the hotel lobbies are stocked with the same giveaway newspapers you can get at the track.

For the four days of Fasig-Tipton's yearling sales, you see a lot of the same faces you find at Keeneland—from Kentucky, Virginia, Maryland, and overseas—and the prices aren't far apart. As a warm-up for her trip to the Bluegrass, Queen Elizabeth sent her trainer, Ian Balding, who followed in Boyd-Rochfort's footsteps, over to Saratoga in '84, and the old casino that had been shut for forty years was opened up to celebrate with a dinner dance for charity.

Provided you're somebody on a guest list kept down to about five hundred, you can step out at the Museum Ball on the Monday after the first weekend. If you're somebody who's not, you can stand outside on Union Avenue across from the clubhouse entrance to the track and watch them drive up in Rolls-Royces, Mercedes, and Continentals before they get onto the floor of a big striped tent for the biggest social whirl on the calendar.

Your name has to be on a shorter list, fewer than a hundred men and a handful of women, to get admission to the round table of the Jockey Club that meets during the second week to talk about how to hold to its standards when new money and new methods are changing the nature of the business faster than anybody in the Old Guard ever expected.

Grade-one people used to turn up in Saratoga in their private railroad cars, with a chauffeur waiting for them at the station. Some of those automobiles still travel the streets, and so do horse-drawn carriages, but the society trade is more likely these days to drop in by helicopter from Newport and Long Island.

Prices keep climbing here, just like everyplace else. A paper cup of lemonade sold by a kid on the sidewalk has gone up from a nickel to a dime to now half a dollar. Oats, hay, and straw for all my horses cost eighteen thousand dollars a month. Tack bills add twenty-five hundred dollars on top of that; medicines, vitamins, cotton, and bandages another fifteen hundred. The bill for renting rooms for the whole crew of us gets closer year by year to the charges you face at the Waldorf-Astoria, but the regular billing to the owners of those horses stays put at forty-eight dollars a day. So I have to reckon on August in Saratoga seeing a bigger outlay of cash than I'd been used to earning for a year's work. Without a few good wins, I'd end up drowned in red ink.

The calls on your time are heavy. The owners like to walk around the barn and socialize. Sportswriters and photographers wait at your elbow. When the auctions get under way, you have to be there to inspect the stock. And the invitations never stop: come to this reception, that ceremony, somebody's party every night of the week. I've gone home so tired I could barely crawl into bed or get out of it in the morning.

But Saratoga does give you the opportunity to meet people who want to do business when they know you're doing all you can to run first-class and you're willing to spend any kind of money to take good care of their animals. If you decide to make space to fit another one in, you have to consider weeding out what you've already got, maybe by telling an owner the truth, that he'd do better running his horse outside of the major tracks because he isn't going to make it in the big time.

In 1979 a filly was brought to my barn by a man who'd never

owned a horse before he bought her at Saratoga. She meant something special to me because she'd belonged to John Olin, and Mr. Olin was somebody I'd remember all my life for his kindnesses. I hadn't seen him lately—he'd been too sick and too wrapped up in his business and politics ever to get to the track. And then, all of a sudden, he was gone for good, and his horses were put up for sale.

The filly's new owner, Henryk deKwiatkowski, put Kennelot in my hands on the recommendation of E. P. Taylor, who'd known me ever since he and Mr. Olin bought a couple of nice colts together, which I took for training. Henryk K. knew nothing about the game, but he had some firm opinions about how to play it. I could have shot myself after the first few times we talked. I said to Lucille, "Where did I run into this character?" It seemed unlikely we'd ever respect each other.

Maybe we never would have come to terms if Mr. Taylor didn't tell him: "You leave Woody alone. Don't interfere." And another friend of mine gave him the same advice: "You keep your fingers off his neck." Things would have been difficult if I'd let him have his way, but I didn't.

It was easier to call him Henryk, and that was the name that stuck. Once we got on the right terms, I liked him for his big smile, his confidence in the judgments I made, and the stories he told about himself, some of them calculated to curl up your eyebrows.

He was a Polish boy, he explained, one of the three sons of an officer in the Army there who'd been killed leading a cavalry charge against German tanks when they rolled across the border in September of '39. Henryk made his getaway going east instead of west, but the Russians grabbed him and sent him to Siberia to work in the kitchens of labor camps for two or three years.

Somehow he got out of that and traveled three thousand miles south to reach Iran. He boarded a British ship there, the *Empress of Canada*, with the hope of sailing to England, but a German U-boat torpedoed her off Sierra Leone on the west coast of Africa.

Only seven of them escaped alive, Henryk by swimming through the oil slick that covered the water so he wouldn't be eaten by sharks. He must have been picked up by some other ship, because he did get to England to achieve his ambition, which was to join a Polish squadron of Spitfire fighter pilots in the Royal Air Force. By his account, he was only fifteen years old. His two brothers had done the same, but both of them died in combat.

Listening to him, you had to believe every word. He speaks practically every language in Europe, and he's a mine of information who taught me a lot of stuff I'd never have known otherwise.

When the war was over, he said, he won a scholarship to King's College at Cambridge in England, to take up aeronautics as an engineer. After Pakistan split away from India, he organized the Pakistani airline. Then he went off on a different tack, carving statues in Florence, Italy, before Pratt & Whitney hired him as a step to making him European salesman for their airplane engines.

When he concluded he'd learned enough about selling to go into business for himself, he raked up three thousand dollars to get started, looking for buyers of secondhand surplus planes and working as a broker. He claimed he never made a payoff of any kind, which I believed, because he's always been aboveboard in his dealings with me.

His big killing came just before the weekend he brought Kennelot to my stable, one of five thoroughbreds he paid a total of a couple of million for. He had met the Shah of Iran through an introduction from one of Pahlavi's sisters. Then Henryk proceeded to sell him nine Boeing 747s in a deal worth one hundred and fifty million dollars. The Shah wrote out a check for ninety million of that as a down payment. Henryk's fee was 10 percent of everything.

Over the years, I've been his top trainer, and we've spent some time together, mostly in Saratoga. He's one of the last of his kind, a horseman starting from scratch and building up a stable that's been lucky enough to bring him big money in purses and in syndication, with syndication a long way ahead of winnings.

His wife was an American, Lynn, whose father was one of Henryk's lawyers, and he had six children with her before the marriage broke up. It seemed to us around the stable that she liked horses for their own sake a lot better than he did, but in the matter of charm and getting along with people they were pretty much alike. Since Lucille fit in that mold, too, the two ladies enjoyed having lunch together.

When Henryk and I reached agreement about who was boss around the barn, he wanted me to buy him more horses. The names he chose for some of them clued you in to where he'd come from and what was important to him in his life.

A yearling I found for him for three hundred thousand was registered as Danzig for the city on the Vistula River that the Poles and the Germans fought over when he was a kid. Siberian Dancer was linked to another early turn in the long road Henryk had traveled.

Conrad, his older boy, shared the name with a colt, and Nicole, a daughter, shared hers with a filly. Michele, another daughter, had a filly called after her, Michele Mon Amour. A third girl, Alexander, got remembered with a filly, Alexander My Love, and the youngest in the family, Stephan, with a colt, a really good one, Stephan's Odyssey.

Sabin was the name of a girl he'd once been engaged to, and also the name he registered the filly I bought for him for three quarters of a million dollars. De La Rose, bid in at half a million, had a girl's name attached to her, too, but he didn't let on who she was.

He didn't care about money, but he had the talent and the luck to keep piling it up in this new business as well as in his old one, where he had a network and agents and contacts keeping him in touch with opportunities around the world. He sold off a fleet of outdated 707s for TWA on 7 percent commission. He talked about going into China. He worked on deals for the Saudis and for Hilton International hotels.

Buying and training horses was left in my hands. "I don't make decisions without Woody" was what he told anybody who asked. "He calls the shots. If he says we don't run a horse, we scratch him."

If there was any stumbling block, it was put there by his wife, Lynn's, good nature. When you find you've a horse that isn't coming up to expectations, you like to get it out of your stable. But Lynn grew too fond of them for that. She wanted to hold on until they'd lost their value and you had to come close to giving them away.

I had De La Rose in one stall and Heavenly Cause in another, in training for Jim and Eleanor Ryan of Columbia, Maryland. Henryk's filly was a candidate for the vote of champion juvenile of 1980, but Heavenly Cause beat her out of the title. Although De La Rose had licked her twice on the grass, I thought the Ryans might take a crack at next year's Kentucky Derby.

The advice I heard from some quarters was to keep De La Rose on turf, since she seemed to prefer it. "I go by what you say," Henryk told me, but I didn't see any grass races for her coming up on the calendar. I put both horses as an entry in the Kentucky Oaks, run the day before the Derby, which the Ryans had decided wasn't the right race for Heavenly Cause. When a trainer puts in two horses with different owners, that's a single entry according to the rules, though the full purse goes to whichever of them wins. Where one of them is intended to set the pace for the benefit of the other, the trainer has to let the stewards know ahead of time.

This didn't apply here; I thought both of them had a fair chance at it, and the Oaks was a race I'd done well in, with four previous winners—White Star Line, Sally Ship, Make Sail, and Hidden Talent, the first of the three in Harry Guggenheim's silks.

Heavenly Cause wasn't the favorite, although she'd just pulled off the Fantasy Stakes at Oaklawn Park, Arkansas, with an added value of two hundred thousand which made it the richest run for three year olds anywhere in the country until the Breeders' Cup came along in 1984. That win at Hot Springs had put an extra $133,890 into the Ryans's account and brought the filly's lifetime earnings up to $421,111.

Laffit Pincay had ridden her then, as he had done on four other outings, and he figured she was getting bigger and stronger every day. As I boosted him aboard her for the Oaks, I told him, "Just let her run. Get that big stride going. Don't restrain her, but don't push her, either."

There were four other fillies in the field besides my pair, but they were the finest any stable had to offer. Heavenly Cause broke sharp, and at the first turn she was just a length behind the leader. At the far turn, Pincay moved her wide, and she stuck her head out front. It looked like an easy score for her when De La Rose with Pat Day in the saddle took up the challenge.

Pincay smelled what was coming, and he moved his mount out to the middle of the track, where Pat was running neck to neck with him at the sixteenth pole. Heavenly Cause dug in again when she spotted her stablemate. At the wire, she won by inches. I had saddled my forty-second winner of a stakes worth a hundred thousand or more, and Jim and Eleanor Ryan of Ryehill Farm had clocked up their twenty-eighth stakes victory in five years of racing.

A sore loser is nobody you want as an owner when you're running a public stable, and there's been nobody in that category on my list. They all come to appreciate that you don't have a hope of winning them every race, which is important for everybody concerned to understand. De La Rose had delivered a brilliant performance, and I went on buying and working more horses for Henryk.

I saw a colt I liked at the Saratoga sales, bred in Florida, sired by Mr. Prospector. I thought he had a classy look about him, a nice, well-mannered animal, and I was surprised to get him at that kind of money when the bidding stopped at a hundred and fifty thousand. Henryk dipped into Spanish to name him Conquistador Cielo, which means Conqueror of the Skies.

I went about getting him ready for his first outing on the track, just hating to abuse him too much, him or any other horse. At this stage he wasn't quite tight enough, and he finished second, beat three quarters of a length. For his second start, I ran him in Maryland, where he outclassed everything else in the field and broke his maiden by nine lengths.

We went back to Saratoga for the Special, and he won that. After his rider, Larry Saumell, got off him, he said, "Woody, he did it easy, but there's something hurting this colt."

I looked Conquistador over in the barn and found a small knot developing on one of his shin bones. I didn't think too much about it because he wasn't sore, and it isn't anything rare in a racehorse. I thought it would just level off and probably go away.

I entered him in the Sanford, and he was beaten by a head. Now he had two out of four to his credit, but the knot was getting bigger, and he was beginning to hurt.

We X-rayed him, and the vets studied the pictures and called it a saucer fracture. They have varying opinions about the treatment for these. One feller advised, "Let it heal on its own." Another wanted to drill a little hole into the knot so maybe more blood would circulate through it and cure it that way, which was the route we took.

On the X-ray plates, a saucer fracture looks like a small, narrow *V* on the surface of the bone; it's something that's tough to deal with properly. One of the vets, Dr. Reid, went in with a drill and made a hole the size of a toothpick into the spot. We were told it would take ninety days for it to get well.

I gave Conquistador those ninety days just walking around with a saddle on his back, no rider. Then we took him to Hialeah to start training again, and he seemed in good shape. He was a colt with a lot of sense. One morning I was working him, his bridle broke, and he went off like a shot around the track. I thought we were in for trouble, but he pulled himself up at the gap and just hung around there. I rode my pony alongside him, put the pony's bridle on him, and walked him back home as calm as you'd wish for.

At Hialeah, I noticed that once in a while he'd take a step that wasn't 100 percent; he was still a little bit sore, but I ran him over seven furlongs there, and he broke the track record. Two days later, he was lame again, and I wasn't sure what to do about it.

Then I remembered hearing about something I labeled "the blue boot," and I bought one for eighteen hundred dollars. It's one of the gadgets that's shown up in the past few years designed for the treatment of horses: no drugging, no disguising the problem, no discomfort to the horse.

You can get hold of equipment today that works with a laser beam to help nature heal bowed hocks and bucked shins. The breeders sometimes use sonar machines to check on the progress a foal is making before it's born, just the way doctors do for a woman who's expecting a baby.

A blue boot is made up of two curved plates, which are charged with electricity when you plug them into a household socket. It works by sending a weak current through the area of the fracture. I strapped it around his leg and kept it on him for two hours every day, following the recommendation not to do much with him for the first ten or twelve days. Then, when he showed signs of improvement, I started him galloping again, but not working him hard for maybe three or four weeks.

After that I entered him in the Flamingo but changed my mind and scratched him, to bring him to New York to begin training him to be ready to run around two turns, a distance he'd never tackled before. He tried that when I sent him to Maryland for the Preakness prep at Pimlico. He won it easy.

I was still faithful in using the blue boot and putting him in ice every day. When I got to work in the morning, I'd train him on the track, then stand him in warm water for an hour, take him out of the tub, and strap on the gadget for the two hours prescribed.

My mind was set by now on the 1982 Metropolitan at Belmont Park, a hundred-thousand-dollar stakes for three year olds and up. He ran awfully well in the prep, so I decided to go for the handicap. He was as good a horse as I'd ever trained, excepting maybe Bald Eagle, and a good stick horse who'd fight back off the stick.

He won the Metropolitan with the fastest mile there ever was for the race, a minute thirty-three seconds, to win by seven and a half. That was on Monday, and I had him in for the Belmont five days later. Some friends of Henryk's were telling him, "There's no way Woody will bring this horse back in form by Saturday. It isn't even worth trying. No chance."

I said flat out, "I can, even if the whole damn world's against me."

"I'm going with Woody," Henryk said.

The colt was eating well, and he had a perfect disposition. Running a horse in races close together had never bothered me if the animal was in condition for it. I'd done the same with De La Rose, and she had proved herself both times. There wasn't a shadow of doubt that Conquistador could pull it off, and I loved it.

Wednesday came, rain turned the track sloppy, and Lucille stayed home from the races that afternoon. She took a call from Laffit Pincay in California: "If anything should happen and I don't have a mount Saturday, I'd love to ride Woody's horse." She mentioned that Eddie Maple was already booked on him for the Belmont.

On Friday, in the seventh race, a filly that Eddie was riding came down at the eighth pole, broke a leg, and pitched him off onto the track. He got to his feet, and I guessed he went home. I called him that evening, but his wife answered. "He's in the hospital, with eight cracked ribs." So now I had the horse but no rider for tomorrow.

Lucille said, "Remember Pincay left a message for you." I stayed by the phone to talk with him in Los Angeles.

He said, "I'm named on six horses tomorrow. I don't know if they'll let me off of them or not."

I hung up, then dialed Marge Everett, who's the boss at Hollywood Park, to tell her where I was hanging. "I'll get back to you in twenty minutes," she said. She was as good as her word. When the phone rang again, it was Marge: "Laffit's on his way." He had never won a Belmont; now he had a chance that looked like a certainty.

The strategy for doing it needed some thinking about. The Belmont is run over a mile and a half, and Bill Shoemaker, who'd be up on board Linkage, was a crack rider at that distance. There was a big speed horse, Aloma's Ruler, who'd have a sixteen-year-old apprentice in the saddle, and I'd have to take account of him carrying a beginner's advantage in weight.

I said to Pincay in the paddock, "Go to the first turn wide, like you're going out." This way, we might have a surprise for the kid jockey, Jack Kaenel, and fox him into committing Aloma's Ruler. As for Linkage, he didn't worry me much; Pincay would have more horse under him.

The whole thing ticked along like a clock. Pincay took my colt so wide at the first turn I heard people say he was trying to get out. It spooked Jack Kaenel into forcing Aloma's Ruler, who ran out of steam, and Linkage didn't fire at all. With a grin splitting his face, Laffit and Conquistador captured the Belmont, fourteen lengths, as easy as taking a walk in the country.

The colt's next shot was at the Dwyer at Aqueduct, the "Big A," where a breezy day turns the chute into a wind tunnel. He was a star of the sports pages now and the one-to-ten favorite in a field of six. Soon after the start, Eddie Maple, with tape around his ribs, took one look under his right arm and another over his shoulder to see if anybody was anywhere close behind him. There was nothing, so he eased up to preserve his mount and let Conquistador finish any way he liked.

Henryk let the word go out that he was considering the colt for syndication. Seth Hancock was only one of the men who got busy nailing together a proposal. I'd sent Conquistador to be broken at Claiborne as a yearling, and Seth reckoned he'd never seen better. The question was how much more than thirty million was this horse likely to bring as a stallion.

We went to Saratoga, where he won the Jim Dandy and stayed on there for the Travers, a mile and a quarter and a two-hundred-thousand-dollar stakes. Then some things began to go wrong. I wondered whether we should have saved him to run against older horses in the Woodward for the same amount of money. And Eddie had gotten into a little trouble and been suspended for a few days.

When that happens to a rider, he can get an extension, which Eddie had asked for, and he thought it was agreed. But twenty-four hours before the start of the Travers, he was told he'd have to begin serving his days. He asked me whether somebody could maybe pinch-hit for him.

"If you don't ride him, nobody will," I told him. The racetrack management wouldn't have wanted to hear that, either. So Eddie got a judge to put off his suspension days again.

You don't make excuses in this business, but I do like to look for explanations. We went into the Travers with a lot of pressure on us, and the horse lost, but I wouldn't have changed a thing about him. Coming up to this race, he'd won seven in a row and earned $474,328, this colt I bought for less than a third of that figure.

I never raced him again, although I thought he was sound enough to have gone on winning. Instead, Seth put together the toughest deal he'd ever handled, thirty shares at $910,000 apiece for a record of $36,400,000, with Henryk getting an extra ten shares for himself. At the close of '82, Conquistador went to stand at Claiborne Farm in retirement with Danzig and a couple of dozen more stallions.

Henryk wasn't impressed or scared by money. He said, "That's a lot of rubles, but it won't change my life. I'm rich already." He's invested big in mares to breed to Conquistador and Danzig; at present, he owns something in the neighborhood of fifteen of them.

The first crop of young horses were babies in 1984. The first foals were to be broken and trained the following fall, and some of them would be mine. When they get to the races, they could set the world on fire, if their sires prove to be the kind of stallions I think they are, and Henryk deKwiatkowski will be a top name in racing.

Some of Conquistador's gold dust rubbed off on his mother. He was the first foal of a stakes winner, K D Princess, from an old Calumet Farm line. She wasn't rated as much before her son came out on the track. After he went to stud, she fetched a million and three quarters at a Florida auction.

There was the other side of the coin to be seen during the golden days of Conquistador. Henryk's wife told me they were having trouble in their marriage. But when they split, they still went around together, and they had one of their sons with them when Henryk flew Lucille and me in his private plane to the Matchmaker in Atlantic City just before Saratoga opened in August of '84.

And on the same dark side again, I split with my brother Bill. I was getting ready to send him to South Carolina with some young horses. He called me and said, "I've decided not to go."

"Just where are you going to go?" He hung up on me. I felt he'd turned himself away, and I didn't know why. I didn't think he was jealous, but that was my sisters' conclusion. They said, "He's been jealous of you for a long time."

He spent a year with no work to do at all. Then he started training in Ocala, Florida. It's been a while since I heard directly from him, but I understand from other people that he's behaving himself and believing in himself, happy in his job and keeping those he works for happy with him.

As things stand with us today, I can't do much more than wish him the best. Most all the time, the tide flowed stronger for me than it did for him. But I'm a firm believer in that old saying, "The best is yet to come," and he's got an edge of nine years over me.

14

You Don't Win 'Em All

We've had a lot of good years but never a better one than 1983 brought us. I'd take a walk through the barn and see more nice horses than I'd ever had in the stalls at the same time.

In the spring, Chumming and Caveat both looked like prospects for the Kentucky Derby, both ridden by Eddie Maple in their Triple Crown preps because I hadn't wanted to race them together. He picked Chumming as his mount in the Derby, so the other colt was under Laffit Pincay. Chumming got hurt, but Caveat broke through a wall of horses and was really rolling when he finished third.

Five weeks later, in July, I ran him with the same rider in the Belmont wearing the scarlet and maroon silks of August Belmont IV, a grandson of the founder of the track; he owned Caveat in partnership with two other men, James P. Ryan and Robert Kirkham.

The colt got bounced off the rail twice, then bumped by Au Point with Angel Cordero in the saddle. But my horse made a rush from far off the pace, and it was all his after the turn for home. Conquistador last year and now Caveat—two Belmonts back to back was something to feel good about. Mr. Belmont was seventy-four years old, and he'd just had surgery on his heart. Watching him hand himself a trophy when he was giving them out was a pretty nice feeling, too.

I had Henryk's Sabin in training and Miss Oceana from Newstead Farm, a daughter of Alydar, who was on her way to piling up eight firsts and three seconds in her eleven starts, which in my opinion qualified her for an Eclipse Award as champion two-year-old filly of '83, but she lost it to Wayne Lukas's Althea, her half-sister also sired by Alydar, who'd done most of her racing in California. The purses are bigger there than in the East, and money talks in deciding the Eclipses.

Morning Bob was in my stable, sore in the legs and owned by Elizabeth Moran, who'd had some jumpers in the past, but she was new to flat racing. He wasn't a quick horse, which is the type I like, and I couldn't see him as a stud. But I found people who did. I vanned him to Delaware to take advantage of the tax break. I'd bought him for sixty thousand; he sold for a million and a half.

Altogether I was training thirty or forty horses, and I like plenty of help to take good care of them. So I'd hired two more assistants to share the load with Phil Gleaves and me.

Billy Badgett, following his father in the business, was an ex-groom who came with me as top exercise boy before he got promoted; Sandy Bruno had a different background, a school teacher with a master's degree.

Sandy was holding down two jobs, teaching and working nights as a waitress, when she asked me in Florida if she could come to Saratoga. "Sure," I said, "I'll give you something to do." She started as a hot-walker, bottom of the ladder, but she was ambitious to get ahead. She had a really good touch with a horse, and she got along with all kinds of people.

After three years of watching her work part-time, I asked her, "What will it take to interest you more in horses than in teaching?" We discussed it, and I made her a proposition to be stable foreman. She told someone later if she wasn't with me, training, she wouldn't be around the tracks.

So now there was an extra reason for thinking this year was something special: I had first-class help at the top in Sandy and Billy. Phil Gleaves would be checking out shortly to train for a

Canadian owner, Frank Stronach, but I knew I had to hold on to quite a few horses to be able to afford to keep good assistants on the payroll. If they wanted to bring in one or two of their own, that would be okay by me. And if I ever decided it was time to rack it up, they could either take over or I'd place them elsewhere at the level they deserved.

I'd always had some nice fillies to train, but it's the colts that draw more attention from the racing crowd. I was happy to see three colts led off the vans in Hialeah for me—Vision, Swale, and Devil's Bag, a son of Halo foaled at Windfields Farm. Alice Mills, who's a du Pont and rich like the rest of that family, had spotted him as a yearling there in Maryland and advised her husband, Jimmy Mills, to buy him at Keeneland in the summer of '82 with a final bid of $325,000.

By the time spring came, it was clear that Devil's Bag held the biggest promise of the three, and I called Mr. Mills to tell him what I thought. I worked the colt alone one morning with Phil in the saddle. "Try to go three quarters in fourteen." The stopwatch showed he did it in twelve. Now I *knew* I had a good horse.

I decided not to get in too big a hurry with him, so I shipped him to Saratoga, where the money is made in August. I waited until the last week there in a six-furlong maiden. On his looks alone, he went to the post the three-to-one favorite, and he scored by seven-and-a-half lengths in a minute ten-and-three-fifths, a second and more faster than the twelve I clocked him at before.

Eddie Maple was on board, and all he had to do was smack him on the shoulder to get him into the lead. "His attitude was exactly right," Eddie said. "He just kept looking around when we finished, like he knew what he had to do."

The first win raises your hopes and provides some clues, but it leaves a lot you still have to learn. I brought Devil back down to Belmont Park to give him another easy race before I tried him in a big stakes. Eight days later on a sloppy strip he scored again, five lengths and a quarter.

I picked the Cowdin as his first outing in a stakes, a popular race over seven furlongs, which was one more than he'd tried so far. He answered every call that Eddie made on him and beat Dr. Carter by three lengths in a record time of a minute twenty-one and two-fifths. As long as I'd been around, I never saw a colt equal that.

You come to know a horse the way you do a man or woman, step by step. You can't learn by listening, only by watching close, judging him by what he does and how he goes about it. Devil's Bag was so smart he seemed to understand how you wanted him to perform.

Now he began to be something special to the world as well as me. Two weeks after the Cowdin, I ran him in the Champagne, grade one and an extra furlong, stretching the distance to a mile. This time, he beat Dr. Carter by seven, running the fastest mile in the history of the racetrack, faster by a fifth than Seattle Slew's seven years earlier. Eddie felt sure the colt could have kept on going. "He wasn't quitting at all," he said. "I was just sitting there without even cocking my whip."

Four out of four set off everybody talking about this horse. I took him to Maryland, and he captured one more, the Futurity at Laurel by five lengths and a quarter at odds of one-to-twenty. I had a last race in mind for him before the end of the year, the Remsen Stakes at Aqueduct, but he stepped on a small stone and got a slight bruise on his right rear leg. Enough was enough; it was time for us to head for Florida.

The amount of attention the Devil was getting left some other horses of mine standing out in the cold, where they didn't deserve to be. Sabin was one of my sweethearts, a tough little filly with an urge to lead the pack and hold on all the way to the finish. Whether it was dirt or grass didn't bother her, but on the grass she was one of the best. I ran her thirteen times that year, and she got beaten in only five of her outings.

Miss Oceana, owned by Gus Schwab and Mark Harding's Newstead Farm, kept up her form and looked like a candidate for the Breeders' Cup races that were already in the works for Hollywood Park in the year that lay ahead.

And I had Swale, the two year old that never seemed quite sure of himself when he stood quiet as a cat in the shadows at the back of his stall, head to the wall. But he was a good, consistent colt, improving every time he was out and snatching a victory in three big races in a row.

I had a lot to be grateful for when my seventieth birthday turned up on the calendar. Five hundred people were there to celebrate and make it quite a party. My mother, who had turned ninety-three, stayed in her house in Lexington, set on living alone without the nurse I wanted her to have because we were scared she'd take a fall and hurt herself some day. But I called her, and we talked on a telephone hookup with the whole crowd joining in.

The entertainment end was in charge of Cab Calloway, still singing his *hi-di-hi* and *ho-do-ho* at the age of seventy-six, a man I'd known from the night Lucille and I walked into the New York club called the Zanzibar, where he was performing with his band, and he introduced us to a singer who was on stage for the first time there—Pearl Bailey.

For the birthday party, a big screen was set up for movies of some of the best racing days of my life. We did some eating and drinking and dancing in the cause of having a good time, and listening to Cab got me thinking about some other friends I'd made in his line of business over the years.

Cab was and is a visitor at my stable in Belmont Park and a steady horseplayer at the track. Harry James, who played the horses as well as the trumpet, used to stop by, too, and I'd let him sleep on the couch in the cottage. His wife, Betty Grable, loved the game as much as he did. They had a few horses of their own, and I guess they both went for a bundle of money.

When I had Caveat in the Derby, Harry called me: "Woody, I can get fifteen-to-one on one of the books in Vegas on this horse. Do you want to take a few dollars?"

"Take a few; a little of it."

After the colt won the Belmont, he called again; he'd backed the wrong horse: "Pincay had him at the quarter pole, but when he went into the lead and opened up three—*now* I'll take him." I thought a lot of Harry and his wife.

There were days I hung around with guys like Pat O'Brien out of Hollywood, Joe Namath, Joe DiMaggio. Billy Martin came in the office at Hialeah one day when Guggenheim was away, so I put Billy in his box to see the races. I would have spent more time with people like them if I'd had more time to spare.

A couple of months after the party, the news was out that Jimmy and Alice Mills had syndicated Devil's Bag for thirty-six million, the highest figure ever placed on a two year old, the third biggest in all the records of racing. Conquistador had topped it by four hundred thousand, and the '82 Irish Derby winner, Shareef Dancer, by four million.

Seth Hancock put the deal together: twenty-six shares in the Devil at a million apiece, with Robert Sangster mentioned as one of the buyers; ten more held on to by Hickory Tree Stable, owned by Mr. and Mrs. Mills. Each share entitled the buyer to breed one mare to the colt after he retired to the stallion stable at Claiborne at the end of next year's season. Meantime, control of his racing was left to me, and the shareholders would get a cut of his earnings.

"I'm better off not knowing the details," I said. "Let me just keep racing him."

Jimmy and Alice Mills had been sending me their horses for any number of years. Terpsichorist, Trove, Dame Mysterieuse —these were a few I'd been lucky with. Mrs. Mills's family had been in the racing game all their lives, and she and her husband were a great couple to train for. They once sent a picture of a mare with a nice-looking foal at her side, and a note: "Save a stall for this little feller." That was Believe It, and I went on to win some big races with him, including the Wood Memorial.

They weren't the kind of people that got stirred up over anything. They didn't say much when they won, and they didn't say much when they lost. They just went with it both ways, up or down, and this applied all the way along with Devil's Bag.

That winter I was at another party, a fancier affair than the birthday celebrating. The Empire Room at the Waldorf was filled to the doors with people, and Jimmy Mills bought a fistful of tickets to be there when they handed out the trophies of the Eclipse Awards to the best horses, owners, trainers, and jockeys of the year, agreed on by the votes of the National Turf

Writers, the Thoroughbred Racing Associations, and the *Daily Racing Form*.

The writers had gone for Miss Oceana, but the two other groups voted them down and chose a French filly, All Along, as the finest of her sex. Devil's Bag walked away with it as champion two-year-old colt, which was no surprise after he'd done everything right. The proprietor of the farm where he was foaled, E. P. Taylor, had a trophy coming to him. And I picked up mine as the trainer. I felt I was on top of the world in 1983.

A good two year old is about as dependable a horse as you can wish for, bursting with energy, eager to deliver his best, not trying to save his legs like an older horse will from the aches and pains that can come from pounding down the track. If he's been trained right, he shouldn't be balky or spoiled by hard handling. With a colt as healthy as Devil, who'd never known a day of sickness, you look forward to improving him further in his third year, getting him up to the top of his class to stay there for another two or three seasons until he starts to lose his sharpness. I gave Devil an easy winter, taking it easy because I reckoned that was what he'd thrive on.

In February, I ran him over seven furlongs in the Flamingo Prep Stakes at Hialeah, his first start since the end of October. I'd been schooling him to wait if somebody wanted to cut a faster pace in front of him, and that's exactly what he did, breaking out next to last, then settling down behind the lead horse, until it was time to take over and win by seven lengths, without even a flick of the whip from Eddie. "He was running so strong that last eighth it floored me," he said.

The Devil had done it in one minute twenty-one and three-fifths seconds, with no more damage to be seen than a little hair burned off his back heels. Then it was six starts, six wins, and earnings to date of $373,185.

But I really wasn't happy with this race. I thought it was taking him a bit longer to get rid of his competition than it had in New York. Then I let it slip my mind, because something else had come up that called for more attention than any job.

My mother was sick and giving no sign of recovery. She just couldn't get a hold of herself, and she died that February.

So 1984 was off to a bad start, and it ran downhill for some long months after that. The pressure was building again. I thought I'd put so much time into the game that I could take anything that came my way, but I was wrong. It wasn't easy to get through to the summer, and I doubt I would have made it without Lucille.

I flew back from the funeral in Lexington to get the Devil ready for the three-hundred-and-fifty-thousand Flamingo Stakes at Hialeah, the first of the seven grade-one races leading up to the Kentucky Derby on the fifth of May. The colt's name was all over town. A "Devil's Bag" made of canvas sold for two dollars across the souvenir counters, or you could get a paper one at the track for free. The cars were plastered with bumper stickers, "The Devil's at Hialeah." The billboards called it "the race of the century," and ads saying the same thing rolled across the TV screens every day.

He'd been rated the best young thoroughbred since Secretariat in the Experimental Free Handicap, which isn't a race at all but a ranking of performance by two year olds drawn up by a group of the tracks' racing secretaries, whose regular job is to assign the weight a horse carries when you run him. The greater the weight they decide on in the Experimental, the higher they value the animal.

I came out one, two, three. They gave the Devil one hundred twenty-six pounds, five more than any one of a hundred other colts, with Swale next behind him at one hundred twenty-three, and Miss Oceana top of the fillies at one hundred and twenty.

I was babying the Devil, not working him hard, but he made the fastest mile in the whole winter campaign four days before the race, with Eddie never asking him for anything. I hadn't noticed any competitor to worry me. The track had advertised a guaranteed purse of five thousand dollars for every finisher, and that had pulled in three more entries to fill out a field of eight, but none of those three latecomers was a classy horse.

Dr. Carter was supposed to be the colt to watch. The Devil

beat him twice the year before, but the Genter Stable horse had scored twice since then, in the Remsen and the Dan Chappell Handicap, and his trainer, John Veitch, was joking about printing his own bumper stickers saying, "The Doctor Will Cure the Devil." Only one other entry looked like amounting to much in the competition: Time for a Change, the Everglades winner owned by Ogden Phipps, who had bred him at Wheatley.

On the morning of the race the managers of Hialeah Park canceled all show betting, afraid that so much money would go down on the Devil to finish third or better that they'd be pushed into the red just to pay off the minimum two dollars and ten cents for every two dollars pulled in at the window. My stable crew laid on a champagne dinner to celebrate what we all counted on as a surefire victory, but it turned out that we were counting chickens before they were hatched.

We got beat. The track was fast, and the finish was close, but Devil's Bag wasn't part of it. I'd told Eddie to go for the lead if nobody else did, because I thought the colt had the stamina as well as the speed for it. That's where he was, with Time for a Change and Dr. Carter stalking him, for the first three quarters of the mile and an eighth distance. And then he began to fade before he could draw away. When they turned for home in the stretch, the tiger was all burned out of him. Dr. Carter kept driving for the wire, but he fell a neck short of Time for a Change. The Devil finished seven lengths behind them, one behind Rexson's Hope, who was a real long shot.

A fourth instead of a win. Phil Gleaves downed a glass of champagne and said, "If I don't, I might start to cry." Sandy popped more aspirin than she'd give a horse. Eddie said, "It's too bad to be true." But he wanted to give the colt another shot at proving himself, like everybody else.

That was a night when I got no more than an hour of sleep. Maybe I'd trained this colt too soft and robbed him some of his sharpness. Maybe he'd fooled himself up to now into believing he could eat up other horses without extending himself, so I'd have to get him used to working under pressure. Or maybe he was off color because of some medical problem.

The next morning, Sunday, I had him checked out. Nothing sore about him. Normal temperature. Eating well. We didn't have the answer yet.

I spent the next couple of weeks concentrating the best I could on getting him sharp again, with Phil riding him as before, which would have been a step down for the average assistant trainer, who expects to leave that to exercise boys. But Phil was as determined as I to get to the bottom of the problem.

We were due to fly the Devil with eight more horses to New York to run him in the Gotham at Aqueduct, but the weather up there was nasty, so I put off the trip by a week. That gave me time to hold down expenses and come to a deal with John McCabe, who was prepared to take the horses cargo class in an old Electra at $1,880 a head, with Phil, the grooms, and Roscoe, my pony, traveling on the house. My intention was to follow them later.

The rain over New York had slowed down our leaving, and then I took a turn at slowing down myself; I slipped on the floor of the bathroom at our place in Miami Lakes and broke some ribs on the tile. The year was staying sour every mile of the way.

If I'd been looking for consolation, I might have found it in what the rest of the stable was doing. With ten stakes wins and more than half a million in earnings already, we'd made a better start this year than last, and I had half a dozen sound horses pointed for big races this spring. But Devil's Bag preyed on my mind, and I was damn tired for lack of sleep.

On the books in Vegas, he ranked first on the list of nominees for the Derby at odds of three-to-one, and the list covered more than three hundred horses. Swale stood way further down after finishing a poor third in the Fountain of Youth, where a forty-to-one shot beat him. I was keeping Swale down there in Florida for a crack at the three hundred thousand Florida Derby, run at Gulfstream Park on the last day of March.

Meantime, I'd shipped Vision, a nice little filly, for the Jim Beam Stakes at Latonia, which is borderline to Cincinnati. On

Saturday afternoon, dragging my tail, I checked into the Netherlands Plaza in Cincinnati to grab a couple of days of rest. I watched the Florida Derby on TV in my hotel room.

Eddie had noticed on his last outing that Swale had run out of fuel as a result of getting his tongue over the bit in his mouth, which caused a breathing problem. This time, we guarded against that by tying his tongue down. Where he'd been skewered in the Fountain of Youth, he roasted Dr. Carter in the fire on the stretch and took it by a length over the six-to-five favorite in the third fastest time in thirty-three years. A good night's sleep couldn't have done more for me.

Snow, rain, and sleet kept coming down on New York City, and puddles were closing in around the Belmont Park cottage. The Gotham was scheduled for the first of April, but it had to be postponed a week. The main track at Aqueduct was a mud bath, so the race would be run on the inner one, which is treated with some sort of antifreeze to protect it from frost. I didn't like that idea, nor the fact it was a track I didn't know too well.

But I was happier to wait seven days than take a chance running a good horse on a bad track. It wasn't what I'd rather do, because the Devil was ready to go, but it shouldn't make a world of difference, although the weather was so contrary he had to be galloped indoors, eight times around the three-hundred-thirty-yard ring in the training barn to make it a mile.

After Swale's performance in the Florida Derby, some rethinking had to be done. Until I'd seen the Devil in the Gotham and then in the Wood Memorial at the same track later on in the month, it would be a mistake to decide which of the colts was more likely to be a Kentucky Derby winner when the Devil hadn't raced in New York since the Champagne five months back.

The rain never let up; I got to rechecking the condition books to see where else I could run the Devil in a Derby prep, which depended on the dates that nominations closed. Most of them fell too early or the distances were too long for a horse who'd had to miss getting a real workout every day. If he was to go to the head of the class again as the favorite, he needed at least one more win.

Two days before the Gotham, I pulled him out of it, and out of the Wood Memorial, too. The Aqueduct track spooked me. There was no telling what might happen to him if he ran there, and though the syndicators weren't on my neck, that thirty-six million was. I felt sorry about the hole it would leave by withdrawing my horse from two programs, but he had to get first place in my thinking. I vanned him to Kentucky to join Swale at Keeneland Race Course. The more I considered it, the surer I was this was the right thing to do.

I was beginning to feel I was rowing against the tide so far as health was concerned, still missing out on sleep, appetite gone and pulling me down toward jockey weight, breath as short as it was when I was smoking heavy. I snatched a few days of time out in Florida to see whether that might help to keep the show on the road. Mike Griffin, Seth's yearling manager at Claiborne, lent a hand and took over the stable while I was away from Keeneland, and Phil ran the shop in New York.

Swale was the early favorite, one-to-ten, when he went out in the slop in the Lexington Stakes with Pincay in the saddle, but he finished a poor second in this final prep for the Derby, eight lengths behind a mediocre colt that carried a dozen fewer pounds than the Claiborne horse. The crowd hooted and hollered, but he'd never been a mudder, and we were glad he didn't get bent out of shape.

Two days later, Eddie climbed on board Devil's Bag for the Forerunner Purse on the same track, which was dried out some but still slow. "If we can't beat these donkeys," I told him, "we're in for bad trouble." He broke second, led by two-and-a-half at the halfway mark, and after a tap of the stick from Eddie he was fifteen ahead at the wire and still strong.

He looked like his old self again, but it was only seven furlongs, a long way from the mile and a quarter of Churchill Downs that were waiting for him sixteen days from now. His last prep would give us a better idea, the Derby Trial, run over one mile.

I wasn't there to see it. I was going to bed crying, and Lucille told me, "You're going to have a breakdown if you don't do something about it." My digestion was so out of whack and my breath so short after the colt took the Forerunner that I stayed home for three days, sicker than a dog.

Lucille got hold of a doctor who's one of the family. My cousin Dr. David Richardson drove out from Louisville to Lexington to check me over and send me to the hospital with a heavy case of pneumonia. If I'd waited another twenty-four hours, he said, I might have been pushing my luck too hard. The trouble I was in was mostly my own doing for fretting over the passing of my mother and then the ups and downs with the horses. He knew something about them as a result of going out to the track now and then with me.

He put me on antibiotics to treat the pneumonia that was complicated by emphysema, and he barred all phone calls to my room. Late one afternoon the operator came on the line. "Woody, I turned down a hundred people today who wanted to talk to you." I said, "I'm glad I didn't get them. If I had, I'd have been dead."

Milk shakes put some weight back on me, but I missed the drinks of scotch. I was allowed to make a few calls out, and most of them were to Mike Griffin, who was staying on with Swale, the Devil, and three other horses I had in Kentucky. The doctor reckoned I was "responding well to treatment" and I'd maybe get to the Downs on Derby Day to saddle both the colts, but he wouldn't give any guarantee.

I couldn't be there to give Eddie a lift up in the paddock for the Derby Trial, so I called him in the jockeys' room. "Ride him to win, like he's sure to run big in the Derby." Seth was ready by now to raise some questions about the Devil's prospects. "If he does win the Derby," he said, "he should never lose again."

Devil's Bag captured the race by two-and-a-quarter, but it took a lot of whipping from Eddie, who doesn't like to do that, and the colt was bearing out down the stretch, looking as if he was either tired or hurting from something. I couldn't tell from personal observation because I was tied down in the hospital, where I'd watched him on a TV screen.

I talked with Steve Crist of the New York *Times*, who'd been around for months writing about the colt. "Everything that horses do," I said, "they do for a reason. You just have to hope you find out soon enough." Maybe Swale was the horse to beat now.

Then Seth and I had a talk about what to do with the Devil, who didn't look like a winner on his present form. We figured on holding him out of the Derby in favor of the Preakness Prep and then the Stakes after he'd been X-rayed. Dr. Gary Lavin took the first set of pictures a few hours later. I didn't get to examine them myself, but he said they showed calcium on the right knee, from damage to a bone two or three months earlier. In other words, before the Flamingo.

My cousin, the doctor, said he'd let me out for an hour or so, and he drove me to my barn on the backstretch at Churchill Downs to face the reporters and the cameras. I'd been ten days in the hospital, and I wasn't feeling any too sharp. "He's out of the Derby" was about all I could say about it.

A good horse runs and does his best even when he's hurting; a cheap one whines and complains about it. I had to find out what was bothering Devil's Bag, which meant getting a second vet's opinion. But first off I had to be discharged from the hospital to saddle my one remaining hope for the Kentucky Derby—Swale.

They let me go twenty-four hours before the race, twelve days after they put me to bed. Sitting with Lucille in front of the TV in the directors' room watching the colt pound home was one of the sweetest moments of my life. Swale had done it for me; come out of the shadow cast over him by the Devil; made me feel like a whole new man. Lucille said it all later: "You see, you always do have to look on the bright side, because if you don't, it makes you sick."

Next day, Sunday, I ran my hands over the Devil's legs and felt some heat in his left front shin. I called the second vet, Dr. Alex Harthill, to shoot more X rays at nine o'clock Monday morning. An hour after he was through, he came back with a print: the colt had a small, loose chip of bone in his right leg, which was why his left shin was sore—he'd been putting his weight on it to favor the right.

Where he got the chip and how long he'd had it we'd never know. But the syndication contract said he would go to stud in '85. If we'd have taken it out—and we could have done that—I was sure he'd have come back 100 percent sound, but that would have taken four or five months, and the contract stood in the way.

At Hickory Tree Farm in Middleburg, Virginia, Mr. Mills said, "If a horse isn't 100 percent, he shouldn't run." At Claiborne, Seth said much the same thing: "You can't run a thirty-six-million-dollar horse on a bone chip." We decided to retire him.

The van came a week later to take him over the seventy or eighty miles from Louisville to Claiborne Farm. I walked with him to the loading ramp. It wasn't the first time I'd known a horse to chip a bone, but for a while this colt was the best, the very best since I was fifteen years old and green as grass. I was glad he wouldn't be running again on his class and his guts alone, and he was going home a winner.

I headed Swale for the Belmont Stakes in July, and he took it again for me, three in a row, 1982 through 1984—Conquistador, Caveat, and then Swale. He was far and away the best of the three year olds. I was itching to take on older horses in the big stakes that were coming up in the fall. But he had just nine more days of life left to him.

The grief caused by his going, dying like a dog in the yard, stayed with me for quite some time. Then Lucille set me straight. "There'll be more ups and downs," she said, "but we'll live through them," and I had to believe her.

15

The Big Money

Sometimes, when the phone's not ringing, we get to talking, Lucille and I, about what she calls "the almighty dollar," what it's done to the game we've spent most of our time in, and where it's likely to go next. We don't reach a lot of firm conclusions, because it would take an army of accountants to calculate what's come about so far and a crystal ball to take a look into the future.

When I started racing, you started low on the ladder, kept there by people who thought too much too soon would ruin you, and at two dollars a mount a jock had to work his tail off to make enough to eat on. Today, the best of them are millionaires.

The trainers knew more about horses than anybody else in sight, which is still true, but the surest route for a man to earn a decent living was to hire out with an owner and stick with him, unless you had the nerve of a tightrope walker and campaigned a public stable.

The owners of stakes-class thoroughbreds were mostly rich in their own right and happy enough to lay out heavy money on a sporting chance to get some of it back in purses and at the betting window. The seasons were short, and entries were more or less regional when shipping horses cross-country took a week of travel time.

Apart from his morning workouts, a horse got most of his

training from running against other horses in real competition. And when the purses in general were small, the owner kept his animals racing year after year, because syndicating them to stud farms for millions of almighty dollars at the age of three was something unheard of as yet.

Stamina as much as speed was what the breeders were after in those days before distances got shortened so more races could be fitted into an afternoon program. A few hundred dollars was your average stud fee, and it was a sunny day when a yearling fetched a five-figure price in the sales ring.

The only place to get down a legal bet was at the track. It was made a lot easier for the horseplayers to unload their money and for the management to collect their cut of it when the tote came along with its perfectas and quinielas and twin doubles—and the track dipped 15 to 30 percent out of the pool.

Then the lawmakers in the state houses got into the act, and offtrack betting (OTB), with a state tax skimmed off the proceeds, pulled in a bigger audience of gamblers. But it didn't sell more admission tickets to the racecourses, so it took a while for the managements to stop complaining and accept the change that was inevitable. There's still some hard feeling when the commissioners sell a race outside their own state lines, specially where an outside course gets paid a piece of the home state's offtrack action, which Hialeah did when Devil's Bag ran in the Flamingo.

With the game turned into an industry and reaching out in all kinds of directions, an awful lot of people dig in their heels and want to hold on to every possible dollar, and any change from the ways of the past seems like bad news to them.

The New York Racing Association tried out something new at Saratoga in '84—simulcasts of the races there showed up on closed-circuit TV monitors in the Kelso Room at Aqueduct, where seven thousand fans went in to watch at two dollars a head and the betting topped a million dollars. That sent some ripples through the OTB corporations, who could see the time coming when simulcasting would put a dent in their daily handle that stands close to three and a half million dollars without that kind of competition.

Cable TV met with the same sort of mixed reception. Some track managers went for it because it would bring in extra money by way of fees, and so did the governments of states like Kentucky where gambling is legal: it seemed to them that cable would stir more interest in racing, which would increase the take at the betting windows, with the tax collector getting his share of it.

The owners and the breeders were left out of the setup, without a crumb off the cake. The men who owned one or two horses argued that this was the handwriting on the wall and they'd be forced out of racing if the crowds faded away from the bush-league tracks because they could stay home and bet on the programs they were watching on cable from Belmont Park or Santa Anita.

There were breeders, too, that saw the red light beginning to shine. Seth was one of them, and John Gaines another. If cable and OTB worked hand in hand, the number of big racing centers in the country might be cut down to as few as five—Kentucky, New York, Florida, California, and Chicago. "The Kentucky breeding industry," Seth said, "would virtually be wiped out. Fewer tracks would mean fewer horses."

The industry turned to razzle-dazzle to protect the market for breeding and selling high-class horses at prices that went up instead of down. Magazines of the business, like *The Thoroughbred Record* and the *Horseman's Journal*, were stuffed with pages of color ads praising the virtues of the stud farms' stocks of stallions, mares, and foals.

The stakes had never been higher. The total inventory, the animals in the barns and paddocks, had to be valued in the billions when a weanling filly could fetch $750,000, a Northern Dancer yearling over $1,000,000 and Nelson Bunker Hunt of Dallas, Texas, was willing to pay $5,250,000 at Keeneland for Producer, a seven-year-old Nashua mare in foal to Nijinski II that hadn't as yet borne a foal of racing age. But he felt he had to have her to add to the band of stakes-winning mares at Bluegrass Farm that he promotes in sales catalogs as fancy as anything put out by Neiman-Marcus or Saks Fifth Avenue.

These sky-high prices brought Wall Street into the picture

for the first time in the records of racing. Up through the 1970s, the bulk of the best thoroughbreds were owned by individuals with fat bankrolls or by syndicates made up of a few people who could afford a million or so for a share. If you liked to play the horses, there was no way of doing it on the stock market. From 1980 you could, by investing a few dollars with a public company trading over the counter.

After nearly thirty years in the private hands of Leslie Combs, Spendthrift Farm in Lexington went that route, with a share selling in the six- or seven-dollar range. In the last six months of '83, Spendthrift showed a profit of a million seven hundred thousand.

Other outfits broke into the field in New York and New Jersey, none of them with the long experience in breeding and trading of the old man who liked to be called "Cousin Leslie," all of them maybe a safer investment than wildcatting an oil well but riskier than a stake in IBM when profits hinge on how a horse performs on the track and at the farm.

The commercial value of one performance can't be measured above the other. The reputation of a horse is made on the track. If he's retired as a winner, then the syndicate that's bought him looks for its profits from stud fees and the sale of his foals as yearlings, with the purses he has earned making up only a tiny fraction of the deal. There's no way around it. A yearling bought for ten million would have to win big stakes races for the next fifty or sixty years to pay off the purchase price.

Some such thoughts were in my mind when I took Lucille with me to see the latest notion the breeders had come up with to make a bigger impact on the racing business. We were on a flight to Los Angeles, the place we'd first set eyes on nearly forty years back in the company of Jule and Ethel Fink.

I had no more than a single entry in the lineup for the Breeders' Cup races at Hollywood Park: Miss Oceana in the million-dollar Distaff for fillies, run on the dirt for a mile and a quarter. Henryk had talked about entering Sabin against a field of colts in the three-million Classic, but I could see problems with that: namely, weight, the track, and the starting fee.

She'd gone to Belmont Park in July with five wins in five starts during the year so far: the La Prevoyante at Calder, the Columbia and the Black Helen at Hialeah, the Orchid at Gulfstream Park, and the Gamely at Hollywood. Altogether in her lifetime she'd scored twenty-four out of thirty-two, ten out of thirteen on grass.

At Belmont in the Sheepshead Bay Handicap, she'd never been better. She was bigger and tougher now she was a three year old, digging in all the way under Eddie Maple's urging, winning by an easy two to put an extra $71,880 in Henryk's pocket. This was on the grass; I couldn't remember any filly being as good on that kind of footing.

But the deadline for the Breeders' Cup program had gone by a month ago. The rules required a fee of 20 percent of the purse to enter her now, which was six hundred thousand dollars in the Classic. If she beat the colts, she'd earn half of the posted three million, but one hundred and fifty thousand would go into a pool for Cup awards at other tracks. Her rider would get 10 percent of what was left, and so would I. Henryk's six-hundred-thousand-dollar entry fee could return him four hundred and twenty thousand at best. We'd have to be lunatics to risk it. On top of that, the Classic would be run on the dirt, and she'd be carrying one hundred and twenty pounds, a crazy weight for the little filly.

"Let's stay out of it," I said to Henryk, and he went along with me.

The Breeders' was dreamed up by John Gaines in the first place, and it had been more than two years in the making. The smartest part of his idea was to make it pay for itself by way of nomination fees, charged in advance if you wanted to run a horse in the series. The biggest charge was for stallions—the same price as a breeder got for stud service that rose as high as two hundred thousand for a sire in the class of Northern Dancer.

That payment qualified all his sons and daughters to be entered, two year olds and three year olds at five hundred a head, an older horse for twenty-five hundred. On the fifteenth of June, the books were closed. After that, the cost of entering shot up to between 12 and 15 percent of the total purse of the particular race you wanted to run in, one million dollars in five of the seven events on the card, two million in the Turf, three million in the Classic.

The target was to raise twenty-two million ahead of time, but they fell a couple of million short when nominations were counted for over a thousand stallions and about eighteen thousand other horses. Ten million was allocated for the purses on what was billed as "Racing's Greatest Day" and ten million as bonuses in four hundred stakes races run at other tracks during the year, extra win, place, and show money for horses that were already paid-up members for the Breeders' Cup. As things turned out, there weren't enough of them to collect all the premiums, so about five million stayed in the pool to be given out later.

It added up to an unbelievable wad of money raised without much pain. The breeders themselves could write off the nominating fees as legitimate tax-deductible business expenses. Or they could have a stallion cover one extra mare and pay up that way to get in. Accountants and lawyers had provided the prescription, and a lawyer from Lexington, Gibson Downing, took over as president of Breeders' Cup Limited after Mr. Gaines stepped into the chairman's place on the board of five to put an end to some early squabbling.

Four of those five were Kentucky men: John Gaines, Seth, Brownell Combs of Spendthrift, and Brereton Jones of Airdrie Stud at Midway, where I used to hoe tobacco. Odd man out was Charles Taylor, E.P.'s son from Windfields Farm, which is split between Maryland and Ontario, Canada.

John Gaines's original plan was to shoot most of the wad on a single "Super Saturday" at a track that Breeders' Cup would pick, since it was the company, not the track, that would own all the races. Seth and Brereton Jones walked out on that one, Seth because he thought the wealth should be spread around by having fifty Breeders' days at all the tracks in the country, Brereton Jones because he wanted more people given a voice in making decisions.

The walkouts went back in after Mr. Gaines found his replacement as president and it was agreed that 50 percent of the up-front money should go as premiums to other tracks. Seth still reckoned the first of the Breeders' series ought to be held in the East at Belmont Park, but most of them, like Bunker Hunt, head of the selection committee, were inclined for California.

The choice of dates for a Super Saturday was tight. It had to be arranged for the fall when the season was over at Belmont Park, where provisions for heating in cold weather are on the cool side of the thermostat. It also had to be on a day to fit the schedule of NBC, the National Broadcasting Company, that came in to sign a three-year contract covering the first series and two more to come.

Without television and millions of people watching it, there'd be no point getting the show on the road. The Cup was designed as a high-powered shot at making racing a sport as popular on TV as pro football and the Olympics, with the overall effect of drawing bigger crowds at the ticket windows.

Up till now, races had been shown one at a time for the most part, like the Derby and the Preakness. But the horses run no longer than a couple of minutes and a few seconds, which was tough for filling out a TV time schedule. The seven Cup races were due to get four hours on the network, which was a real challenge. So was the job of finding the right Saturday clear of competition from other sports on rival stations. The first choice was for late October, but it had to be pushed into November to keep it out of contest with the World Series running late.

There was more arguing over which track should play host for Super Saturday, Oak Tree-Santa Anita or Hollywood Park, when both of them were eager to have it, although the expenses they'd be compelled to carry would take care of any profit. Oak Tree offered to put up a hundred thousand of its own as promotion money. Marge Everett of Hollywood Park topped that by donating two hundred thousand to Breeders' Cup to clinch it for the track where she's the boss and Cary Grant sits on the board.

Marge, whose stepfather owned Arlington Park in Chicago,

watched races there as a schoolgirl and worked there when she dropped out of college. Then she sold out the share in it that she inherited when he died, and she bought a piece of Hollywood Park.

It used to be advertised as "The Track of Lakes and Flowers"—a lot of lakes, a lot of flowers, palm trees, and the trademark, the Goose Girl with a flock of them in the water. Marge was already giving the plant an eight-million-dollar face-lift when she won the contest for Super Saturday, but she poured in more millions to get the place ready. She was a dynamite woman, quick on the trigger, and I wasn't the only one to tell her so.

A ten-minute drive from Los Angeles airport gets you to Inglewood and Marge's race course. Lucille and I took a guided tour. There was so much to turn your head it was hard to know where to start when I doubt there's a track anywhere in the world like this one in existence today.

It's reckoned that no more than 10 percent of people have ever been to the races, while the rest stay away, thinking of a racetrack as a hangout for gamblers and railbirds. Her ambition was to make the Park a place where a man and his wife would go with the kids to have a good time.

She had most of the infield lakes drained and sodded with grass, then in the bend of the first turn she put in a playground with swings, slides, monkey bars, and supervisors to look after the kids so their parents could concentrate on the track.

She lengthened the straightaway and redid the whole course by mixing in thousands of yards of screened sand to lower the content of clay to improve the drainage when it rained and to keep it from hardening like concrete in the California sun.

We took a turn through the brand-new "Pavilion of the Stars" with luxury suites and a hundred boxes, all built with Super Saturday in mind at a cost of thirty million. The old grandstand got a new paint job, orange and white, and on a brick wall across from it there were big blue letters saying "Racing's Greatest Day."

This was the front side, done for the benefit of the fans, but the spending hadn't stopped there. To me, because of the business I'm in, it was the backstretch that was the real knockout. At Belmont Park, it looks like a country village with its shade trees and dirt roads lined with shingled cottages and low-roofed barns. At Hollywood Park, tomorrow had already arrived.

The great big concrete barns could hold more than two thousand horses in stalls twelve-feet square with fireproof doors of metal that a cribber couldn't chew on. Sprinklers and fire alarms and loudspeakers were all hooked into the PA system.

This was for the benefit of the horses; for the stable crews there were improvements on the same scale. At both ends of every barn, the buildings rose a story higher, tack rooms with ceiling heaters and smoke detectors on the ground floor, living quarters upstairs with washrooms and showers; it was more like a modern motel than the tenement rooms the grooms live in at most other places. It struck me as being a good setup: everything self-contained, so if a night watchman needed help, he could get it from the boys up there in a matter of minutes.

On Super Saturday, we sat in a box on a hot and humid November morning, wondering what we might expect to see. The Pavilion of Stars had its fair share of them, and the TV cameras were roaming around looking for them. They picked up Fred Astaire, who was a horseman in his day, and Jack Klugman, an actor and horseplayer who can afford to lose.

They got Elizabeth Taylor and then Linda Evans to say a few words into a mike about which horse they fancied on the card, but Cary Grant and Gregory Peck were only faces in the crowd, like David Cassidy and Gerald and Betty Ford.

We knew we were in for a long session when Tom Durkin, the race caller, would have work to do only about once every half an hour. But a high school band and drill team got the ball rolling, and anybody watching this TV special on one of the monitor screens had plenty to keep him occupied.

Over in Europe, there's no shortage of big companies willing to put money up front to sponsor races as an investment to promote whatever they put on sale for the public—beer, a hotel room, or a bet in a chain of bookmaking shops. A company that sold furniture bought itself a horse that Lester Piggott rode to get it voted European Horse of the Year.

On this side of the water, sponsorship has been slower in catching on. Budweiser has promoted the Million at Arlington, the Marlboro Cup gets its name from a brand of cigarettes, and in Canada another brand antes up half the purse for Rothmans International that was a win for Eddie Maple in '82 on board Majesty's Prince.

But NBC found a full deck of backers for the Cup, and commercials outnumbered the races on the order of maybe three to one. The monitor screens showed them plugging everything from diamonds to cough syrup, shampoo, credit cards, flashlights and light bulbs, two kinds of beer, and two makes of automobiles. A familiar face kept coming and going—Earl Scheib, turned down once by me on a hundred-thousand-dollar horse deal, was putting in his own pitch for his car-spraying business.

Another man threw a line of his own into the stream, with shots of him at Grand Coulee Dam, in the cockpit of a helicopter, and some other unlikely places for a Wall Street broker to be. Robert Brennan's normal workday has him wearing two hats, one as president of a New York venture capital company, the other as founder of International Thoroughbred Breeders of New Jersey that sells over-the-counter stock in breeding and selling horses, insuring them and racing them, for a profit of better than two and a half million a year.

Mr. Brennan also snapped up Garden State Park, the racetrack in Camden County, New Jersey, that had fallen on hard times. The price was fifteen and a half million, and then he raised another hundred and twenty-five million to rebuild it as a showplace like Marge's Hollywood Park.

His message in the commercials, and in his magazine ads, talks about "growth industries" as a good thing to get into, and he thinks racing will be one of them. Come Grow with Us is the motto where he's concerned.

Robert Sangster was part of the program, too, interviewed in front of the cameras in between the starts in much the same way they showed mares with their foals at Gainesway and a stallion covering a mare at Windfields. If I'm the Vincent O'Brien of America, then Mr. Sangster might be the closest thing England has to Robert Brennan as a young man who's breezed ahead in the horse business.

The Englishman, who took the millions he had invested in secondhand cars for sale and switched to buying thoroughbreds, has something in common with another American: like Bunker Hunt, he took a Derby double, the Epsom Downs, and the French, in a period of less than a week.

Mr. Gaines also turned up on the screen to say a few words about his dream that came true. It was another TV program that got him steamed up enough to try, a piece about juicing horses with drugs on *60 Minutes*. He was made so mad by it, he said later, that he concluded he had to convince the public that the number one question in racing was "Who's got the best horse?"

But in the matter of drugging, New York has the jump on California. The rules are as different as white and black. In New York, they're stated as plain as your old Aunt Jane: "No horse will be permitted to start who has received medication for any reason after being entered in a race." In California, bute and Lasix are both on the approved list, and there's no obligation to announce which horses are getting them.

So before the first of the post parades, I was wondering what the Breeders' would add up to, except maybe a flash in the pan that would burn itself out. I speculated about how many people would stay glued to the TV when most of them think racing begins and ends with the Kentucky Derby and the Triple Crown.

I asked myself whether the regulations made it too complicated and expensive to bring in anything but a mixed batch of horses, some good and some not too bad, most of them flown in to run on a tricky track that was new to them against horses that might have been medicated to step up their speed.

And if Super Saturday did make a hit, what would the impact be? It could mean that Breeders' Cup got to hold more power than the Jockey Club. Or that Super Saturday got more attention than the Kentucky Derby. What was going to happen to races like the Washington International at Laurel when the purses there fell so far short of the money available here that might be won by inferior horses? Maybe Seth was right, and the game was on the wrong road that could only end in a ditch for all except the superstars of racing. I didn't have any answers to such questions, but I was willing to learn. If this was the wave of the future, I was ready to row with the tide.

The way things turned out, some of my worrying had been wasted. I said, "It was a good go," which Marge Everett deserved to hear for a certainty. The crowd at the track wasn't the eighty thousand they hoped for, but sixty-four thousand was a good turnout for a show that the people who make movies out there couldn't have improved on even if they'd been trying ever since Elizabeth Taylor played in *National Velvet*.

We saw an odds-on favorite, Chief's Crown, a son of Henryk's Danzig, win the first race, the Juvenile, paying $3.40 on a two-dollar bet and moving into the lead at the sixteenth pole on a track that was a bit slower than it used to be before it was done over.

Four-year-old Princess Rooney sewed up the Eclipse title as best filly of her age by taking the Distaff, sponsored by an oil company. Life's Magic closed for second, which clinched her award as best three year old of her sex. Her only rival had been Miss Oceana, but she bled and was left last in a field of seven. I decided the best we could do for her was send her into retirement.

One aim of the organizers was to get more attention for female horses to give a boost to filly racing, which doesn't have the same popularity as the male events. More and bigger stakes for the fillies would jump up their value along the route to the farms. Robert Sangster had a good day in that respect; he watched his Irish-bred Royal Heroine set an American record in the Mile on the grass against a field of nine male horses.

We were up on our feet for the finish of the two-million-dollar Turf when an outsider, the Aga Khan's Lashkari running at fifty-three-to-one, won by a head with the Frenchman Yves St. Martin in the saddle.

I had some doubt about the soundness but not the speed of a

son of Mr. Prospector entered in the Sprint, but Eilo, Florida-bred, flew away with it.

We sat it out while the hassling went on over who won the Juvenile Fillies, which was bumper to bumper for a while. Fran's Valentine was first at the wire, but the stewards placed her last for interfering and gave the race to Outstandingly, Louis Wolfson's entry trained by an old friend of mine, Pancho Martin.

All through the afternoon, I kept saying to myself, "If only I had those two colts, the Devil and Swale, how they would *shine.*" With the marbles they could have picked up here, I might have had the first stable ever to make five million in just one year.

And then in the last race, the Classic, the dice got another roll. A lot of the sportswriters had given columns of space to Slew o' Gold, owned by Mickey Taylor and Dr. Jim Hill, who've a name for switching trainers in midstream like Elizabeth Graham used to. Gate Dancer, with all his headgear on, was in this field, and so was another long shot, Wild Again.

In the stretch, Slew o' Gold was having trouble grabbing hold of the track. He got sandwiched in between a couple of other horses, and Angel Cordero had to take up. Gate Dancer was lugging in against him, while Pat Day had Wild Again on a course straight along the rail. With the finish coming up, Gate Dancer knocked Slew o' Gold in his hindquarters, and when they all got off their mounts, the stewards, at a wall full of TV monitors, had to run and rerun the film clips to settle the question of foul.

They disqualified Gate Dancer and gave first place to Wild Again and show to Slew o' Gold, who had been third at the wire. Winning a purse this size would have pushed Gate Dancer over the top as champion three-year-old colt of the year. By disqualifying him, the stewards left that title open for a different horse to take, a dead horse, Swale.

During the next couple of weeks, I put in more flying time over the miles between Los Angeles and JFK, going back to Hollywood Park to saddle Sabin, who'd won three out of six this season in California. She was entered for an invitational, the four-hundred-thousand-dollar Yellow Ribbon, to run against Robert Sangster's Royal Heroine.

Then it rained, and Henryk had me scratch her. I needed to have a talk with him. "If you and I hadn't been taking chances, you'd be stuck in Poland and I'd still be in Kentucky hoeing tobacco. She's going to stud, anyway, and you're never going to sell her. She won't like the soft track, but let's go back in."

He went with me 100 percent. Sangster's filly beat her to the wire, but Sabin slogged on to run third, to give Henryk another thirty thousand in the bank and carry her earnings before retirement to a million and a quarter.

I wanted something to take away the taste of disappointment that came from not even having placed in the Breeders' Cup. Stephan's Odyssey supplied that for me. I entered him in the Hollywood Futurity, to be run on the same track some days later. With a $1,140,000 purse, it was the richest run for two year olds ever held anywhere in the world, and the colt took it like a hero.

"Richest," mind you, is a word you have to be careful with when megabucks are bringing such changes to our game. Nobody would ever have guessed that six months after the Breeders' series poured millions of dollars into the business, Robert Brennan would pull ahead at his Garden State Park with the biggest payday in racing history, making it possible for Spend a Buck under some powerful driving by Pincay to earn $2,600,000, a win by a neck over Creme Fraiche, a gelding out of my barn, with Eddie Maple in the saddle.

Super Saturday in 1985 was scheduled to bring super purses to Aqueduct; the November date of the Breeders' calls for heat for the crowd, which Belmont Park can't provide enough of, and opening up Belmont for just one more day of racing when the season there was over didn't make sense.

After I'd seen what Marge Everett had done to Hollywood Park, I just didn't know how Aqueduct could handle that upcoming Saturday without spending a carload of money. But I expected they'd manage it somehow, and I counted on being there if I could with some entries from my stable.

16

One of These Days

"I'm getting older," I told Henryk. "It's time you start looking for a younger trainer because you're getting big in the business."

"You look for him," Henryk said.

"One of these days you're going to need maybe a private trainer."

"I don't want to listen," he said.

"The time will come when I'm going to have to go."

"You've got a lot of years left," he said.

So he didn't look for another man, and nor did I. Lucille didn't put up an argument or claim we'd come to the wrong conclusion, but she still liked to talk about the day down the road when I'd finally decide to rack it up. Meantime, I kept going hard the way I had all my life, so it was nothing new. Anytime you're going for a stakes worth a quarter of a million or more that you'll win or lose in a couple of minutes—that's never easy. But nothing good is easy, regardless of the game you're in.

I knew Henryk had learned at least this much from me: when you lose, you go home, and when you win, you go home, and there isn't much more to it than that.

Lucille, who's a religious person, kept getting on me about the things I should maybe do just as she does; she hasn't got an enemy in the world, and she tries to be as good as she possibly can be to people.

Our doctor said, "You ought to cut this down some now," and I tried to please him, too, by taking a little more care of myself, but it's hard to break old habits. There was a month just recently when I flew fifteen thousand miles to and fro across the country to saddle horses.

Sometimes you feel you're the only one with that certain touch. I shouldn't be that way, but I do like to saddle them myself. I was forty years on the racetrack before I let an assistant do it, and then I fretted about whether it was done right and the saddle was sitting the way it should.

"I'd be scared to quit," I said to Lucille. "I might be unhappy, which is something I've never been. I've learned to row with this thing, and it's good for everybody to keep going."

"But you never even take a Sunday," she said.

We turned again to discussing what might happen if I did let go. Maybe build a house on the two acres we had bought in the Bluegrass? I reckoned it was too late for that, but we could think about getting a little place ready-made and go there to live.

"Then I wouldn't have to work too hard," I said. "Just keep looking around, and if I saw something Henryk wants to do, I'd do it. Buy a chance horse once in a while, and if he turns out good, then fine, and if he doesn't, Henryk wouldn't be putting out much."

Lucille would like a small farm close to where we keep our five brood mares; there are the six stallions I trained and raced as champions before they retired to stand at Claiborne; and there're another three at Windfield in Maryland.

With the rights that are mine to horses like Danzig and Conquistador guaranteeing a live foal every season, I might have their sons and daughters from my mares coming into my own stable. Or I could take up other breeders' offers to buy those rights that keep the phone ringing in the spring; running even a small farm calls for work a lot harder than training, and I've done my share of hard labor.

Nobody I know works as we did when I was a kid, and that's

something I remember clearer than what it was I had for breakfast. We'd house the cut leaves of tobacco in the barn to cure in the fall, then strip and grade them before we took them to the market in Lexington. Back in those days, there were very few trucks, and we didn't have one.

I'd see my father load five or six thousand pounds of the stuff on a big, flat-bedded wagon ready to set off down the road we called the Hard Pike. It would sit all night under a tarpaulin, sometimes with snow and sleet coming down on it. Next morning, early, he'd hitch a team of mules with calks on their feet to get them through, and he'd climb up to drive sixteen miles into town. He'd sell his tobacco at the auction, and that was what we lived on. One other choice for him would have been to go up into the mountains and work just as hard for no more money hiring out in a sawmill.

"You'll have to turn out someday," Lucille says, but staying put in any one place wouldn't be easy after all our years of pick up and pack.

We might go to Florida in December and stop there until March or April, ducking those nasty six o'clock mornings by not getting out of bed before eight, when the sun's up and you can see the golf course and the blue water from your windows and you think about going fishing.

In the spring, we'd go to the place in the Bluegrass we still have to find, where we could drive off on an afternoon to take a look at the only babies we've ever had, the foals and their mothers. Kentucky's where I came from and where we'll go back someday.

There's racing all through the year, and I've been around long enough so it doesn't haunt my mind when I lose. I could go to the sales and run a few horses of my own, with a manager put in charge of the stable. Then in July we'd go up to Saratoga, where there'd be plenty to see and do as a change from what we'd done before—fighting off people and working the horses.

I'd be curious to see what racing might do in Texas, where I was a guest of the breeders at a dinner in San Antonio in '84, part of a campaign that went on for years to get the state back into the business. But the lawmakers stuck their heads in the sand on the assumption they'd keep gambling out if there weren't races to bet on.

I'd like to add Texas to the list of places I've saddled stakes winners in—something like a hundred and twenty horses and better than three hundred wins, according to the count I don't keep but that the sportswriters do.

But I've been too busy or else too lazy to move out of our little house in Franklin Square, where we can go downstairs and watch reruns on the Betamax. Lucille thinks the house is too small, but I don't know how much room you need when there's only two of you, and the more house you have, the more tax you pay.

She says, "I'd like to have some place to display all the trophies and pictures," which would need space in a museum. That's where they'll go in the end, back where they came from, to racing, when the closest to a son or a daughter we have are nieces and nephews, who wouldn't want them anyway.

There's another one in the family that falls in that same category—the little Yorkshire terrier we call Muskie, who sticks with me all day when Lucille happens to be away. For him I go in the kitchen to fix a hot dog or a hamburger, some chicken or turkey.

I used to think I could never leave New York. For some reason, I've always been able to win here. Whether I just picked up the way to do it, I don't know. But once I arrived, I went on to make money and do better than I ever thought I could. My family seemed proud of that.

Good horses made me, and I've made some good horses. They keep coming, and you don't often find an empty stall in the barns. There isn't a whole lot I can do with a horse or a horse can do for me that I haven't lived through before. If he runs a poor race, I'll try to get to the bottom of it so he might do better next time out.

The owners understand who calls the shots, and they've been beautiful people to work with, one of them for half the time I've spent living and breathing: John Morris, who lived into his nineties, was still a friend right up to the end who liked to watch the races at Belmont Park.

When you talk to owners about this business, you've got to make them appreciate you know what you're talking about. If they lose that confidence in you, you're gone. But I've got a good crew there at the stable, and I can say, "They'll have to race without me today," and the owners know it's true when I tell them, "We do the best." I don't have to pressure myself the way I used to, not when *nobody* can say, "Woody's still got a lot to learn."

One thing I wish I could fathom is what brought about the end of Swale, although I don't expect ever to hear the answer. People say, "It's over and done with, so what's the point?" But it wouldn't be right to let go of it, so far as I'm concerned. Seth was an owner willing to lay out money for the labs and the vets to do their best to find out why. They couldn't, because there are too many holes in their knowledge.

A lot can go wrong with a horse that gets the same good care as Swale did, but some owners don't do more than collect the insurance, if they carry any, and they've no more interest in the case because they think of the animal as a machine on four legs that they hope will make them money. I've never had a stall available for people of that kind, and I never will, nor have to.

Dr. Fritz, who was the vet who looked after the colt, said something after the autopsy about the need to research the causes of the trouble. Mickey Taylor, who owns a piece of Seattle Slew, picked up on that later and promised he'd make a start at filling the need. He'd donate the proceeds from a breeding season of the horse and some of the offspring to studies by veterinarians. So there's just a slim chance there'll be more to learn about Swale.

I don't change much, and I like to hold on to the help in my barn, so there's not too much change there. Unless there's some big reason they have to go, they stay. When it doesn't work out, I'll say, "If you're unhappy, come on—let's get you out of here."

Without good help, you can't run a good stable, which is

what I've always known was the only way for me. I remember Royce Martin saying when Harry Guggenheim was dickering with me, "Don't ask what he's going to pay you. If the job's any good, the money will be there."

So I'm a believer in paying bonuses to grooms because I could hire men who knew a lot more than I did when I started running a public stable. If you hold tight today, you can have a ten-million-dollar horse in the hands of a two-hundred-a-week groom, and he's going to resent it in ways the owner will never suspect.

I can only guess the reason they come to work for those wages. It has to be because the track is one of the very few places left where a man without the price of a fresh shirt on his back can get to talk on level terms with a millionaire. It's only the horses that bring them together, and something along the same lines maybe happened to me.

In my case, it was the idea of love and caring that got me into the game, and the money came as a result of that. I started green, but I stuck on to get the experience, and without it I'd have fallen on my face.

Today, it's different. Big money has changed the game so much, and the changes can only go on—for owners, trainers, everybody alike.

They're not likely to be prepared to put in time to wait for the best, because it takes too long and it's more expensive. If they all get hasty and greedy, they're not going to last too far down the road. They're going to break down the horses, and we'll get a different kind of horse. The boys of the old school started for love and ran into money. But those days are gone.

This lifetime experience of mine was good, because you really knew practically all the horses, the families they came from, what to expect of them, how they liked to be ridden. If I was wrong in my judgments, I wouldn't try the same thing again.

Now, some of them want to be trainers overnight. They want it without the foundation it took me fifteen years to build, so they last a couple of seasons, and then they're gone.

Someone on the racetrack said to me the other day, "Woody,

do you think it's going to be harder for me than when you were starting?"

I said, "Jack, I don't think you've got a chance. When I started, I could hire men that could lose me, grooms who knew a lot more than I did. You can't find help like that anymore."

But if I could turn my life around, there'd be no other way to turn it. You've got to kind of like what you choose to do, and if you're a loser, you can't be a winner. I like what I've done, and I wouldn't want to change it. I've lost some of the drive I used to have, but I think I still do a good job.

So in the mornings, when the sets of workouts are over and the horses are back in cooling off, we get together in the little office of the cottage at Belmont Park, and between the ringing of the hot line and the traffic coming and going through the door I discuss with the crew the lineup for the day ahead.

I might start with something like this: "I just talked with Chicago. He's got a filly with me today. He doesn't think she's really high-class, but let's see what we can do with her."

"There's a five-horse field. I talked to the jock. We've got a good chance," says Sandy.

"The track was still a bit soft this morning after that rain yesterday."

"It dries out slow this time of year."

"Jule thinks the filly can take an easy lead."

"Look," I'll say. "We're on the outside course. Suppose we follow them around the first turn?"

"I think we've got to go in and set our own pace."

"Who's the hurry-up rider in there?"

"Nobody," says Bob Frieze, who's Eddie Maple's agent.

"Then what if we sneak along for a bit before we go to the lead?"

"Okay. That's what we do."

"I called Pat Day and told him what Eddie said about the colt."

"I'm going to try him one more time on the grass."

"We got anything in the fifth today?"

"Nothing. There's a new rider in there, imported from Maryland," says Sandy.

"Has he ever rode that horse?"
"I'll ask around and find out."
"Kelly scratched in the fourth."
"I'm glad he got his ass off that fence."
"There's a race here the twenty-first that I might run the bay in. If I did, I'd call Chris. Bob, can you call about the other horse and check his papers out? I want to know so I can call up and get that squared away."
"Will do."

And that's about the way it goes, give or take a little, most days of the year until noontime's getting close and I head off to the house to stretch out on a sofa for half an hour, then shower, spruce up, and come back for more.

The crew often kids me, "Woody, you've got a memory a hundred years old." If I have, it's been put to the test in these pages, and I couldn't figure how to get them to the finish line except on the racetrack. So I decided to try for the grand finale by taking a shot at the 1985 Belmont, to see if I could make it not three but four in a row.

The only other trainer who'd won three back to back is named in the records as "D. McDaniel." He pulled it off in the 1880s, when the annual crop of thoroughbreds was five thousand, not the fifty thousand we have nowadays. And the story goes that in one of McDaniel's Belmonts there were only three runners, two of them his, which probably improved his chances some.

"Wouldn't that be something," I said to Lucille, "if I made it four? It would be one more mark to be remembered by. With all the changes that have come about in the game, it's likely nobody could match that in a hundred years."

"You can say a thousand years if you're really counting changes."

The Belmont Stakes is known to some people as "the test of the champions," a hard mile-and-a-half distance that measures their class and character. I didn't have a colt of quite the same talent as Conquistador Cielo or Caveat or Swale, but Stephan's Odyssey came close, and I entered him.

Then I got to thinking about covering myself with a kind of

insurance policy—a second starter, so I could play both ends against the middle. There was a little bay in my barn that weighed no more than nine hundred pounds. Creme Fraiche was owned by Elizabeth Moran from Chester, Pennsylvania, who bought him as a yearling for $160,000 at the Keeneland summer sales. He turned out to be an unruly youngster tough to train, so he had to be gelded.

Mrs. Moran got into flat racing after seven thin years with steeplechasers that gave her just four wins. Creme Fraiche did much better than that for her, finishing second in five major races before the Belmont in '85, winning the Churchill Downs Derby Trial in the mud in May, which when added to his juvenile starts gave him four victories in a dozen outings. He was an honest little animal that kept going no matter what happened. I made him my second entry in the Belmont, my ace in the hole in case the weather turned to rain on race day and made mud of the track.

It was agreed that Lafitt would fly out on the red-eye from Los Angeles to ride Stephan's Odyssey, hoping to make it four Belmonts in a row for himself as well as for me. Creme Fraiche would be Eddie Maple's mount, and he'd be riding to win sure as fate after what had happened to him in the past three years —injured the day before Conquistador Cielo took the race in '82; in the saddle of Chumming instead of Caveat in '83; aboard Devil's Bag not Swale through '84.

The weather haunted my mind during the early days of June while I worked to keep a sharp edge on Henryk's colt and Mrs. Moran's gelding. First thing every morning, I'd tune the radio to get a forecast as I drank a cup of wake-up Sanka. I had some doubt about Stephan's Odyssey's ability in mud; that discourages a lot of horses when it's kicked up on their faces. It wouldn't bother Creme Fraiche, but there was something else to be considered and then dismissed: geldings had been barred from the Belmont for forty years prior to 1957 because the breeders had no use for them, and no gelded horse had ever captured the race. If I could get this one first at the wire, there'd be an extra reason to holler.

On Saturday morning, the eighth of June, the rain came

down like it was on special order, then stopped comfortably short of post time, leaving the Belmont Park track wet but fast. Lucille was wearing a nice red dress and I was rigged out in a suit when we left the house, to find we had to park by my barn because there was no space anywhere else.

We knew a mass of people would be rooting for us, not forgetting Jimmy the Greek, who likes to play the horses, some of mine in particular. He was right about all three of the previous Belmonts, and today on CBS television he was going for Stephan's Odyssey and Creme Fraiche because he thought well of the trainer.

I had much the same thing to say to both the riders: "Keep him in reserve for half a dozen furlongs; start your move before the second turn." The strategy had worked with Caveat. I was pretty sure it would work today.

I was sitting in the box with Henryk when a symphony orchestra played *The Sidewalks of New York* as eleven horses were loaded into the starting gate. With two entries to watch, the deal made with Lucille was that she'd keep her eyes on one while I focused the glasses on the other.

The field broke clean, and both jockeys followed the plan to the letter, Lafitt holding back in last place, Eddie just ahead of him. The mud wasn't doing much to slow the pace. Nearing the second turn, the two riders started their advances, Creme Fraiche angled to the outside, Stephan's Odyssey along the inside. As they entered the stretch, Lafitt was riding so close to the rail that his left boot got gashed and scraped with white paint.

Eddie was gaining ground to challenge him, and his mount was in love with the track. At the sixteenth pole, a crazy notion skidded through my head: "It's going to finish in a dead heat; not four Belmont wins but *five!*"

But in the end, Creme Fraiche took it by half a length over his stablemate. Eddie, who's normally a quiet, family man, felt so great he tossed his whip up into the air and lost it. When Lucille went to give him a kiss, she got mud all over her face. What he told a TV interviewer was true about a mount that was mostly regarded as second string: "He's a first-string horse now."

"Why, that little feller would have gone another turn and still kept going!" said Lucille, who always thought well of Creme Fraiche.

Outside my barn, the celebrating continued long into the night, fifty or sixty of us helped along by cases of champagne and buckets of beer. Mrs. Moran, a good, family lady, brought some of the refreshments in the van that would take her home to Pennsylvania.

It was midnight before we'd finished, and the partying went on again for days, including the one Eddie threw next Monday. The phone rang itself off the hook. The telegrams and letters kept on coming. One of them, from an old friend, stuck in Lucille's mind: "Dear Woody—All I can say is you remind me of old bourbon. You simply get better with age."

At present, I'm thinking along these lines: "A one-two sweep of the Belmont in 1985 and the first gelding ever to win it . . . Damn it, the next time I go to Florida, I'll pick a young horse to make it five in a row for me."

Woody's Stakes Winners
(More or Less Complete)

HORSE	RACE	TRACK	LOCATION
	1944		
Saguero	Excelsior	Jamaica	Jamaica, NY
	1948		
Hal's Gal	Miss America Handicap	Atlantic City	Atlantic City, NJ
Page Boots	Kent Stakes	Delaware	Wilmington, DE
	Leonard Richards	Delaware	Wilmington, DE
Sports Page	East View Stakes	Jamaica	Jamaica, NY
	1949		
Halt	Blue Grass	Keeneland	Lexington, KY
Lady Dorimer	Test Stakes	Saratoga	Saratoga Springs, NY
Tall Weeds	Ashland	Keeneland	Lexington, KY
	1950		
Away Away	Cowdin	Aqueduct	Jamaica, NY
	1951		
Marta	Ladies Handicap	Belmont Park	Elmont, NY
	Molly Pitcher	Monmouth Park	Oceanport, NJ
	1952		
Armageddon	Ventnor	Atlantic City	Atlantic City, NJ
Blue Man	Dwyer	Aqueduct	Jamaica, NY
	Flamingo	Hialeah Park	Hialeah, FL
	Preakness	Pimlico	Baltimore, MD
	Yankee Handicap	Suffolk Downs	Boston, MA

WOODY'S STAKES WINNERS

HORSE	RACE	TRACK	LOCATION
Boot All	Columbiana	Hialeah Park	Hialeah, FL
Marta	Vagrancy	Belmont Park	Elmont, NY

1953

Marta	Top Flight Handicap	Belmont Park	Elmont, NY

1954

Brother Tex	Breeders' Futurity	Keeneland	Lexington, KY
	Sanford	Saratoga	Saratoga Springs, NY
Goyamo	Bahamas	Hialeah Park	Hialeah, FL
Marta	Vagrancy	Belmont Park	Elmont, NY

1955

Traffic Judge	Jerome	Belmont Park	Elmont, NY
	Ohio Derby	Thistledown	Cleveland, OH
	Withers	Belmont Park	Elmont, NY
	Woodward	Belmont Park	Elmont, NY

1956

Blessed Bull	Queen's Handicap	Jamaica	Jamaica, NY
Missile	Flash	Saratoga	Saratoga Springs, NY
Traffic Judge	Laurel Turf Cup	Laurel	Laurel, MD

1957

Jota Jota	Ashland	Keeneland	Lexington, KY
Lucky Dip	Kent Stakes	Delaware	Wilmington, DE
	Leonard Richards	Delaware	Wilmington, DE

1958

Merry Hill	Frizette	Jamaica	Jamaica, NY
Nile Lily	American Beauty	Jamaica	Jamaica, NY
One-Eyed King	John Macomber	Suffolk Downs	Boston, MA
Red God	Roseben Handicap	Belmont Park	Elmont, NY
Sports Page	East View Stakes	Jamaica	Jamaica, NY

HORSE	RACE	TRACK	LOCATION
Victory Morn	Dwyer	Aqueduct	Jamaica, NY
	Excelsior	Jamaica	Jamaica, NY

1959

HORSE	RACE	TRACK	LOCATION
Bald Eagle	Gallant Fox	Aqueduct	Jamaica, NY
	Suburban	Belmont Park	Elmont, NY
	Washington, D.C., International	Laurel	Laurel, MD
Heavenly Body	Matron Stakes	Belmont Park	Elmont, NY
	Princess Pat	Arlington Park	Arlington Heights, IL
Hidden Talent	Ashland	Keeneland	Lexington, KY
	Kentucky Oaks	Churchill Downs	Louisville, KY
Make Sail	Schuylerville	Saratoga	Saratoga Springs, NY
One-Eyed King	Dixie	Pimlico	Baltimore, MD
	Donn	Gulfstream Park	Hallandale, FL
	Lincoln Downs Handicap	Lincoln Downs	Lincoln Downs, RI
	Long Island Handicap	Belmont Park	Elmont, NY

1960

HORSE	RACE	TRACK	LOCATION
Bald Eagle	Aqueduct Handicap	Aqueduct	Jamaica, NY
	Gulfstream Park Handicap	Gulfstream Park	Hallandale, FL
	Metropolitan	Aqueduct	Jamaica, NY
	Washington, D.C., International	Laurel	Laurel, MD
	Widener	Hialeah Park	Hialeah, FL
Make Sail	Alabama	Saratoga	Saratoga Springs, NY
	Kentucky Oaks	Churchill Downs	Louisville, KY
One-Eyed King	Arlington Handicap	Arlington Park	Arlington Heights, IL
	Green Valley Handicap	Gulfstream Park	Hallandale, FL

WOODY'S STAKES WINNERS

HORSE	RACE	TRACK	LOCATION
	1961		
Battle Joined	Saratoga Special	Saratoga	Saratoga Springs, NY
Make Sail	Post-Deb	Monmouth Park	Oceanport, NJ
	Top Flight Handicap	Belmont Park	Elmont, NY
	1962		
Battle Joined	Lawrence Realization	Belmont Park	Elmont, NY
Dead Ahead	Roamer Handicap	Aqueduct	Jamaica, NY
Never Bend	Futurity	Belmont Park	Elmont, NY
	Champagne	Belmont Park	Elmont, NY
	Cowdin	Belmont Park	Elmont, NY
	1963		
Never Bend	Flamingo	Hialeah Park	Hialeah, FL
	Yankee Handicap	Suffolk Downs	Boston, MA
Sally Ship	Ashland	Keeneland	Louisville, KY
	Kentucky Oaks	Churchill Downs	Louisville, KY
	1964		
Iron Peg	Suburban	Belmont Park	Elmont, NY
	1966		
Bold Bidder	Amory Haskell	Monmouth Park	Asbury Park, NJ
	Charles Bidwill Memorial	Hawthorne	Cicero, IL
	Hawthorne Gold Cup	Hawthorne	Cicero, IL
	Monmouth Handicap	Monmouth Park	Oceanport, NJ
	Washington Park Handicap	Arlington Park	Arlington Heights, IL
Missile	Dover Stakes	Delaware Park	Wilmington, DE
	1968		
Eaglesham	Miami Beach	Tropical Park	Coral Gables, FL
Mrs. Peterkin	Chrysanthemum	Laurel	Laurel, MD

WOODY'S STAKES WINNERS

HORSE	RACE	TRACK	LOCATION
	1969		
Eaglesham	Assault Handicap	Arlington Park	Arlington Heights, IL
	Lexington Handicap	Belmont Park	Elmont, NY
Gunite	Pinafore Stakes	Suffolk Downs	Boston, MA
Hibernian	Pan American Handicap	Gulfstream Park	Hallandale, FL
Meritus	Adirondack	Saratoga	Saratoga Springs, NY
	1970		
Jungle Cove	Canadian Turf Handicap	Gulfstream Park	Hallandale, FL
Meritus	Spinaway	Saratoga	Saratoga Springs, NY
Missile Belle	Coaching Club Oaks	Belmont Park	Elmont, NY
	Gazelle	Belmont Park	Elmont, NY
	La Troienne	Churchill Downs	Louisville, KY
Proudest Roman	Hopeful	Saratoga	Saratoga Springs, NY
	National Stallion	Belmont Park	Elmont, NY
Top Round	Distaff	Belmont Park	Elmont, NY
	Margate Stakes	Atlantic City	Atlantic City, NJ
	1971		
Cohasset Tribe	Sanford Stakes	Saratoga	Saratoga Springs, NY
	Tyro Stakes	Monmouth Park	Asbury Park, NJ
Kittiwake	Firenze	Aqueduct	Jamaica, NY
	Margate Stakes	Atlantic City	Atlantic City, NJ
	Princeton Handicap	Garden State	Cherry Hill, NJ
Missile Belle	Indian Maid Handicap	Arlington Park	Arlington Heights, IL
Northfields	Hawthorne Derby	Hawthorne Park	Cicero, IL
	Kent Stakes	Delaware Park	Wilmington, DE
	Louisiana Derby	Fair Grounds	New Orleans, LA

(220) WOODY'S STAKES WINNERS

HORSE	RACE	TRACK	LOCATION
	1972		
Kittiwake	Matron Handicap	Arlington Park	Arlington Heights, IL
Lucky Bidder	John Macomber	Suffolk Downs	Boston, MA
Summit Joy	Little Silver Handicap	Monmouth Park	Oceanport, NJ
	1973		
Cannonade	Aqueduct Handicap	Aqueduct	Jamaica, NY
	Kentucky Jockey Club	Churchill Downs	Louisville, KY
	Great American	Churchill Downs	Louisville, KY
Dance A Lot	Matron	Belmont Park	Elmont, NY
	Selima	Laurel	Laurel, MD
Judger	Florida Derby	Gulfstream Park	Hallandale, FL
Kittiwake	Columbiana	Hialeah Park	Hialeah, FL
North Broadway	Jersey Belle	Garden State	Cherry Hill, NJ
	Chrysanthemum	Laurel	Laurel, MD
	1974		
Cannonade	Kentucky Derby	Churchill Downs	Louisville, KY
Circle Home	Kentucky Jockey Club	Churchill Downs	Louisville, KY
	Heritage	Keystone	Bensalem, PA
Judger	Blue Grass Stakes	Keeneland	Lexington, KY
North Broadway	Sheepshead Bay	Belmont Park	Elmont, NY
	1975		
Ascetic	Bahamas	Hialeah Park	Hialeah, FL
	Everglades	Hialeah Park	Hialeah, FL
Bravest Roman	Paul Revere	Suffolk Downs	Boston, MA
	Saranac	Belmont Park	Elmont, NY
Gull's Cry	Columbiana	Hialeah Park	Hialeah, FL
	Gallorette	Laurel	Laurel, MD
	Vineland	Garden State	Cherry Hill, NJ
Harbor Springs	Breeders' Futurity	Keeneland	Lexington, KY

HORSE	RACE	TRACK	LOCATION
		1976	
Bold Royal	Gardenia Trial	Garden State	Cherry Hill, NJ
Fable Monarch	Lexington Handicap	Belmont Park	Elmont, NY
Jabot	Suwannee River	Gulfstream Park	Hallandale, FL
Logical	Saranac	Belmont Park	Elmont, NY
Lucky Bidder	John Macomber	Suffolk Downs	Boston, MA
Mrs. Warren	Matron	Belmont Park	Elmont, NY
	Schuylerville	Saratoga	Saratoga Springs, NY
	Spinaway	Saratoga	Saratoga Springs, NY
One-Eyed King	Magic City	Gulfstream Park	Hallandale, FL
Sail To Rome	Cowdin	Belmont Park	Elmont, NY
Sensational	Astorita	Belmont Park	Elmont, NY
	Colleen Stakes	Monmouth Park	Oceanport, NJ
	Selima	Laurel	Laurel, MD
	Frizette	Belmont Park	Elmont, NY
		1977	
Believe It	Heritage	Keystone	Bensalem, PA
	Remsen	Aqueduct	Jamaica, NY
Mrs. Warren	Mother Goose	Belmont Park	Elmont, NY
Quadratic	Cowdin	Belmont Park	Elmont, NY
	Nashua	Aqueduct	Jamaica, NY
Sensational	Ladies Handicap	Belmont Park	Elmont, NY
	Long Look	Meadowlands	East Rutherford, NJ
	Post-Deb	Monmouth Park	Oceanport, NJ
		1978	
Believe It	Wood	Aqueduct	Jamaica, NY
Mrs. Warren	Firenze	Aqueduct	Jamaica, NY
Quadratic	Bahamas	Hialeah Park	Hialeah, FL
	Everglades	Hialeah Park	Hialeah, FL
Smarten	Miami Handicap	Gulfstream Park	Hallandale, FL
	Secretariat	Arlington Park	Arlington Heights, IL
	Senatorial	Laurel	Laurel, MD

HORSE	RACE	TRACK	LOCATION
Terpsichorist	Long Island	Aqueduct	Jamaica, NY
	Rutgers	Meadowlands	East Rutherford, NJ
	Athenia	Belmont Park	Elmont, NY
Too Many Sweets	Concord	Rockingham Park	Salem, NH
	Keeneland	Keeneland	Lexington, KY
White Star Line	Alabama	Saratoga	Saratoga Springs, NY
	Delaware Oaks	Delaware Park	Wilmington, DE
	Kentucky Oaks	Churchill Downs	Louisville, KY
	Test	Saratoga	Saratoga Springs, NY
1979			
Bends Me Mind	Hill Prince	Aqueduct	Jamaica, NY
Poppycock	Athenia	Belmont Park	Elmont, NY
Smart Angle	Adirondack	Saratoga	Saratoga Springs, NY
	Frizette	Belmont Park	Elmont, NY
	Lucky Penny	Bowie	Bowie, MD
	Matron	Belmont Park	Elmont, NY
	Selima	Laurel	Laurel, MD
	Spinaway	Saratoga	Saratoga Springs, NY
Smarten	American Derby	Arlington Park	Arlington Heights, IL
	Illinois Derby	Sportsman's Park	Cicero, IL
	Pennsylvania Derby	Keystone	Bensalem, PA
	Woodland	Pimlico	Baltimore, MD
	Ohio Derby	Thistledown	Cleveland, OH
Terpsichorist	Violet	Meadowlands	East Rutherford, NJ
	Sheepshead Bay	Belmont Park	Elmont, NY
1980			
Akureyri	Pilgrim	Aqueduct	Jamaica, NY
Dame Mysterieuse	Holly	Meadowlands	East Rutherford, NJ
	Treetop	Meadowlands	East Rutherford, NJ

WOODY'S STAKES WINNERS

HORSE	RACE	TRACK	LOCATION
De La Rose	Remsen	Aqueduct	Jamaica, NY
Heavenly Cause	Frizette	Belmont Park	Elmont, NY
	Marlboro Nursery	Bowie	Bowie, MD
	Selima	Laurel	Laurel, MD
It's True	Louisiana Downs Handicap	Fair Grounds	New Orleans, LA
Smart Angle	Poinsettia	Hialeah Park	Hialeah, FL
	Poinsettia	Hialeah Park	Hialeah, FL

1981

HORSE	RACE	TRACK	LOCATION
Akureyri	Fountain of Youth	Gulfstream Park	Hallandale, FL
Conquistador Cielo	Saratoga Special	Saratoga	Saratoga Springs, NY
Dame Mysterieuse	Black-eyed Susan	Pimlico	Baltimore, MD
	Forward Gal	Gulfstream Park	Hallandale, FL
	The Mademoiselle	Keystone	Bensalem, PA
	Old Hat Stakes	Gulfstream Park	Hallandale, FL
De La Rose	Diana	Saratoga	Saratoga Springs, NY
	Lamb Chop	Aqueduct	Jamaica, NY
	Long Branch Stakes	Monmouth Park	Oceanport, NJ
	E. P. Taylor	Woodbine	Toronto, Can.
	Athenia	Belmont Park	Elmont, NY
	Saranac	Belmont Park	Elmont, NY
	Hollywood Derby	Hollywood Park	Inglewood, CA
Heavenly Cause	Acorn Claiborne	Belmont Park	Elmont, NY
	Fantasy	Oaklawn Park	Hot Springs, AR
	Kentucky Oaks	Churchill Downs	Louisville, KY
	La Torienne	Churchill Downs	Louisville, KY
Miswacki	Charley Hatten	Belmont Park	Elmont, NY
Trove	Star Bright	Monmouth Park	Oceanport, NJ

(224) WOODY'S STAKES WINNERS

HORSE	RACE	TRACK	LOCATION
	1982		
Bemissed	Miss Grillo	Pimlico	Baltimore, MD
	Natalma Stakes	Woodbine	Toronto, Can.
	Selima Stakes	Laurel	Laurel, MD
	Japan C. Handicap	Laurel	Laurel, MD
Bravest Miss	Colonia	Meadowlands	East Rutherford, NJ
Caveat	Prince John	Belmont Park	Elmont, NY
Conquistador Cielo	Belmont Stakes	Belmont Park	Elmont, NY
	Jim Dandy	Saratoga	Saratoga Springs, NY
	Dwyer	Aqueduct	Jamaica, NY
	Metropolitan	Belmont Park	Elmont, NY
Larida	Boiling Springs	Meadowlands	East Rutherford, NJ
	Columbiana	Hialeah Park	Hialeah, FL
	Hill Prince	Aqueduct	Jamaica, NY
	Wistful Stakes	Belmont Park	Elmont, NY
Number	Firenze	Aqueduct	Jamaica, NY
	First Flight Handicap	Belmont Park	Elmont, NY
Smart Heiress	Very One	Laurel	Laurel, MD
	Garden City	Belmont Park	Elmont, NY
	Mount Washington Handicap	Belmont Park	Elmont, NY
Trove	Forward Gal	Gulfstream Park	Hallandale, FL
	Prioress	Belmont Park	Elmont, NY
	Wistful Stakes	Belmont Park	Elmont, NY
What's Dat	Cowdin	Belmont Park	Elmont, NY
	1983		
Caveat	Belmont Stakes	Belmont Park	Elmont, NY
	Derby Trial	Churchill Downs	Louisville, KY
Devil's Bag	Champagne	Belmont Park	Elmont, NY
	Cowdin	Belmont Park	Elmont, NY
	Maryland Futurity	Laurel	Laurel, MD

WOODY'S STAKES WINNERS

HORSE	RACE	TRACK	LOCATION
Larida	Orchid	Gulfstream Park	Hallandale, FL
Miss Oceana	Arlington-Washington Lassie	Arlington Park	Arlington Heights, IL
	Frizette	Belmont Park	Elmont, NY
	Selima	Laurel	Laurel, MD
Mistretta	Black Helen	Hialeah Park	Hialeah, FL
Morning Bob	What a Pleasure Stakes	Calder	Miami, FL
Number	Hempstead	Belmont Park	Elmont, NY
Quixotic Lady	Anne Arundel Stakes	Bowie	Bowie, MD
	Cotillion	Keystone	Bensalem, PA
	Honey Bee	Meadowlands	East Rutherford, NJ
	Monmouth Oaks	Monmouth Park	Oceanport, NJ
	Oaklawn	Oaklawn Park	Hot Springs, AR
	Post-Deb	Monmouth Park	Oceanport, NJ
	Prima Donna	Oaklawn Park	Hot Springs, AR
Sabin	Boiling Springs Handicap	Meadowlands	East Rutherford, NJ
	New York Handicap	Belmont Park	Elmont, NY
	Saranac	Belmont Park	Elmont, NY
	Sheepshead Bay	Belmont Park	Elmont, NY
Swale	Breeders' Futurity	Keeneland	Lexington, KY
	Futurity	Keeneland	Lexington, KY
	Saratoga Special	Saratoga	Saratoga Springs, NY
	Young America	Saratoga	Saratoga Springs, NY
Vision	Pilgrim	Aqueduct	Jamaica, NY

1984

Born a Lady	Pearl Necklace	Meadowlands	East Rutherford, NJ
Contredance	Adirondack	Saratoga	Saratoga Springs, NY

WOODY'S STAKES WINNERS

HORSE	RACE	TRACK	LOCATION
	Washington-Arlington Lassie	Arlington Park	Arlington Heights, IL
Creme Fraiche	What a Pleasure	Calder	Miami, FL
Devil's Bag	Derby Trial	Churchill Downs	Louisville, KY
	Flamingo Prep	Hialeah Park	Hialeah, FL
Dinner Money	Biscayne	Hialeah Park	Hialeah, FL
Endear	Miss Grillo Stakes	Pimlico	Baltimore, MD
Herat	Buckpasser	Hollywood Park	Inglewood, CA
	To Market Stakes	Belmont Park	Elmont, NY
Jubilous	Eatontown Handicap	Monmouth Park	Oceanport, NJ
Miss Oceana	The Acorn	Belmont Park	Elmont, NY
	Bonnie Miss	Gulfstream Park	Hallandale, FL
	Forward Gal	Gulfstream Park	Hallandale, FL
	Gazelle	Belmont Park	Elmont, NY
	Hibiscus	Hialeah Park	Hialeah, FL
	Maskette	Belmont Park	Elmont, NY
Morning Bob	Pennsylvania Derby	Keystone	Bensalem, PA
	Tropicana Derby	Calder	Miami, FL
Sabin	Black Helen	Hialeah Park	Hialeah, FL
	Allez France	Hollywood Park	Inglewood, CA
	Columbia Handicap	Hialeah Park	Hialeah, FL
	Gamely	Santa Anita	Arcadia, CA
	La Prevoyante	Calder	Miami, FL
	Matchmaker	Atlantic City	Atlantic City, NJ
	Orchid	Gulfstream Park	Hallandale, FL
	Sheepshead Bay	Belmont Park	Elmont, NY
	Yellow Ribbon	Santa Anita	Arcadia, CA
Stephan's Odyssey	Hollywood Futurity	Hollywood Park	Inglewood, CA
Swale	Belmont Stakes	Belmont Park	Elmont, NY
	Florida Derby	Gulfstream Park	Hallandale, FL
	Hutchison	Gulfstream Park	Hallandale, FL
	Kentucky Derby	Churchill Downs	Louisville, KY

HORSE	RACE	TRACK	LOCATION
Vision	Secretariat	Arlington Park	Arlington Heights, IL

1985*

HORSE	RACE	TRACK	LOCATION
Creme Fraiche	American Derby	Arlington Park	Arlington Heights, IL
	Belmont Stakes	Belmont Park	Elmont, NY
	Derby Trial	Churchill Downs	Louisville, KY
Sabin	La Prevoyante	Calder	Miami, FL
Stephan's Odyssey	Dwyer	Belmont Park	Elmont, NY
	Lexington	Keeneland	Lexington, KY

* As of July, 1985.

Major Events in Woody's Career*

Voted into the Hall of Fame		1976
New York Racing Association hosts seventieth birthday party		1983
Six consecutive Eclipse Awards:	Sensational	1978
	Smart Angle	1979
	Heavenly Cause	1980
	De La Rose	1981
	Conquistador Cielo	1982
	Devil's Bag	1983
Voted Champion Horse (before establishment of Eclipse Awards):	Bald Eagle, Never Bend, Bold Bidder	
Two Kentucky Derbies:	Cannonade	1974
	Swale	1984
Four consecutive Belmont Stakes:	Conquistador Cielo	1982
	Caveat	1983
	Swale	1984
	Creme Fraiche	1985
Two Metropolitans (fastest on record):	Bald Eagle (1:33.1/5)	1960
	Conquistador Cielo (1:33)	1982
Two Washington, D.C., Internationals:	Bald Eagle	1959
	Bald Eagle	1960

* As of July, 1985

Widener track record (unbroken to date):	Bald Eagle	1960
Champagne Stakes track record:	Devil's Bag	1983
Five Kentucky Oaks:	Hidden Talent	1959
	Make Sail	1960
	Sally Ship	1963
	White Star Line	1978
	Heavenly Cause	1981
Two La Prevoyantes:	Sabin	1984
	Swale	1985
Two Florida Derbies:	Judger	1973
	Swale	1984
Six Selimas:	Dance A Lot	1973
	Sensational	1976
	Smart Angle	1979
	Heavenly Cause	1980
	Bemissed	1982
	Miss Oceana	1983
Four Dwyers:	Blue Man	1952
	Victory Morn	1958
	Conquistador Cielo	1982
	Stephan's Odyssey	1985
Six Cowdins:	Away Away	1950
	Never Bend	1962
	Sail to Rome	1976
	Quadratic	1977
	What's Dat	1982
	Devil's Bag	1983
Five Frizettes:	Merry Hill	1958
	Sensational	1976
	Smart Angle	1979
	Heavenly Cause	1980
	Miss Oceana	1983
Trainer of the Year (Eclipse Award)		1983